Points In Between

Points In Between

An Anecdotal History

Ignatius Fay, Ph.D.

ISBN: 978-0-9809572-1-1

Canadian Cataloguing-in-Publication Data:

Fay, Ignatius 1950-

Points In Between
An Anecdotal History

1. Anecdote   2. Personal History   3. Growing up   4. Northern Ontario

1. Title

Design and layout by: Ignatius Fay, PhD

Published by: Ignatius Fay, PhD and Lulu.com

Copies of this work may be purchased online at:
http://www.lulu.com/product/paperback/points-in-between/18464439

for Kathryn and Danielle,
the two best justifications for my existence

Contents

Acknowledgements

I probably never would have committed these episodes to paper if not for the encouragement of my daughters, Kathryn and Danielle, who grew up listening to them. Their assistance during the tedious editing phase is greatly appreciated.

My sisters, Christine and Rosanna, and close friend, Susan Ritchie-Comery, were kind enough to proofread earlier drafts of the manuscript and caught me with my pants down several times. My sisters, including Gerarda, also served as a valuable check on my memory of the very early years.

To all I am sincerely grateful and indebted.

Any errors or omissions are strictly my responsibility. These anecdotes are based on my memories of the events and I apologize in advance for any perceived or real lapses.

Introduction

Points In Between

Non-Autobiography

AT A BUS DEPOT, when announcing a boarding bus, the voice on the P.A. invariably lists the major stops along the route, almost always ending with the phrase 'and points in between,' to include all the smaller stops. Looking back on the 'bus trip' of my life, I find the more memorable parts of the trip involved the smaller stops along the way. The major centers may have served to anchor the route, but the scenery, the background details that gave the trip its unique flavor, were encountered at the points in between.

Thus, my intention in writing this account is not autobiographical. Instead, I have undertaken to write a series of anecdotes recounting those events in my life that I find particularly interesting. I have shared many of these stories with my daughters over the years and they have been encouraging me with increasing frequency to get them down on paper. *This is for them.*

A few paragraphs of biographical information seem to be in order, if for no other purpose than to supply reference points. Without them, comments about my frailty, for example, would leave the reader with a lot of unanswered questions.

I was raised in the small mining town of Levack in northern Ontario. The town was literally owned by Inco, the nickel mining giant: our houses, schools, commercial buildings, utilities, medical clinic, sanitation facilities—everything.

My first recollections are of events in our house at 86 Poplar Street. Born in 1950, the second of five children (Margaret, me, Gerarda, Christine, Rosanna), I was the only male. I was a sickly baby that grew into a sickly boy. When I got older, doctors would determine that I was severely asthmatic from birth or, at least, before the age of one. The doctor in Levack, a Dr. Jessop, employed by Inco at its medical clinic, did not put that label on my illness until I was old enough to exert my individuality. Like so many doctors in that era, he believed asthma was psychosomatic. In an effort to justify his diagnosis, some of his explanations for my illnesses were convoluted indeed.

For example: when I was seven or eight, after another asthma attack requiring a trip to the clinic for adrenaline, my dad asked Dr. Jessop why so many of these attacks happened on Friday. Jessop's response was that my bouts could be attributed to my dad's staunch Catholicism.

"Luke, you are a faithful member of the Catholic Church and adamant about adhering to Catholic doctrine. Among other religious observances, you make a point of ensuring no one in the family eats meat on Friday, as dictated by the Vatican. Your son is rebelling against your strict religious teachings by getting sick on those days. When he becomes more comfortable with your beliefs, these bouts will subside."

Somehow, they both missed some pretty obvious facts. I was made to attend church every Sunday, coerced into being an altar boy, required to help dad clean the church after hours and had to participate in any number of other religious holidays. Yet I did not display this same rebellion on any of those occasions. And the bouts always happened at supper time. Years later, tests would show my worst allergy is fish—on the menu most meatless Fridays!

Just the smell of raw fish or fish being cooked triggers a serious asthma attack. Luckily, I never got to the point of actually eating or even touching the fish. As it turns out, contact causes me to go into anaphylactic shock, lethal without immediate injection with epinephrine. Contact with peanuts or alcohol does the same.

I am detailing this incident only as an example of how my illness was mismanaged on the advice of Dr. Jessop. I had multiple bouts of pneumonia before the age of five, causing the onset of Swyer-James Syndrome. The affected part of the left lung stopped growing: the tissue, the bronchial tree, the alveoli and the blood supply remained that of a 5-year-old. In short, that area of the lung no longer functioned, serving only to collect phlegm, and breed and harbor infectious organisms. My health deteriorated until removal of the left lower lobe and lingula was required at age 36. Dating from a year after that surgery, I have been disabled on 24-hour oxygen therapy and devoting my life to maximizing the length of my stay on the planet.

Throughout my education, I spent a lot of time home or in hospital with pneumonia. I missed a lot of school and time with my friends. As a result of my fragile health, physical activities were severely restricted. I endured many mustard plasters on my chest and back until I suffered first-degree burns as the result of a particularly potent treatment.

When I was almost nine, the understanding of asthma at the Inco medical clinic had advanced sufficiently for them to recognize that the molds and mildews growing in the corners of the basement of our house were very likely contributing to the frequency and severity of my bouts. Dad applied through the Inco office to be assigned different housing and we were given permission to move to 13 First Avenue. The move had a positive albeit small effect on my health.

Not long after the move, my mother started complaining of chest pains and miscellaneous discomforts. Dr. Jessop found nothing wrong. In his opinion, my mother was a bored housewife. She needed an interest outside the home, away from the kids, to take her mind off feeling sorry for herself. My dad, accepting the judgement of the professional, encouraged her to find diverting activities.

Mom deteriorated over six months and, after repeated trips to the clinic, dad finally took her into Sudbury to see specialists. She was diagnosed with cancer of the left lung and shoulder, and shipped to Princess Margaret Hospital in Toronto. She died there in September 1961 at age 42.

Dad was grief stricken, of course, his faith in the medical profession seriously shaken. In years to follow, when he learned how badly my health had been handled, he would lose what little respect for the profession he had left.

Most important to all our futures, dad panicked. He had been left with five children, one under a year old! How was he going to care for them? Raise them? He couldn't do it alone. His kids needed a mother and he needed a wife.

As the fates would have it, he ran into Isabelle, the woman who used to live next door to us on Poplar Street. She was a widow of two years, with three girls similar in age to my sisters, and working as a newly graduated Public Health Nurse in Sudbury. Conveniently, they fell in love and married in July 1962. To my benefit, she quickly impressed upon my father the fact that asthma was not psychological and arranged testing at the Hospital for Sick Children in Toronto. We came home armed with the knowledge that I had hundreds of severe allergies. She and dad were both smokers and, when told how allergic I was to cigarette smoke, they both quit cold turkey, leaving their unfinished packages in the waste basket at the hospital. I remember half a carton of Peter Jackson sitting in the hall closet at home for months before someone finally heaved them.

My step-mother taught me how to avoid allergens, to cope with the asthma attacks, to resist the tendency to panic and to take medication regularly to control my breathing problems. I have to admit, when it came to my health, she was unstinting. Finally, I gained a little stability for a few years. But the damage had already been done.

I went to Laurentian University in 1968 to study towards a Bachelor of Science and was asked to withdraw a couple of years later due to nonperformance. I had taken a job at Cortina Pizza, my first real job, and was working too many hours and having too much fun to concentrate on school. I bought into the Cortina franchise system in 1972, eventually owning three in partnership with my dad's youngest brother, Henry, three months my junior.

I was married to Joanne in 1973, enrolling as a mature student at Laurentian in 1975, the year my first daughter, Kathryn, was born. I kicked the snot out of my studies! I sold my franchises in 1977, the year Danielle made her appearance. Then, in 1978, I moved my family of four west to Saskatoon for graduate school, earning my PhD in paleontology in 1983. I spent a year as the first Curator of Invertebrate Paleontology at the then under construction Royal Tyrrell Museum of Paleontology in Drumheller, Alberta.

Then my health went to hell and I began being hospitalized for increasing lengths of time fighting life-threatening pneumonia. We moved back to Sudbury in 1984 and I haven't worked since. In 1986, I had lung surgery and got divorced, both victims of my illness. The girls stayed with me except during my extended sojourns in hospital.

Today, my daughters have grown into wonderful, successful women of whom I am extremely proud. I do computer graphics to keep myself stimulated and write haiku poetry as a form of expression.

But enough about me. Let's meet some of the characters who populated my life.

Early Family

Points In Between

Sisters

I WAS HARD ON my sisters. Having me for a brother must have been a trial. The closeness that the younger three and I share today is entirely attributable to their tolerance and understanding.

I was going to start this section by saying I was mischievous in my younger years, but I feel that may not be entirely true. I don't remember ever being motivated by maliciousness, although I often stepped beyond the envelope of acceptable behavior and, I must admit, some of the things I did were the result of distinctly poor judgment. And mitigating everything was my inquisitiveness. I had a very active mind and I was always trying to find out how things worked, what would happen if, why shouldn't/can't we do such-and-such. However I try to slice it, my sisters put up with a lot!

§

TRITE AS THIS MAY sound, Christine is my soulmate. As she once commented to one of her physicians, "Iggy and I are twins who happened to have been born four years apart."

We have always been of the same mind, sharing interests, attitudes, opinions and outlook. She is the only person, until my daughters reached appropriate ages, to whom I ever loaned my records or whom I allowed to use my stereo. For me, that's trust! From the beginning, without discussion, we knew we would always be able to rely on each other. We knew, when the chips were down, the other would be there, unquestioning and non-judgmental. Our commitment was, and is, unconditional.

I could ask Christine to do anything and she would do it, no question. That was not necessarily always a good thing. Like me, she has always been a seeker of experiences driven by an inquisitive mind. In discussion preparatory to writing this section, she assured me that, even at a very young age, she never felt real maliciousness in any of my actions.

"You always struck me as motivated by a need to know. Which was an echo of something inside of me. That's why I had no problem standing in for the guinea pig. And don't forget, you used yourself as guinea pig far more often than you used others."

She's right, of course. My bruises, scrapes and broken bones easily outstripped the number and severity of anything I inflicted on others.

That is not to say I do not take responsibility for my actions. The fault, if any, is all mine.

Remember when you were a kid and about to do something with an electrical appliance, some adult telling you, "Don't do that, you'll get a shock!" Does it ever occur to parents to actually explain that statement? To describe what a shock is and its potential side effects? Do they ever consider the possibility that just saying the words does not impart understanding? Especially to a child?

When we lived on Poplar Street, my sisters had a toy clothes iron that really worked. A little aluminum replica of a real iron, it warmed when plugged in and they would pretend to iron doll clothes. The cord eventually began to fray where it entered the iron itself and mom told them they couldn't use it anymore because they could get a shock.

Ping. What's a shock? Why is it bad? I went straight for the iron first chance I got. I plugged it in and the iron warmed. Fiddling with the cord, I couldn't get the iron to act up, aside from cooling somewhat when I held the cord just so. I unplugged the cord from the wall and began to take this pseudo appliance apart.

Christine happened along about that time and asked what I was doing and could she help. I let her participate in the usual capacity of a child between four and five, pretty much just holding pieces for me as I took them off the iron. When done, I was no more enlightened than when I started, but we were surrounded by pieces of iron and an electrical cord with a plug on one end and bare wires at the other.

"Here, hold this," I told Chris, handing her the bare wires. When she had a good grip on them, I stuck the plug in the socket. We heard a zzzt sound, her arm jerked independent of the rest of her body and she let go of the wire. I suspect the jerk pulled it out of her hand, as opposed to her voluntarily letting go. A look of surprise and fear flashed across her features, gone before they could settle.

"Ow! That hurts!"

Hmm. A fact was thus catalogued. A shock hurts, but seems to be more unpleasant than dangerous. Nothing to fear, really. I more than half believed that, even after being taught differently in my teens, until I got a hell of a jolt repairing a t.v. as a newlywed.

§

I TRULY REGRET to this day one unpleasant situation to which I subjected Christine. She holds no rancor, thankfully, but that does not remove my culpability. The Christmas just before I turned ten and just after we moved to First Avenue, I received a remote-controlled gorilla. It stood 30 cm tall and walked forward, swinging its arms up and down, and roaring, while its eyes flashed red. A long wire connected it to the control unit that essentially just turned it on and off.

Not long after Christmas and already bored with a gorilla that just marched and roared, I had one of my 'I wonder…' moments. With classically poor judgment, I put the gorilla in the depths of my closet and strung the wire out the door along the wall where it would be unobtrusive. Then I called Christine.

"I have a surprise for you. I put it in the closet, so you have to go and get it."

Excited, she opened the door and went in, looking for her surprise. She found it, too.

I closed the door so she was in the dark and hit the 'on' button. I tried it myself later and it truly was a scary sight—those disembodied red eyes glowing above the reddish shadows of flailing arms, everything seeming to jerk in midair as it tottered forward. And the roar!

Christine screamed louder than the gorilla and, if I had not opened the door, she may well have knocked it off its hinges or kicked right through the hollow core structure. She ran, terrified.

For as long as she can remember, Christine has suffered from claustrophobia. I wonder where she got that!

§

GERARDA TOOK A LOT of crap for me, too. She had a significant impact on me long before I affected her life, though. She is 14 months younger than me. Until she was born, I was the baby and garnered all mom's attention. That dried up as soon as Gerarda arrived and, apparently, my young nose got quite out of joint.

My highchair was the type with the hole in the seat and a potty attached underneath. Toddlers have a tendency to empty as they fill up, so this cut down on the diaper changing. Apparently, I was so jealous of Gerarda that mom had to go back to feeding me by hand for a couple of weeks. If left to feed myself, which I had been doing for a while, I didn't eat. I took the food by handfuls and stuffed it down between my legs into the potty! I really don't think that jealousy played a role five or six years later, but who's to know?

When Gerarda was about five, Margaret (my older sister by 25 months) and I decided to give her a haircut. All we had were those dull children's scissors with the rounded ends. We were in the corner of the basement cutting pictures from an old catalog, mom working upstairs, when we made the decision. Gerarda didn't complain, just sat there and let us work. With the dullness of the scissors, we pulled out nearly as much as we cut. Mom, keying on the fact that we were 'too quiet down there,' decided to check on us. She was aghast! It took more than a couple of months and as many trips to the barbershop (all young girls went to the barber) to get Gerarda's hair in some sort of presentable order. No wonder months passed before we were allowed to use the scissors unsupervised again.

§

ANOTHER OF THE incidents involving Gerarda occurred in winter. I know it was winter because we were just home from school and had not had supper, yet it was already dark. Snow isn't part of the memory, but the rest yells 'winter' in my mind. We were playing in the basement of our Poplar Street home, same venue as the haircut a couple of years earlier. Gerarda was still wearing her school uniform, required for girls at Levack Public. Presently, mom called down to say it was time to come up and wash for supper. We headed upstairs, Margaret in the lead with me bringing up the rear behind Gerarda. Two or three steps up, she froze.

"Dutchy, what's on the back of my leg?" she asked in a shaky voice. I looked closely and saw that a thread was hanging from the hem of her uniform skirt and making contact with her leg. Did I tell her that? No!

"A spider."

I was sorry the second the words were out of my mouth. She nearly came out of her skin trying to get away. She screamed as if she was being tortured, her face turned red and she ran upstairs. The screams got louder and more hysterical with each step that brought the dangling thread back into contact with her leg. She was sheer panic when she reached the kitchen and mom.

Mom needed quite a little time to calm her down and convince her there was no spider, just a loose thread. Supper was a considerably late and subdued affair that night. Good thing dad was on afternoon shift.

Aunty Rita

LET'S START WITH a little something about names. Well, my name, actually, and its permutations.

I was named after a woman who would later become my favorite aunt on my mother's side. Aunty Rita was mom's youngest half-sister (same dad, different mother). In her mid-teens, she entered the Order of the Sisters of St. Joseph and has been a nun ever since—60-plus years and counting! When she took her vows, as was the rule in those days, she took a saint's name as her own. She had a thing for St. Ignatius, so she took the feminine form and became Sister Ignatia. When I was born, I was named Ignatius, after her.

Many years later, when the rule was abolished by the order and she reverted to Sister Rita, she apologized for saddling me with the name. I assured her I had become quite attached to it and felt no burden. To this day, I wouldn't think of going anywhere without it.

From my earliest memories until my mom died when I was eleven, her side of the family called me *Dutchy*—and they still do. Apparently, Uncle Peter, mom's oldest brother who had lost an arm in Europe during World War II, made a comment once that my early gibberish sounded like Dutch. And a nickname was born.

I have had others. Some grew out of kids struggling with pronunciation, others from maliciousness. And still others, from a sense of humor. So, I have variously been called *Iggy* (still the most common), *Iggy Piggy, Ignag Faghead* (believe it or not, this was a term of endearment), *Ignition* and *Igneous* (this from 'creative' geology students). Recently I learned that my niece's husband refers to me around their house as *Uncle Igger, the Dinosaur Digger*, a humorous reference to my being a paleontologist.

To paraphrase George Bernard Shaw, it doesn't much matter what you call me, just don't ignore me. That being said, I find that, as I get on in years, I increasingly prefer good old *Ignatius*.

§

FOR A TIME, I thought of Aunty Rita as the aunt with the hole in her head. When she took her final vows, the family had a formal portrait taken of her in her new habit. The vintage being mid-fifties, the photo is black-and-white. I have always thought that photo seems so contradictory. The nun, a symbol of righteousness, piety, simplicity and humility posing at the bottom of this pretentious, phony replica of a spiral staircase.

I was the proud recipient of one of these portraits. Having limited resources, she only framed two photographs, which she gave to her mother and to her sister, Azilda, my mom. I had to resort to using a thumbtack through the top edge of the photo to fasten it to the wall above my bed.

Many nights, in bed but not ready to sleep, I'd sit up, legs parted and bent, to form a series of hills and valleys with the bedsheets. These would serve as either terrain for battles between my toy soldiers or as off-road courses for races between my small plastic cars. Every now and then, I felt the need to talk to Aunty Rita. I'd take her picture down, climb back into bed and talk to her.

With all this un-tacking and re-tacking, the hole became enlarged and eventually tore right off the top edge of the photo. So I had to move the pin, creating a new, slightly lower hole. The third hole, I think, had to be placed through the forehead of Aunty Rita's habit. Hence, the aunt with the hole in her head.

§

FROM THE BEGINNING, Aunty Rita was my biggest fan. She supported me in everything I did. Recognizing early on that I was quite bright, she encouraged me to push myself intellectually, possibly as compensation for the frail body I had been issued. She sang my praises at every opportunity and counseled me on how to make improvements when I did something wrong or did not perform up to my potential. She always had something positive to say, no matter the situation.

She encouraged me to read, to read critically, to make up my own mind, to ask questions and seek answers. Ironically, the independence of thought that she nurtured in me eventually led to my movement away from the Catholic Church. With her as a role model and my dad's devout wish that I become a priest, I had decided at eight years old that one day I would join the priesthood. So I read everything that I could about altar boys who had been sainted (I served at my dad's suggestion for a short time) and the lives of particularly holy monks, priests and lay people. And I read the bible.

I felt like I was swimming against the tide. One of the strongest currents opposing me was the way most of the members of our parish conducted their lives. They continually proved themselves to be inveterate sinners who put on a pious mask on Sunday morning or when trying to impress someone. I tried to convince myself their failings were because they were weak, only human. I wanted to believe that the basic underlying doctrines were sound and, if I resisted temptation, I could be a good Catholic.

Unfortunately, the more I read, the shakier the foundation of the belief structure seemed to get. With time, I came to the conclusion that the teachings and dogma of the Catholic Church were illogical, unsupported by fact, full of inconsistencies, made absurd claims and suggested a less-than-forgiving God. In short, it was all crap.

I did not tell my dad to his face until many years later, the day I graduated with my Ph.D. He lamented that I had become a scientist and lost the faith. I responded that I had become a scientist and gained enough self-confidence to tell my dad he was full of it!

In fact, the only person of authority that I *did* tell was Aunty Rita. And you know what? She didn't give me grief about it. Not then, not ever. She respected my conclusions and said I should follow my heart, that being a good person was much more important than uncritical belief. Her one request was that I try to maintain an open mind and not condemn or judge others with different beliefs. I've tried to do that. I truly don't judge individuals, but over the years my beliefs have extended to all formal religions.

Damned if I know if there is a god. But I'm definitely anti-religion. As far as I'm concerned, organized religions are simply money/power structures concerned with the control of the masses.

§

FOR ALL THAT SHE HAD a hole in her head, Aunty Rita was a pretty 'together' nun. She had a practical understanding of human nature and, although idealistic in the sense that she believed anyone could better themselves if willing to make the effort, she had no delusions. She knew that both weakness and true evil ruled the souls of some human beings. Aunty Rita was pretty quick on her mental feet. She adapted to local conditions quickly.

Just after my wife and I bought our first house in the summer of 1974, we were entertaining two other young couples. You know, a few beer for them, do the barbecue thing, listen to some tunes. Our house was in a small rural community, Blezard Valley, about 25 kilometers outside of Sudbury. Our backyard butted against a huge potato field. Very rural, very peaceful.

After a tour of the local scenery and a once-through of the new house, one of the husbands, Ken, pulled out an 8mm porn flick that he had just acquired. These films were extremely rare and illegal contraband in those days, so the illicit titillation was the biggest attraction. He suggested we check it out. I dug out my projector and in short order the wall of the living room was writhing with the images of sex. I have to admit we grew bored very quickly; after all, sex is a participation sport, in my view. For a laugh, I turned on the t.v., dialed the picture to black and focused the film on the screen. It was hilarious. Listening to the audio while watching the graphic sex, it was uncanny how often dialogue on t.v. could be interpreted as veiled comments about the action taking place.

Right in the midst of this silliness the doorbell rang. I flipped the projector off and went to the door, which opened into the living room of our little bungalow. There stood Aunty Rita.

"Hi, Dutchy. I happened to be in the area and thought I would stop for a minute and say hello, maybe get a look at your new home. I hope I'm not interrupting anything."

"No, no, Aunty. We were just sitting around watching a bunch of porno movies."

Well, what a reaction! Not from Aunty Rita, from my wife. She went beet red and said, "Iggy! As if you just say that to a nun. My God, what will she think!"

Aunty Rita, on the other hand, laughed and asked, "Are they any good?" She's always had such an open, hearty laugh.

After introductions all around, she informed us that she really only had a few minutes. Her ride would be back shortly. We gave her a quick tour of the house, chatted a bit, then her ride was waiting for her.

As she was about to leave, she turned to Ken, whom we had identified as the source of the film, and asked, "Do you watch a lot of porno films? Because I can put you in contact with a fellow in White River that supplies them. I'm told his prices are quite reasonable."

Remember, this coming from a nun in full habit. Ken, a little nonplussed, quickly assured her that he didn't, but thanks for the offer.

"Well, if you change your mind, have Dutchy get hold of me." With that, and kisses for my wife and me, she was out the door.

§

AUNTY RITA WAS a truly remarkable woman. She's one of a few people that I would even consider describing as holy, if that very term doesn't demand the existence of a god. She worked for years at L'Arche House in Sudbury, a home and community center for Mentally Retarded adults. No one could have been kinder, more supportive, more genuinely loving than my aunt. She never seemed to run out of patience and encouragement.

At the other end of the spectrum, she was one of only three women who could verbally put my dad in his place. Precious few even dared try. The other two were my dad's sister, Gertie, and my mother, but I'll get to them in the next section.

My father was six-foot-three and, after putting on some beef by working in the mine for a while and getting married, pretty solidly built. He was no man-mountain, mind you, but he wasn't a weakling either. Add to that his unshakable Catholicism, his black-and-white view of right and wrong, his personal discipline and his overblown sense of responsibility, he presented a formidable opponent. One that few of either sex were willing to challenge.

I'm not familiar with how the system operates today, but when my aunt entered the convent, rules were quite strict. New members of the order, until their final vows, could leave the convent only in extreme circumstances and could not receive visitors outside the immediate family. Even family could only visit on a very few specific dates. These new recruits left the convent only under supervision. After final vows, the new nuns were still restricted for several years. They could go to visit family, unaccompanied, for a few days once a year.

> *As far as I'm concerned, this was all about control. Once a girl had been drawn into the fold, the power structure wanted to minimize contact with the outside world until she had been well indoctrinated. More freedom was extended as they became confident the propaganda had taken firm root. End of rant.*

A year or two after taking her vows, a young Aunty Rita arranged a few days away from the convent to visit members of her family at their cottage. Other members were invited to drive out and visit her there. Please forgive me. I do not recall which lake or even which relatives. This was August of 1956 and I was six years old.

My parents took my two sisters at the time and I to spend an afternoon at the cottage with Aunty Rita. The sky was overcast and rain had been falling intermittently since the previous afternoon. Everything was damp, a little clammy, but the temperature was pleasant enough that a sweater was plenty.

As is usual for kids of all ages, after the initial attention from the adult relatives upon our arrival, we soon bored of the adult conversation. We asked if we could go outside. Dad checked to make sure it wasn't raining, then delivered the requisite lecture about not getting our clothes dirty and staying away from the water. Naturally, once out of his sight, we almost made a beeline for the water's edge.

The cottage didn't have a beach. The water was, actually, a couple of feet deep where it met the shore. A wall of railway ties had been erected to protect the embankment from erosion. We spent some time skipping stones out into the lake, chasing each other around playing tag and looking for birds' nests. Then it was time to walk along the top of the wall of railway ties.

Sure, you see it coming. The rain had made the wood very slippery. Even though the ties were plenty wide for my little feet, I had taken only a couple of steps along the wall when my feet went out from under me. Odds being what they are, it was fifty-fifty that I land on the ground or in the drink. Splash! I went in sideways so I was drenched head to foot. When I got my feet under me, the water was only up to my chest. One heave and I was out. Total elapsed time about 8 seconds.

I drifted my way back to the cottage, trailing that wonderful squishing sound from my shoes. I was in no real hurry to meet my fate, so I took my time. Dad, informed by my sisters who had run ahead, greeted me on the porch. He was so angry, he started to tear a verbal strip off me. You know, the patented parents' rant that starts,

"Didn't I tell you not…" *or*

"What part of don't go near…" *or*

"Look at your good clothes…" *or*, especially for me,

"All we need is for you to get pneumonia on top of ruining…"

Before he could get too far into it, Aunty Rita came out with a blanket, wrapped me in it and escorted me in to sit by the fire. My dad didn't skip a beat.

"We'll get you out of these wet clothes and keep you warm here until they are dry," Aunty Rita said softly. Then, turning to dad, she said, "Okay, Luke. Enough! Look at him. I'm sure he gets the point."

My dad, obviously still angry, opened his mouth to continue, but she cut him off.

"Luke, he's a little boy. And you're a grown man. Act like it! It's only water, for heaven's sake. Let it go."

Then she added in sterner, threatening tones, "Or do I have to tell Dutchy some of the many stories about the trouble you knowingly got into at much older ages than his?"

Dad looked like an inflated doll that had sprung a leak. His attitude was subdued toward me for the rest of the visit and I *did* get a short lecture in the car on the way home. But for a while I enjoyed the warmth of the fire and the warm tea with lots of milk that Aunty Rita made me.

§

IN THE YEARS immediately following the death of my mother and my dad's subsequent remarriage, Aunty Rita was reassigned to Marymount College, the English Catholic girls' high school in Sudbury. Although we could drop in to see her anytime, with a little notice, the administration much preferred that local family members use the specific days each month set aside for visitation. In addition to the regular classrooms, the college had a number of small rooms where music lessons and practice took place and smaller rooms yet for personal instruction. Visitors were assigned one of these rooms based on the size of their group.

I remember one visit on a Sunday in the winter of 1963 when I was thirteen. The family was shown to one of the larger music rooms, since all ten of us were there: dad and his five, step-mom and her three. We had quite a pleasant visit, albeit a little hard on the Fay kids. We were always quite active and didn't respond well to sitting quietly for very long. And that's what these visits were for the kids—a few hours of sitting quietly in our good clothes on chairs that were not very comfortable.

Dad was just beginning to make noises about it being time to leave when a nun quite a bit younger then my aunt knocked and stuck her head in. She smiled and waved at us, and beckoned to my Aunty Rita. She conferred with my aunt at the door and then left. The young nun was the younger sister of Dave Keon, a star NHL hockey player for the Toronto Maple Leafs. We had met her a number of times before. Knowing that my dad was a huge Leafs fan, she had stopped by, with her brother's permission, to invite the two of us to go next door and meet him.

Aunty Rita sat down beside me and asked if I'd like that and I grinned, saying I sure would.

"Okay. You and your father come with me," and she got up.

My dad quickly nixed the idea. "Mr. Keon is here to visit his sister and we are not going to intrude on his time with her."

"Luke, we will not be intruding. He would not have agreed and extended the invitation if he didn't want to do it."

"Rita, you know he was just being polite and accommodating his sister."

"I know no such thing. But I do know his sister. She would never impose on her brother. Her coming to invite you means that it's okay. So, come on." She reached and took me by the hand.

"Rita, I just said we're not going. Dutchy, sit down."

Aunty Rita stiffened, still holding my hand, and looked him square in the face. "I don't remember asking your permission," in clipped tones. "Stay here, if you want. Come on, Dutchy."

And away we went. Of course, dad stuck to his guns and stayed behind.

I got Dave Keon's autograph. You know, he was a lot smaller than I had imagined.

Aunty Gertie

JUST A YEAR YOUNGER than my father, Aunty Gertie had an extremely close relationship with him, not unlike that between me and my younger sister, Christine. They shared similar interests and attitudes, particularly a love of music, were equally disciplined and hard-working, and were unconditionally supportive of each other.

She was a great lady, one tough broad and my favorite aunt on dad's side of the family. In truth, she was like a female version of dad and, as with him, you didn't want to come up on the opposite side from her on an important issue. She'd run right over you. She was very feminine, but when need be, she had no problems getting her hands dirty. During the Second World War, she worked underground alongside my dad, as a miner.

Because of their relationship, she could speak her mind with impunity and she didn't let him get away with anything that she considered to be bull. She would correct him, challenge him and even dress him down when she felt it was necessary. Dad might argue his case, but was never offended by what she had to say, knowing how it was intended.

§

AUNTY GERTIE WAS one of the kindest people I've had the pleasure to know. She was always helping someone, particularly family members. She took care of me a lot during my mother's illness and for a short time after her death. I remember her bringing me a different flavor of milkshake each day for lunch when I was sick in bed. At the age of eleven, I was old enough to stay home alone, but she checked on me a couple of times a day. She lived just up the street. The visits were a little dicier when she was at work, but Mr. Palumbo, her boss at the Levack Drug Store, was a good friend of my mother's and made allowances.

I was home with pneumonia yet again two weeks before Christmas, mom having died that autumn. Pneumonia being relatively serious, I couldn't be left alone, so I spent the days at Aunty Gertie's and dad picked me up on his way home from work.

She was wrapping gifts that particular afternoon. She always seemed to know the exactly right gift for anyone on her list. When she was just about finished, she hauled out four huge dolls, almost three feet tall, and told me I had to keep them secret. Two of the dolls were for her twin daughters and the other two were for my sisters, one a year older than me and the other a year younger. The dolls made noises, blinked their eyes and they walked beside you if you held their hand as you walked. My sisters were going to love them!

The first thing I did when I got home, of course, was tell them what they were getting from Aunty Gertie for Christmas. I swore them to secrecy and stressed that they had to act surprised when they opened them. They were so excited, they had a hard time going to sleep at bedtime. You'd think it was Christmas Eve.

Two weeks later, Christmas morning, I was much recovered and, after opening gifts at home, we went to Aunty Gertie's. Dad was already feeling morose, it being our first Christmas without mom, and was anxious to get out of the house.

Standing across the room from me, Aunty Gertie watched as all the kids unwrapped their gifts. When my sisters received their huge gifts, they tried, but neither had any talent as an actress. Even I wasn't fooled and my aunt most certainly wasn't. Her face went slack as she realized I had given up our secret. She slowly raised her eyes and stared at me without emotion. She didn't say a word. She didn't have to. I felt like such a worm. I had betrayed her trust and I had absolutely no excuse. If I could have shrunk out of existence, I would have. I've never been so ashamed.

Dad noticed the nonverbal communication and asked what was up.

"Don't worry about it, Luke, this is between Ignatius and me." She used my full name! Dad and I both understood how serious the situation was and he recognized pursuing it with her would be fruitless.

In all the years since, neither of them has ever brought the incident up. And I can honestly say never once, since that time, have I divulged something that I knew was a secret, no matter how seemingly insignificant. It became a matter of principle.

Mom

THE ONLY OTHER WOMAN who seemed to have influence over my dad was my mother, Azilda. She had a much more reserved character than Aunty Gertie, unobtrusive, tending not to make waves. But when something ran afoul of her belief systems, she could be every bit as stubborn as my dad. Being raised by such a pair, it is no wonder that my sisters and I have more than a little stubbornness of our own.

Anyway, one thing mom couldn't abide was a man that drank too much and, as a result, treated his wife and family poorly and shirked his responsibilities. She had no intention of allowing that kind of behavior from her husband, so she nipped in the bud any tendency in that direction. She did not object to responsible social drinking at parties or with family and friends, and she herself enjoyed the odd beer on a hot summer day, but drinking to the point that you could not function was unacceptable.

Once, early in their marriage, my dad stopped for a few beer with the boys after working day shift at the mine. A few led to a few more, then to a few more. According to my mother, when he got home well after dark and long past supper, he was not quite falling down drunk. He had, after all, staggered home on his own (he walked to and from work everyday). He was reeling, however, had difficulty standing, slurred his words and was close to incoherent.

So she refused to let him in the house. She locked him out, telling him to sleep on the lawn, which he did. This was in late September; although not really cold, still quite uncomfortable. He never came home in that condition again.

Mom had another effective weapon, although this one was not necessarily an asset. She had inherited a tendency towards melancholy and moodiness from her father. In fact, her father's bouts of depression were so severe that he eventually took his own life. A younger half-brother, Billy, suffered the same torment, eventually to the same end.

When she became upset with dad, she would first ream him out, then stop talking to him. Ignoring him for as much as a week during one of these episodes was not uncommon. Dad hated that. He was a talker, quite gregarious, and the silent treatment was a real punishment.

§

MOM DIED OF CANCER in September 1961, when I was eleven. Being so young, I can't say I knew her well and I have, sadly, few concrete memories of her. When you are a kid, you are more focused on living your young life than developing a relationship with your parents or chronicling their lives. I think I knew mom better, however, than my sisters did because I spent so much time sick at home.

When you are ill, even if it's serious, you can only rest so much. So she would let me get out of bed for short periods and I would sit and talk to her while she worked.

In my most vivid memories of mom, she is wearing one of her one-piece peasant dresses with the tiny floral motif and a cardigan sweater. She had three of these sweaters almost identical—one pale blue, one gray and one gray-blue. No fashion plate, my mom.

In these memories, she is usually doing something related to food. She might be spreading Kraft Velveeta® process cheese in celery sticks, rolling dough for pies, preparing cheese and bacon on open hamburger buns for supper. I suppose, linking your mother to food in the days when most meals were made from scratch at home is only natural. While we talked and I watched, I learned a few of her secrets.

For instance, she was making pies one afternoon, don't ask me what kind. I noticed that she always rolled her crust, both upper and lower, quite a bit bigger than needed, leaving her with quite a bit of overlap to trim. The remnants she put off to the side.

"Mom, if you used a little less dough, you'd have less waste when you trim your pies."

She smiled at me and said, "Don't you like pets-des-sœurs?"

For those of you unacquainted with this delicious pastry, it is made by buttering a rolled out portion of dough, covering it with brown sugar and cinnamon, and rolling it together to make what resembled a fat cigar. This was cut into one-inch thick segments so that you ended up with what looked like chunky pinwheels. Then they were baked on a cookie sheet. These little pastries were heaven and we, the kids, didn't just bite into them and gobble them down. We savored the treat, slowly unwinding the coil and eating a bit at a time.

"Mom! Of course I do. You know that."

"Well, they were first invented as a way of using up leftover pie dough. You're not supposed to use fresh dough. So, the less leftover dough, the fewer pets-des-sœurs."

Made sense to me.

She had a number of those sorts of tricks. One of my favorites was the caramel sauce she made from one of her mother's recipes. Very occasionally in our family, a cake lasted longer than expected and went stale. Once it got hard, no one wanted the eat it, except perhaps the icing. The caramel sauce was designed to save these stale remnants from the garbage. It was served hot over the stale cake, soaking and softening. We loved it. Sadly, there never seemed to be enough stale cake!

In the last year or so of her life, stale cake began appearing more often. I really didn't question it, attributing it to the general upheaval in our day-to-day lives caused by her illness. During another bout of pneumonia that kept me home from school, I discovered the reason.

She had developed the habit, every second or third time she made cake, of baking an extra pan that she did not ice. She would put it on the top shelf of the cupboard and leave it there until it was stale enough to need rejuvenating with her magic sauce. What a sweetheart!

§

I ALSO HAVE STRONG memories of playing darts with mom in the basement of the house on First Avenue, while she did laundry, and of shooting my bow years earlier on Poplar Street. The bow memory needs a little explanation.

Since very early childhood, I have been enamored of archery. As an adult, I came to own quite a powerful and sophisticated compound hunting bow, but my first bow and arrows were pretty primitive. I got them when I was eight or nine. The bow was essentially a bent strip of wood with a string, the arrows were simple shafts with elementary fletching and suction cups.

On Poplar Street, my bedroom was directly across the hall from the bathroom—out my door, across the hall, in the bathroom door. The bathtub was against the far wall under the window. Confined to my bed with pneumonia (yes, I really had pneumonia that often!), when I got bored I'd ask mom to bring me the bow and arrows. I'd shoot the three arrows from a sitting position in bed, through the two open doors and stick them on the window above the tub. The arrows didn't stick very well unless I licked the suction cups. Then they made a popping sound when pulled from the pane. The bow was so weak that the window was in no danger. Every few minutes, while going about her business, mom would stop, collect the arrows and bring them back to me. This would go on until one of us tired of the game.

Of course, in my mind I wasn't shooting windows. My arrows impaled a wide assortment of wild animals and bad people, as I variously took on the roles of hunter or avenger.

§

MY MOTHER BECAME ill shortly after giving birth to Rosanna in December, 1960. We were living at 13 First Avenue, which had two bedrooms and a bath on the second floor; living room, kitchen and dining room on the main floor; full basement. My three sisters shared the larger room upstairs, a little crowded, and I had the other. My dad had modified the dining room to make a bedroom for him and mom just off the kitchen. Rosanna came home and moved into a crib set up in my room, the only logical place, and we proceeded to get to know each other.

In the early stages of the illness, the local clinic doctor decided it was psychosomatic, what many doctors pejoratively called 'bored housewife syndrome.' As she got worse and the pain became obvious to everyone, my father lost faith in that diagnosis and took her to see specialists in Sudbury. Over a period of weeks and many tests, they determined that she had cancer of the left lung and shoulder. Both she and dad were smokers.

Mom deteriorated significantly in those weeks. The pain reached a level that she could no longer sleep with dad. Just his rolling over caused her pain, but dad was also prone to body jerks in his sleep, which made the situation unbearable. I was moved out of my double bed upstairs to the couch, so mom could have my bed. That was very strange. I felt privileged that my bed was used to give her some comfort. Conversely, to come home after school and hear her moaning in agony or sobbing from my bedroom was heart wrenching. Sadly, that is one of my most vivid memories of mom.

Midsummer, mom was referred to Princess Margaret Hospital, the cancer specialists in Toronto. There she was subjected to intense radiation therapy. Dad would drive down every weekend to visit her. Half the time he would take some of the kids, the three girls one weekend and me another. Our last trip together was particularly memorable for me.

To begin, we ran into a sudden downpour just south of Barrie, Ontario, the likes of which I haven't seen since. Until half an hour earlier, the day had been beautiful—warm, hardly a cloud in the sky. Clouds rolled in over a matter of minutes and the air cooled noticeably, although it didn't actually get cold. We were on a long stretch of highway hemmed by the straight rows of cultivated young pine trees when we saw the rain.

We could have been in a science fiction movie. Cars approaching at a distance were being consumed from behind by a gray wall of water that towered into the sky. We watched as perfectly dry pavement disappeared into that wall. Not a drop of rain hit our '53 Chev before the wall made contact with the front bumper and we watched that wall of water move steadily over the hood, up the windshield, over the roof and down off the trunk. We couldn't see the hood ornament at the front of the car!

Dad stopped the car right where we were, convinced all the other drivers would do the same, lacking visuals to let them safely pull over. There was no wind, the water falling perfectly straight down. We came out the other side of the storm exactly the same way and watched the wall of water recede into the distance behind us. The highway was littered with vehicles sitting squarely in their lanes and beginning to move again. Ten minutes later, the sun was out and the pavement was dry once more.

We stayed at the home of friends, the McAuleys, in Richmond Hill. Mom signed out of the hospital for the weekend and stayed with us.

Man, was she burnt! The entire left side of her torso, front and back, looked like a slab of well-done beef on a barbecue. I knew it must hurt because I felt pain just looking at it. She was in agony all the time; she even had to sleep in a sitting position because lying down was too painful. Every movement caused her to wince involuntarily.

The McAuleys had a son and a daughter around my age. To ease tension and take my mind off mom for a while, Mr. McAuley suggested that the 'boys' take in a semipro baseball game Saturday night. My first baseball game, I enjoyed it as much as I could, given the circumstances particularly the events earlier in the afternoon. I did, however, come away with the belief that watching the game live was infinitely better than sitting in front of the t.v. To this day, I'm not a fan of baseball on t.v., but get me to the field…

Earlier Saturday afternoon, mom and I had gone for a short walk together. We made small talk about the storm, about how I was doing in school, about how Rosanna and I were doing sharing my room. Even as young as I was, I could tell she had something on her mind, that she was just keeping me talking while she decided what she was going to say. We sat down on a bench in the empty play area of the local public school, her face contorted in pain as she eased down.

"I need to tell you something. You may be too young to fully understand, but I'm hoping in the future it will make more sense to you. I can't do this anymore. Taking these treatments, I just can't anymore. The pain is too much. The pain of the radiation is worse than the cancer. So I quit. I'm not going to fight anymore. I have no more fight left. I wanted you to know. I don't want you to feel I am abandoning you. That's the last thing in the world I would do. But I am no good to anyone like this—not to you, not to your father, not to myself. I have to ask you a favor, though—you mustn't tell anyone else. The girls and your dad especially would not understand. You may not understand right now, but I believe you will accept my decision."

Everything that came to me to say to her boiled down to, "I love you, mom. I know it hurts. And I won't tell anyone." Not entirely true—I told my sisters when I was in my fifties, and then only those I thought would understand.

I wanted to hug her, but I knew how painful that would be. So we sat quietly for a while, holding hands. Then we slowly walked back to the McAuley's. She never took another radiation treatment.

Dad and I drove home on Sunday. The next Thursday, after school, I was in the ball field playing pee-wee with Ricky Cormier when my Aunty Gertie showed up. She had been crying and, speaking in low tones, she told me my mom had died earlier that day and that I should come home with her. I was surprised later, upon reflection, that I didn't cry. On the way home, Danny Hall shouted from up the street,

"Hey, Iggy, wanna come over and play Batman?"

"I can't. I gotta home. My mother is dead."

Just like that, no tears. And through the next week and half, I was dry-eyed through the visits from relatives, the exposure at the funeral home, the funeral mass, the grave-side ceremony and burial, the family breakfast after the funeral. No tears. My dad and my sisters cried nearly nonstop.

Two weeks later, a fine evening after supper, I was playing chess next-door with Ricky Cormier. We were sitting halfway down the steps of the front porch with the chess board between us on the step above. Ricky's parents were sitting on the porch itself, talking quietly and drinking tea. It suddenly occurred to me that I would never, *never* sit on the porch in the evening with my mother again. And just that once, the tears came.

Rough and Tumble

DAD DIDN'T PLAY with us much when we were kids. Not that he neglected us. He put up swings, made a sandbox, that sort of thing, but he didn't play catch or baseball. We didn't go hiking together or biking. And as we got older, old enough to take on responsibilities, most of the time we spent together we were doing some sort of work around the house. The only times I remember him actually playing with us was when we were quite small and still living on Poplar Street. One game, which he seemed to enjoy and played with us repeatedly, I not only remember well, but played often with my own girls to similar effect.

He would come in from work and we'd rush to the back door to greet him, jumping at him and hanging on. He would pretend we were too heavy and fall to the kitchen floor with us all over him. The wrestling match would begin. Climbing all over him, we'd try to pin him down and he would try to get out from under, hold us down and tickle us. When he let go of one of us for a second, we would scramble away. At the last moment, when we thought we were free, he would reach out and grab an ankle, a wrist, whatever and pull us back into the pile.

The roughhousing took up much of the kitchen floor. When he felt it was time to call a halt, the pile of writhing bodies would somehow make its way back to the head of the stairs without us kids noticing.

The stairs on Poplar Street went down four steps from the kitchen to the back door and a landing, where they took a left and went down eight or nine fairly steep steps to the basement. When he had maneuvered us to the head of the stairs, he would contrive to make it look like we pushed him and he'd fall down the stairs. And he never came to rest on the landing. Oh, no! His 'momentum' was always great enough to carry him around the corner and down, all the way to the basement. He would lie there unmoving in a contorted pile at the bottom of the stairs.

This was great fun! Watching him fall so theatrically, we would laugh and go down as far as a landing to watch him. But then he didn't move. In the compressed time frame of childhood, what was only a few seconds seemed like a very long time that he didn't move. The laughter would taper off and we'd begin to call "Dad?" tentatively. Then, we became more urgent and Margaret's face would begin to scrunch up preparatory to bursting into tears.

At that point, my mother would yell from the kitchen, or living room, wherever she was, "Get up, Luke! You're scaring the kids!" And dad would unwind himself and come upstairs, scooping up a bunch of giddily laughing kids on the way.

I always wondered why we didn't clue in, why we always fell for it. Now I attribute it to the naivete and trust of childhood. After all, my girls fell for the same ruse repeatedly in their turn.

Dad and Me

DAD AND I NEVER did any of the father-son things. Sure, he was a busy guy, but I think it had more to do with my frail constitution. As far as my dad was concerned, not understanding my health issues in those days, his son was a wimp.

The two activities we *did* do together of which I have vivid memories, ironically, both involve the church. My dad was a member of a small volunteer group that shared responsibilities for cleaning the church in the evenings. They switched off a month at a time. When it was dad's turn, I went with him. How well I remember redistributing the hymnals, raising all the kneelers, picking up loose trash, sweeping, mopping and, eventually, polishing the floor. Man, I loved using that big electric polisher! As slight as I was, at times there was some question as to which of us was in control.

An integral part of that memory is walking to and from the church in winter. We would go to do the cleaning right after supper, about six or seven, so it was already dark. I can still see us walking down the center of the street, following the wheel ruts in four inches of snow, the snow still falling. In small town Levack, traffic was so sparse, especially in winter, we were in no danger of being run over even that early in the evening. Sometimes we'd be talking about things going on in the family, sometimes about school, sometimes he'd be grilling me in my multiplication tables. It didn't matter what we were talking about, it was great to be just the two of us walking and talking. With the glow of the street lights, it was almost magical.

§

I WOULD ALSO accompany him to choir practice. He was a hell of a tenor, well known and sought-after in the community to sing at all sorts of affairs. I'm sure my love of music, and that of my sister Christine, comes from my dad.

I would sit in the body of the church, looking up into the choir loft. The choir would form a semicircle around the organ and the choir leader. In the early stages of learning a new piece, there was a lot of pausing to discuss intonation, phrasing, pacing, the integration of the various parts and other technical details. Not terribly entertaining. But once they became more comfortable with the selection, the church would resonate with those finely modulated voices. At those times, the building was filled with joy.

I can still see dad, in seventh heaven, concentrating on his part, hand cupped over his left ear so he could hear himself. The only time I ever saw him happier was when he was jitterbugging!

§

SPEAKING OF WHICH, my dad was a phenomenal jitterbug dancer. I didn't get to see him actually doing the jitterbug very often. The dance, being a craze mainly of the forties, had pretty much died out by the time I was old enough to be aware of the phenomenon. I was replaced in the fifties by the jive.

Every now and then, on New Year's Eve or some other special occasion when a lot of the 'old folks' were in attendance, the rug in Aunty Gertie's living room would get rolled up and the jitterbug once again reigned. My dad was far and away the best. The look on his face was sublime. He was in a world of his own, not even aware of anyone or anything beyond his partner and the music. He never watched his partner, or himself for that matter. He moved, he crouched, he twisted, he spun; and whenever he let go of his partner in some sort of twirl, he never looked to find her. He just reached out expecting her to be there—and she was. I've never seen him happier.

I have it on good authority, not the least of whom is Aunty Gertie, that in the forties, my dad and one particular lady among the young dance crowd were regular jitterbug partners that wowwed local audiences. They never dated, but they often showed up at the same dances. When a jitterbug was played, they'd leave their respective dates and find each other. My sources say it was just like in the movies. Everyone else would stop dancing and form a loose circle around the couple and watch them dance. I wish I could have seen that!

Uncle Rene

THE EIGHT MONTHS following my mother's death were very unsettled for us kids. To be sure, things were pretty rocky for dad, as well, but his sense of responsibility would not allow him to share that with us. We didn't know, day to day, who would be watching us when he was at work.

We had a series of daytime babysitters and a couple of aunts took their turns supervising for short periods. Rosanna, the youngest, was even sent to live with family friends for a time.

In February, 1962, my Uncle Rene, one of dad's younger brothers, came to live with us for a time. Rene was a serious alcoholic, as were several of dad's brothers, and had gotten himself into trouble—again. He needed a place to stay for a while. He offered to come and take care of us in exchange for a roof and food. Dad was leery. Rene was notoriously undependable, but dad felt he should help him and certainly needed the assistance with us. So he said okay, as long as Rene stayed sober. The first time he drank, he'd have to leave.

Dad had a bit of a soft spot for Rene. When they were kids in late grade school and early high school, my dad was pretty meek. He was tall, but very thin and absolutely abhorred the idea of fighting; if bullied, he wouldn't defend himself. In the small town of Moonbeam in northern Ontario where he grew up, a few groups of tough kids gave the weaker ones a hard time. My dad got his share of bloody noses, bruises and torn shirts.

Uncle Rene was always in trouble as a kid. Enough so that one time, after getting caught stealing, he was given a choice of reform school or joining the police boys' club. The authorities felt he was becoming too much of a problem and needed some sort of rehabilitation. He chose the boys' club. He was required to attend at a local gym run by police officers a couple of nights a week and on Saturday afternoons. And they taught him, of all things, to *box*!

Perhaps not the wisest move, it was a boon to my dad. For a time, when my dad came home bloodied, Rene would ask, "What happened to you, Luke? Who did this?"

Dad would try to avoid answering, but eventually gave him the information. Rene then went to find the assailant. Apparently he would just walk up to the guy, no matter where he was or with whom, and say, "You hit my brother?"

And POW! Rene would hit him—and proceed to clean his clock. As I say, that only went on for a time. Eventually my dad stopped being hassled.

So Uncle Rene moved in with us. The kids were happy to have him because, sober, he was always fun, he cut us a lot more slack than dad and he could cook. No, really. He could *cook*! For three weeks, he turned our usual simple fare into nightly feasts. It was great. Dad started to loosen up and Uncle Rene was even doing housework.

But as I said, he was an alcoholic. One morning, after feeding dad breakfast and watching him leave for work, he broke into the locked cabinet that held dad's one bottle of rye. He was half in the bag when he fed us breakfast and saw us off to school. When the bottle was empty, he walked downtown and got a couple more. At the same time, he went to the grocery store and arranged to have quite an order of groceries delivered by noon. All of this, the food and the booze, he charged on my dad's name. My dad didn't have a tab anywhere—he didn't buy on credit as a matter of principle. But he was well known and respected, the merchants knew his situation and that Uncle Rene was living with us to help out. They had no problem extending the credit. Of course, they asked and Uncle Rene lied, saying Luke had authorized it.

He came home, dove into the second bottle and, when the groceries arrived, he began to cook. And he cooked all afternoon. We came home to a house that smelled like heaven and the kitchen didn't have a blank horizontal surface anywhere. I have seldom seen so much food in such a small space. And Uncle Rene was hammered.

He told us we were having a party. We had lots of food, so he sent us out to ask two friends each to come for supper. In short order, we had twelve kids eating with Uncle Rene serving. I don't recall most of the details, but I do remember it was delicious and there was lots of it. The feast was topped off by a white cake with boiled icing as thick as the cake itself!

Dad was late that evening, having offered to help a friend change the rear springs on his car. Normally, he came straight home, but Uncle Rene's presence allowed him a little flexibility. Needless to say, he blew a gasket when he saw the aftermath of the gala. And became positively apoplectic when he found out it had been charged on his name. Pardon the pun, but Uncle Rene's being drunk was the icing on the cake. He was gone the next morning when we got up.

Levack

Points In Between

Self-Confidence

CONFIDENCE DID NOT come naturally to me. I can trace its beginnings to an incident in Grade 2 and my teacher, Miss Wall. In those early years I was continually protected by my family, told all the things I could not do because of my delicate constitution and discouraged from doing anything the least bit physically challenging. Not surprisingly, I was afraid of just about everything, easily intimidated and had no confidence.

One afternoon in Grade 1, I raised my hand and asked if I could go to the washroom. Given permission, I left the classroom and headed down to the basement to the boys' washroom. I remember passing the janitor's room on the way down and seeing old Mr Malleau asleep at his workbench. I went into the washroom, did my business at the urinal, did not wash my hands and went out.

I froze, my heart in my throat and pounding so badly that I could hardly breathe. I was in a completely empty and unfamiliar room! I had never seen it before. My God, what had happened!? Where did the stairs go?

I crossed the floor to the only other door and opened it on another room unknown to me, half-full of sports equipment. I was now so scared, I was lucky I had already emptied my bladder. I went and stood with my back against the wall beside the bathroom door, eyes the size of saucers, I'm sure, waiting for something bad to happen to me.

I don't know what made me go back into the bathroom, but that's what I did after 2 or 3 minutes of standing stock still in terror. The minute I reentered, I saw something I had never noticed before—the bathroom had two doors! I had exited through the wrong door. The flood of relief that coursed through my body made me light-headed. Once I went out the other door, I was back in familiar territory and Mr Malleau was still snoring.

My fearfulness came to a head one day in Grade 2. Miss Wall had assigned an arithmetic project for the day—writing all the numbers to 1000. The idea was to get us really comfortable with numbers and their innate repetition and rhythm.

We were issued unlimited foolscap and told to take our time, we had all day, if needed. Miss Wall spent some of the time working at her desk and the rest circulating quietly among us, giving advice. Shortly before recess, when I was only at 200 or so, I began to cry softly. I would never make it! No way I could write all the way to 1000!

While circulating, Miss Wall noticed the tears and came over to ask what was wrong. Now the dam burst and I began crying loudly and openly.

"I can't do it. I'll never get to 1000. It's too many."

She kept me in the classroom while everyone else went out to recess. She talked very calmly to me.

"I have complete confidence in you, Ignatius. I know you can do anything you set your mind to."

Very slowly, she once again explained the theory of numbers. She pointed out that there was no mystery; every 10 numbers, the digits started over again. The same thing happened every hundred numbers. The secret was to decide I was going to do it and stick to it.

Then she said something to me that I've always remembered.

"Any really hard thing you want to do is like climbing a mountain. It seems huge and impossible to climb when you are at the bottom looking up. You have a choice. You can see how tall the mountain is, think about how much effort the climb is going to take and convince yourself that it's impossible. Or you can tackle the climb one step at a time.

"Put your full attention on each step. If you are always looking up at the top of the mountain and worrying about how far away it is, you can't be watching your feet. You have to concentrate on what you are doing at the moment to make sure you don't trip.

"Ignore how far you have to climb and, before you know it, you will go to take the next step and find that you're standing on top of the mountain. And you will be completely surprised that it didn't take as long and wasn't as hard as you thought it was going to be."

From that day forward I stopped letting obstacles in my path intimidate or discourage me. I didn't achieve the turnaround overnight, but it started then and grew with each success. I have used Miss Wall's example many times to bolster the confidence of someone who was struggling.

Ironically, Miss Wall left teaching the next year. I was told years later that she suffered from emotional problems and could not handle the stress. But thanks to her, I can write *way* past 1000 now.

Small Town

THE RAIL LINE running through the center of town was used to transport nickel ore from the mines at the north end of Levack to the smelter in Copper Cliff. The line, in fact, divided the small downtown area on the east side of the tracks from the rest of the town. Most residents, to go shopping, check their mail, go to the movies (in the days before the movie theater closed) or eat out, had to cross the tracks. The tiny police station sat right next to the tracks on the downtown side.

Almost in the center of town, not that far from the police station, was a short rail siding used to store rail cars not in use. It was only long enough to hold perhaps two ore cars.

One summer day, we noticed that a railway hand car sat alone on the siding against the stops at the end. After supper, Brucie Brunelle, Danny Hall, my younger sister, Gerarda, and I decided to see if we could take it for a ride. When we arrived at the siding, we were disappointed to find the hand mechanism had been removed. That didn't deter us for long. We figured, if we could get it on the main line, we could still get it going fast enough for us to hop on and enjoy at least a bit of a ride until in coasted to a halt.

Again, we were frustrated. Turned out, the siding was on a bit of a grade and the car, although only about half the length of an ore car, was far too heavy for us to push onto the main track. Now I look back and count myself lucky we couldn't.

At nine and ten years old, we were sorely taxed to push the car four or five meters up-grade, then hop on for the all-too-brief return trip. Great fun!

After only a few short rides, from behind us, an adult male voice called out, "You kids! Down off that thing and get over here!"

The constable was standing by his cruiser on the street parallel to the tracks. He stood waiting for us, stern-faced and arms crossed.

We got down alright—and ran! No logic, no thought. Just gut reaction. We didn't even consider the idea that we might not be able to outrun him. A glance over my shoulder reassured me a little: he was hurrying to get back in his vehicle. With the adrenalin-boosted speed of fear, in no time we were several blocks away, turning onto our street, no sign of pursuit. By the time he got his car turned around, he must have lost us.

Hearts pounding, we boys started to laugh just as Gerarda began to cry. She had lost one of her shoes a couple of turns back and had been too scared to stop for it.

I had no choice but to go back and retrieve it. Trying to explain the loss to dad was not an option. She told me exactly where she had lost it and, telling the others to wait, I headed back. Her shoe was still lying right in the middle of an intersection just as she had said—and standing right beside it, this time leaning on his cruiser, was the constable.

"Figured you'd come back for it. I could have brought it to your house, but I thought you'd rather talk about this without involving your dad."

I guess the look on my face gave me away because he went on, "Of course I know where you live. You're Luke Fay's boy. Small town."

He lectured me on the dangers of playing around the railway, stressing my responsibility to set an example, being the oldest. After my sincere promise not to do it again, he let me take the shoe back to my sister.

The Escape

YOU'D THINK, after the shoe incident, I'd have learned my lesson. No damned chance! In the forever world of a child's summer, the passage of a week or ten days relegated events to the distant past.

At the bottom of a six-foot slope a short distance beyond our backyard and parallel to First Avenue was an old gravel railway access road now called High Street. Beside that road ran an even older rail line that had long since been pulled up leaving just the rail bed. Next to that, and right on the lip of the much higher wooded slope leading down to the river, was a large rail shed and the stripped relic of a coal-burning railway engine we called *Silver Bell*.

We spent many hours climbing over and playing on *Silver Bell*. To this day, when I think of her, my mind is flooded by her distinctive smell, a cloying mixture of dead, dusty summer heat, rusty metal and fine sand.

One of my more interesting childhood abrasions occurred while playing on *Silver Bell*. Cowboys and Indians was the game that day (damned if I remember which I was) and I was trying to sneak up on an opponent, Wayne Villemere, by crouching along the walkway that ran the length of the boiler housing. This walkway was a 2 x 8 plank bolted to brackets on the side of the boiler.

I was the one that got surprised. He had elected to hide in the hot, claustrophobic space inside the boiler housing. As I drew near, he stuck his head and gun-bearing hand out of the opening and shot me!

I was always one for authenticity. As far as I was concerned, if you were shot while in a tree, you did not climb down from the tree, then lay down dead. You fell out of the tree! I broke my arm once doing just that.

So, considering the engine's location, I was going to fall against the boiler and slide down onto the walkway. Unfortunately, as I staggered back clutching my chest, I missed my footing and slid off the walkway.

The edge of the plank tore my shirt and scraped the flesh off my side from belt to armpit. To make matters worse, I received various other scrapes and contusions as I tumbled halfway down the wooded embankment. Another job for tweezers and that wonderful reddish-orange antiseptic of the fifties, Mercurichrome!

But the focus of this particular anecdote is not *Silver Bell*, but the big shed next to it. One Saturday afternoon, Wayne and I were picking raspberries in the large patch beside the shed. The rail spurs leading into the big doors at opposite ends had been removed with the rail line and the place had been boarded up and well padlocked for as long as I could remember. Admittedly, considering how young I was, the time span involved probably wasn't all that long!

Speculating, yet again, on the building's former purpose, we became absorbed with what it might contain now. Our heads swam with possibilities. We had to find out. The weak point in the security was the chimney-like slatted vent on the roof. If we could pull out a few of the slats…

Up a tree, over to the roof and soon we were attacking the vent—barehanded! So absorbed were we in the adventure at hand, we didn't notice the man who lived right next door arrive home with a pick-up full of groceries. Suddenly, "You kids! Get down from there. Now!"

In short order, we were seated shoulder-to-shoulder in the cab of his pick-up. Having some perishables among the groceries, he decided to get his load into the house first, then we'd all go and have a talk with our fathers.

Not being dummies, the instant he disappeared into the house, Wayne and I disappeared from the truck. We ran for several blocks, cutting through backyards and taking a roundabout route, just in case. Breathless, we arrived at my house only to find the pick-up parked in our driveway. He was smiling as he got out of the truck.

Resigned, I said, "Yeah, I know. Small town." And we went in to talk to dad.

Pay Attention

I REMEMBER BEING cautioned many times during my formative years, "You have to pay attention to what you are doing. Even a moment of inattention can have dire consequences. That's how a lot of people get hurt and even killed. Most accidents happen because someone isn't watching what they're doing. Pay attention!" Not always easy as a kid. But you *do* have to live (if you're lucky) with the consequences.

The family had gone up the street to visit Aunty Gertie, who lived in a duplex on the corner of Church Street and First Avenue. Right there, Church descended a short, steep slope barely levelling off as it met First Avenue. My sisters and I, with Bugsy, the youngest of my aunt's girls, quickly grew bored with the adult conversation and decided to go across the street to play in the trees on the rocky hill. At the end of their short driveway leading to Church Street, Champ the milkman was sitting in the dairy delivery truck checking his orders.

Bugsy was in the lead. She went around the front of the truck, which was facing downhill, turned to look in the driver's window and said, "Hi, Champ."

"Hi, Bugsy," he smiled, always friendly with the kids.

Bugsy headed across the street as Gerarda rounded the truck, turned and greeted Champ, and followed Bugsy. I was behind Gerarda. And that was when I suffered my lapse.

I came around the front of the truck, stopped and said hi to Champ, waited for his greeting, then turned without looking and headed across the street. And some kid barreling down the hill full tilt on his bicycle slammed into me. I didn't hear or see him coming. Instantly, we were both on the ground. Apparently, his only damage extended to bruises and torn clothing. I can't even tell you his identity, if I ever knew; my attention was elsewhere. My left arm was in agony and I had several other minor sore spots. When I got up, I recognized my forearm had an odd kink in it and my little finger dangled, held in place by a narrow strip of skin. I walked into Aunty Gertie's kitchen holding my arm. One look and she said, smiling and shaking her head, "How do you get so banged up when you've been out of the house less than a minute?"

She and my dad rushed me to the clinic to have the broken forearm bones set and cast, and the dislocated finger repositioned, stitched in place and bound.

Of course, I got the, 'How many times have I told you? You have to pay attention?' lecture. Worse than that was the serious crimp that cast made in my active schedule for the next 6 weeks.

The Raffle

IT WAS TIME. I was eight and ready for a bicycle. I just *had* to have a bike! But in 1958, in small town Levack after the longest strike in the mine's history, money wasn't just tight. It was non-existent—for everyone who depended on the mine for their income.

Some group at the church organized a number of fund-raisers to help the families most drastically affected. And damned if they didn't decide to raffle off a bike! Two bikes, actually, one boy's, one girl's.

The bikes were beautiful: a deep plum color, silver fenders, kick stand, bell. Best of all, they were three-speed bicycles with hand brakes. Most kids had ordinary one-speed bikes with regular coaster brakes. Only the financially elite or the dedicated cyclist owned a three-speed, the ultimate in cycling technology for kids in those days.

The bikes would be on display in the vestibule of the church for six weeks, the draw to be made on Dominion Day (now Canada Day), July 1. The raffle tickets were not cheap at 50¢, amounting to two-weeks' pre-strike allowance, which had been suspended for the duration of the lean period. So, I ran some errands for a couple of my aunts and did a little clean-up job in the garbage shed behind the Red and White grocery store to earn enough to buy a ticket. And I went every day to spend a few minutes admiring the bike.

Now, the workings of a child's mind are both wondrous and mysterious. I went through a litany of the kids I knew who had tickets and compared them on the basis of behavior, performance at school, parents' reputations and the like. This was, after all, a raffle sanctioned by the church and could be nothing if not fair and just, right? I can't tell you exactly when in this process I became convinced I couldn't lose, but I did. And I don't mean wanting it so badly that I felt I just had to win it. No. I was certain, no question, at the core of my being that the bike was mine. I even began calling it my bike when talking to other kids about it. I couldn't understand why that attitude upset some of them or why they continued to hold out hopes of winning.

My father cautioned me about becoming too attached to the bike. He spoke of numbers of tickets sold, odds, those sorts of things. He just didn't understand!

The day of the draw, I showed up proudly to accept my new—*my first*—bike. When they made the draw and began calling the winning number, I actually started moving toward the front of the hall because, sure enough, the first three numbers were correct. Of course, I didn't know that the numbers on each roll of mass-produced tickets usually began with the same series of digits. This, plus the color, allowed the organizers to limit fraudulent use of the tickets.

When the fourth number didn't match, I was not just devastated, I was completely numb. Something fundamental in my universe had changed. The Earth had gone off its axis, the sun was exploding or a sudden ice age was descending.

Looking back, I still marvel at how quickly life returned to its routine. The next day, with the resilience and short memory of childhood, I was back to borrowing my cousin Bugsy's bicycle, as usual.

I finally got my own bicycle the next summer.

Downhill

THE FIRST AND ONLY bicycle my parents bought me was a bright red Hiawatha with coaster brakes. It was beautiful! I got it for my ninth birthday, but didn't actually receive it until some weeks later. My birthday is March 30 and my dad, practical man that he was, saw no reason to spend the money weeks before I could use the bike.

When the time came, he took me downtown to Crest Hardware. In keeping with his all-pervading policy of frugality, he picked out the largest boy's bike they had in stock, one with 28-inch wheel rims.

'I know it's a little big, but you'll grow into it with time. If you take care of it, this bike will last you a lifetime.'

Picture this. I was nine and, being sickly, quite small for my age. I could not stand astraddle my new Hiawatha—not if I wanted to touch the ground with both feet. I tried. I ended up painfully hanging with the cross-bar jammed into my crotch and my feet dangling several inches above the ground. This model was one of the few Hiawathas that had the high, straight cross-bar rather than the distinctive curved cross-bar of most of their models. To stay upright, I had to put one foot on the ground with my pelvis twisted upward at a sharp angle, my other leg looped over the cross-bar, the bar at the back of my knee. Very awkward.

Pedalling standing up was an interesting study in motion. My feet only just maintained contact with the pedals at the low end of their arc, and only if I shifted my whole body to that side. So, standing and pedalling, my body and the bike were constantly shifting balance from one side to the other.

Seated, my toes again barely reached the pedals in their lowest position. This could make braking problematic at times. Coaster brakes are applied by trying to pedal backwards, pressing down and back on the rear pedal. This becomes difficult when trying to brake with the pedal at the bottom of its arc. In that position, you have no leverage and very little leg force. Matters become orders of magnitude worst if you have only the slightest toehold on the pedal!

Why all this detail about the mechanics of braking? I want you to develop a vivid mental picture of the event I am about to describe, an event that occurred mainly because my bike was too big for me.

We were preparing to move from Poplar Street to First Avenue, my parents having arranged the move after doctors determined that molds and mildew in the basement were exacerbating my lung condition and contributing to my repeated bouts of pneumonia. So I only had my new bicycle for a few weeks before the move—just long enough to get into trouble.

Poplar Street was one over from Church Street where, of course, St Bartholomew's Church was situated. And across the street from the church was Levack Public School, which I attended. A huge esker, a long glacial deposit of sand and gravel, runs right through the town. Poplar Street sat at the base of the slope and Church street ran up one side and along the top of the ridge. From the backyard of our house, a steep gravel slope led up to the back of the church property. To go to mass or to school, except in dead of winter, we just had to climb the hill.

Often in the evenings or on weekends, my friends and I rode our bikes to the school yard to play. A favorite competition was the race home. We'd cross Church Street, cut through the churchyard and skid down the steep gravel slope to Poplar Street. And I do mean skid. The slope was so steep that we had to ride the brake, back wheel locked, and slide through the loose gravel to the bottom.

One Saturday, racing home for lunch on one of the rare occasions that I was leading, we got quite a surprise. Two of the neighborhood fathers who were backyard mechanics had decided to build a pit for oil changes, grease jobs and various auto repairs into the base of the hill, using the slope of the hill as a natural ramp. Very little digging was needed, just enough to square off the base of the gravel slope, a much easier task than digging a huge six-foot-deep hole. They had spent most of the morning modifying the base of the slope to suit and lining it with railway ties to prevent cave in. By the time we were headed home, they were finished and gone to lunch.

Leading the pack, I came over the lip and headed down slope, jamming the brakes on. But I miscalculated and my feet were out of position. I was forced to brake with only the tips of my right toes holding the pedal at the bottom of its arc. I couldn't let up to adjust positioning without losing control of the skid. As luck would have it, I hit a larger rock with my back tire, jarring my foot loose from the pedal. I was freewheeling uncontrollably. Glancing down, I fought panic and tried to get my foot back on the pedal.

Without warning, my Hiawatha disappeared out from under me and I was skidding on my chest in the gravel. I had slid right into the grease pit I didn't even know was there!

My thin summer shirt was in tatters and I ended up with a pound or two of variously sized gravel imbedded in my skin. My dad and I spent well over an hour in the bathroom, while I tried not to cry or show how much it hurt and he picked gravel out of my chest with tweezers and applied Mercurichrome. (My family went through *a lot* of the orangy-red antiseptic.) I looked like an extra from some gory zombie movie.

I was surprised at the time that dad didn't seem angry and didn't give me a lecture or some sort of punishment. Later, as an adult with my own kids, it occurred to me that he may have figured nothing he said would add to the valuable lesson I had learned the hard way and the days of pain to follow would be punishment enough.

Short Lifespan

MY BEAUTIFUL Hiawatha, the bike that could have lasted a lifetime, regrettably didn't make it through the second summer. In the year that I'd had it, I hadn't grown much, so the bike was still too big. I had learned, however, to compensate and to avoid situations that demanded greater control of the bike than I had. That didn't mean that I didn't find myself on the ground on a regular basis, with the torn clothes and Mercurichrome-tinged patches of scraped skin as evidence of my struggles with the big bike.

Hills were my most difficult challenges. I not only had trouble reaching the pedals at the bottom, but I was too light and a little short of leg strength. Nowadays, that wouldn't be a problem: I'd just gear down, reducing the resistance on the pedals, stay seated and pedal steadily up the hill. But, on my Hiawatha, with its coaster brakes, that wasn't an option. With only one gear, the resistance on the pedals remained constant at all times. As I started up a hill, I had to use more leg power. Like anyone else, when the slope was too steep, I couldn't remain seated and had to stand to pump the pedals, adding my weight to my leg power and pulling down on the handle bars with my skinny arms. Even then, most of the hills on the streets of Levack, no matter how gentle, were too steep for me with that bike. Far too often, half- or three-quarters of the way up a hill, I would come to a standstill, balanced on the pedal, my weight insufficient to push it down. Then I'd fall over, to the chagrin of any driver of a car that happened to be behind me. Such foul language aimed at a kid!

A number of the streets in Levack had been earmarked for repaving that summer of 1960, plus a number of others would be getting their first asphalt surfacing. In the heat of August, the paving company tackled First Avenue, the last to be repaved.

My friends and I could hardly wait. There was nothing quite like riding your bike on freshly laid, perfectly smooth, black asphalt. The work crew was adamant about keeping kids at a distance during most of the process, as much to minimize the nuisance factor as to ensure the personal safety of the public and the crew, I'm sure.

We waited with the limited patience of our age group. True, other streets had already been completed, but all were distant enough from our neighborhood that we were not allowed to venture that far from home. For an adult, the entire town was within walking distance in a relatively short time, but short reins were held on the kids. Most of the time our limits were pretty much line-of-sight, with occasional permission to go a block or two. Tales of biking fresh pavement from kids living in those neighborhoods only served to whet our appetites.

Five or six of us, while riding home from the ball field that fateful afternoon, discovered that completion of First Avenue was imminent.

All of the company's equipment and paraphernalia, save one big machine, had been removed. The last machine, a compactor, was as big as a steamroller. It served the same function, but instead of the huge steel cylinders on a steamroller, it had what appeared to be a row of large bald tires front and back.

We quickly keyed on the fact that the operator didn't seem as concerned about our presence as the earlier crew. Seizing the opportunity, we waited until he got to the west extreme of the new stretch, reversed and started back. The bunch of us fell in behind him revelling in the deliciously smooth ride and the heat rising from the surface.

About two-thirds of the way to the other end, I was talking excitedly to the friends riding beside me and looking at them rather than where I was going. As one, they veered to the sidewalk without warning. Caught in mid-sentence, I started to ask where they were going, but never got it out. The impact! A wrenching motion threw me toward the sidewalk and I was lying face down in a heap, scraped and bleeding, with no sense of transition.

And my bike was almost completely under the machine, a convincing imitation of a piece of abstract art.

The operator, white-faced and shaken, climbed down from his perch and was relieved in the extreme to find I was really none the worse for wear—just a bunch of abrasions not unlike those I achieved in the normal course of playing hard. For myself, I was oblivious to how narrow my escape had been. My mind could only focus on my twisted bicycle!

I carried the wreck home and put it behind the garage. I waited there with it for dad to get home from day-shift at the mine. This was not going to be pretty. Just before he was due, a pick-up with the paving company's logo on the doors pulled into the driveway. The driver got out and climbed the porch steps, knocked and asked my sister if my father was home. I hadn't reached the steps, too curious to stay hidden, when dad walked into the yard.

The man introduced himself as the foreman of the paving crew. He expressed his regret about the accident and how glad he was that I wasn't seriously hurt. Realizing dad didn't know, the man summarized what had happened. He added that the operator had admitted that he had allowed us to follow him and had reversed the compactor without first looking over his shoulder. He had assumed we would stay a safe distance behind the machine. Saying that the company assumed full responsibility, he took out a cheque book and said he wanted to reimburse me for my bicycle and give my dad an amount for damages.

Dad would have none of it. He said payment was not necessary. He added that, as far as he was concerned, I had been riding where I knew I was not supposed to be, so the accident was really my fault and I had to learn to take responsibility for my actions. He repeatedly refused to take any money and, after about twenty minutes trying to convince him, the man shook dad's hand and left.

Picking up his lunch pail and heading up the steps, dad said, 'I hope you enjoyed it. That's the only bike you'll ever get from me.'

And it was.

High-impact Sport

THE BASEBALL FIELD was right across the street from our house at 13 First Avenue. Well, almost. Actually, the outfield butted against the backyard fences of the group of houses directly across the street from ours. Hitting a homer over the fence meant putting the ball into one of those backyards. The one formal entrance to the field, a gravel drive, was located in a lot-sized gap between a single dwelling and a duplex. The gravel extended into the field; not a blade of grass to be seen, not even in the infield. And, aside from grading once in the spring, it wasn't maintained. Predicting the bounce of a ball was more luck than skill!

Unlike most neighborhood ball fields nowadays, the Levack diamond seldom stood empty. In summer, the men's softball league took the field a couple of evenings a week. More importantly, the field played a central role in the year-round recreational activities of most of the neighborhood kids until their mid-teens. Technically a ball field, it served a multitude of uses.

In winter, the central portion of the field was occupied by a large skating rink. Regulation boards were put up late in the fall and fathers in the community spent late nights watering it so we could play hockey and figure skate. The scraping of snow to clean the surface was generally the kids' responsibility—you want to skate, clear the ice. The dads only did it when they wanted to water because watering over the snow made for an uneven, crumbly ice surface.

Most of the hockey played on that rink was shinny. A bunch of kids would show up, we would pick teams and play. As there was no shack, those of us who lived nearby would put our skates on at home and hike through the snow to the rink. Many evenings I'd be having too much fun to give in to cold feet. Too often, I had no sensation in my feet when I arrived home and spent 20 minutes/half an hour in the basement hopping around on bare feet, tears in my eyes, as my feet went through the excruciating process of thawing. I often had to yell up some excuse as to why I was taking so long, so my mother wouldn't know. Being quite sickly, I spent enough time ill that, had she found out, she would have cut off the skating entirely.

In the fall, we played touch football on that field. That is, until they built the high school and its football field. Complete with real grass!

Throughout the warmer three seasons, kids could be found using the field to play peewee, tag, marbles against the backstop fence or racing around on their bicycles.

During the summer, when we were out of school, most mornings and afternoons some group of kids was playing ball on the field. Generally, it was 'first-come, first served.' That rule had a little play in it, though, as the teenagers seemed to think they were exempt and had no qualms about evicting us younger kids. Thus it was one Saturday morning.

There were eight of us, mostly eight and ten years old, both sexes. With only four to a team, half of whom were occupied with catching and pitching duties, the field was pretty sparsely covered. As might be expected, these games involved a lot of running, both on the bases and in the field, and were pretty high-scoring affairs.

Our group did more running than most. We preferred to play with a real baseball rather than the larger softball most of the others used. Being smaller and denser, it was much harder (hence the nickname 'hardball') and tended to travel faster and farther upon contact with the bat.

We had no sooner gotten started that day, when a larger group of older boys, ages 13 to 15, showed up and decided the field was theirs. We took ourselves to the small set of bleachers to wait them out.

That idea quickly palled and we began to discuss other options for the morning. We had just about given up the ball idea when one of the girls suggested we play in the tennis court.

The tennis court was located perhaps 10 meters from the right-field side of the ball field. It was paved and surrounded by a 3 m high fence comprising a wooden frame supporting chain-link. The net was kept in the INCO Employees' Club situated next to the court and the ball field. You had to ask for it if you wanted to play.

We thought playing on the court was a great idea. The fence would limit the time spent chasing the ball in the field and, perhaps, make for a closer game. We had a blast.

Before we knew it, we began to hear mothers on First Avenue calling us in for lunch. (When was the last time you heard *that* in your neighborhood?) I don't recall what the score was, but we decided that the team that scored the next run would be the winner.

We had already put two out when Patrick O'Connor came to the plate. If we could get him out, we'd have a chance at scoring that winning run. I was catcher at the time.

Wouldn't you know, he hit a high fly ball that just seemed to keep going up. I came out of my crouch behind Pat and we all watched to see if it was going to make it over the fence—the first of the day, if it did.

The ball started the downward part of its arc and someone said, "Nope, too high," at the same time that one of the girls yelled, "It's outta here!" Splitting the difference, the ball came down on top of the fence and bounced over. Home run!

The entire opposing team when into cheers of triumph, arms waving, jumping up and down. Pat, as surprised as anyone else, I guess, threw his arms up and yelled. He probably had even forgotten he was holding the bat.

I was standing too close to him and, on the upswing, the bat hit me smack in the right eyebrow. The impact spun me around and the all-encompassing pain drove me to my knees. Suddenly my whole universe was pain. As most people do when injured, I automatically grabbed my eyebrow with both hands, pressing on it, and began to rock back and forth. I remember my head making contact with the fence with each forward movement.

"Oh, Iggy, you okay? Shit! I'm so sorry. I didn't see you. You okay?" Pat pleaded, as he bent over me.

By that time I was surrounded by the rest of the group. "Man, does that hurt! S'okay, Pat. Not your fault. I'm okay, but what a headache!"

Pat asked again if I was alright and I answered again in the affirmative. Leaning back on my heels, I made the mistake of taking my hands off my eyebrow. I have often wondered what would've been different had I kept my hands pressed to my head. But I didn't. From my perspective, it was a strange sight. As my hand moved away from my head, spurting blood seem to keep pace with it. Then there was blood everywhere.

I clamped my hand back over my eyebrow, but once started, the flow refused to be stanched. And now the pain set in gangbusters.

I think it was about then that Pat took off to get my dad. In the time warp of agony, it felt like he was gone forever, yet he seemed to be back almost immediately. Knowing we'd probably be going to the clinic, my dad brought the car, a pale blue '53 Chev. For the rest of the time we would have that car, there would be a huge bloodstain on the passenger side of the front seat.

At the clinic, they didn't stitch it right away, choosing to get x-rays to assess the condition of the skull. The eyebrow was indeed fractured, two main breaks and a few minor cracks and chips. Part of the bone had been pushed back and was resting ever-so-gently against my eye. The small clinic didn't have the facilities to do anything about the fracture without significant risk of damaging the eye and, considering my generally fragile health, decided that getting me stitched and stabilized was the priority. Seven stitches later, we were headed home with a prescription for Frost tablets for pain. We got home just in time for dad to leave for afternoon shift at the mine.

My mother was beside herself. She couldn't do enough for me, but quickly realized that the intense headache was the immediate problem. I spent the rest of the day on the couch in the darkened living room, trying to get some rest and dealing with the blinding headache.

I never had the eyebrow repaired. Although the bone still presses on the eye, it has never given me any problems. Besides, I have this great macho scar and crooked eyebrow as trophies.

Epilogue

This story doesn't quite end here. The stitches were to be removed a week later. The clinic preferred to deal only with emergencies on Saturday and Sunday, so an appointment was made for two in the afternoon on Friday. Mom walked up to the school, signed me out and we walked the two blocks to the clinic. Afterwards, I went back to the school alone.

The next day, Saturday, Tony Armstrong and I, and two of his younger brothers, went to the matinee at the theater downtown. In those days we saw two cartoons, previews to coming movies, the weekly installment of the current action serial and the main feature. That week, we were in the middle of a Batman serial.

Later in the afternoon, in my backyard, we decided to play Batman. Somehow, in the midst of all the rough and tumble, I smacked my forehead on the back of one of the brothers' heads—and split my eyebrow wide open again! Tony has always been amused that the first words out of my mouth were, "There goes another pint of blood."

This time around, my mother was decidedly unimpressed. She had to arrange a ride from my uncle as my dad was on day shift. Then, it took 13 stitches to close the gap this time.

And she was all out of patience and solicitude. There were no offers of cookies and milk, of a blanket to rest on the couch, of drawing the blinds to reduce the glare out of consideration for my headache. I was sent to my room to be quiet and stay out of her hair. And I was only too happy to oblige.

Discipline

MY FATHER WAS a difficult task master and tended toward strict disciplinary attitudes. My mother, the perfect foil, was pretty much a softy. As a general rule, the interaction between the two meant we were held accountable for our wrongdoings, but punishment was seldom as severe as dad would've preferred. That was true, at least, for most first offenses. Particularly blatant or extreme offenses, or repeated transgressions, received the full force of dad's sense of punishment.

The worst punishment, for something truly heinous, usually started with the strap, followed by grounding, deprivation of privileges, assignment of a particularly loathsome chores, etc. But I must give dad a certain amount of credit. He espoused, at least until mom died and he remarried, a quality that I tried to emulate when raising my girls. Once he was sure we understood what we had done wrong and punishment had been meted out, we never heard about it again—*unless we did it again.* None of this bringing up of old offenses every time we did something wrong. When the incident was over, it was over.

A good example—surprise, surprise—comes to mind. One thing that was stressed when we got to school age was the absolutely inflexible rule that we go straight to school and come straight home. If we wanted to play, whether at lunch or after school, we were to come home first, check in and change clothes, and then go out to play. And there was absolutely no stopping to play on the way to school.

Lunch was even more critical because we only had an hour, from noon to 1 p.m., to go home, eat and get back to school. Like most parents, mom and dad explained that if we were late, they didn't know if we were in trouble, hurt, or just off playing somewhere. The rule was intended to minimize temptation and the opportunity for us to be distracted or get into trouble.

Being normal kids, we said we understood and agreed, but seldom went *straight* to school or *straight* home. We tried to keep the lollygagging to a minimum, though. That way, minor distractions did not make us late enough for it to be noticeable and cause problems.

The theory did not always work in practice. Sometimes we got ourselves into situations that required less than optimum solutions to avoid incurring punishment. Like that winter afternoon when I was in Grade 6.

The shortest route to school was through the ball field, past the tennis courts and the Inco Employees' Club, and across Second Avenue. Enough kids took this route that a path was kept open all winter by the tramping of so many feet. That day, David Gillis and I got it into our heads to climb the fence that surrounded the tennis court and walk along the 4-inch wooden rail at the top. We weren't afraid of falling and getting hurt because there was more than three-and-a-half feet of snow on either side of the fence. I made it about two thirds of the way across before I lost my balance. Rather than fall sideways or headfirst, I stepped off and went into the snow feet-first, up to my waist. I struggled for several minutes before I could get free of all that snow, but my rubber boots were lodged tight at the bottom of the leg-holes in the snow. As I began to dig down to get them out, a long job, the five-minute warning bell rang at the school. My choice was to dig out my boots, be late for school and face dad or go to school in stocking feet and get the boots on the way home. You tell me which I chose. Luckily, I had shoes at school into which I normally changed anyway. The walk (run, actually) was cold on the feet, though.

Anyway, back to my example. In early spring of 1961, I'd used up all of my 'Get Out of Jail Free' cards with respect to being late coming home for lunch. I had been warned and punished and still that day I opted to stop in the ball field with a couple of friends to play marbles (we called it 'alleys') for just a few minutes. As you know, time flies when you're having fun and, not having a watch, I didn't realize how long we played there. I got home at 12:40 p.m.

Coming in the door I saw two things: a used tabletop hockey game, with the push rods controlling the skaters, that a neighbor had been promising to give us; and dad, steaming mad. Giving me the benefit of the doubt, he waited for my explanation, then told me to pull down my pants.

He went to the drawer where he kept the authentic leather school strap he had acquired, being a school board trustee. He bent me over his knee and gave me six or eight good ones across the bare buttocks.

And that was the end of it. As I pulled my pants up over my steaming butt, he put the strap back in the drawer. Turning to me, he said, in a completely different tone of voice than earlier, "You've got fifteen minutes to eat and get to school. If you eat your sandwich while we play, I think we can probably get in a quick game of hockey before you have to leave."

It was indeed a short game, more than a little awkward juggling my sandwich while manipulating the push rods. I made it to school on time, my butt still sore.

Writing Lines

I HAVE REPEATED, possibly to the point of becoming wearisome, that I missed a fair amount of school during my days at Levack Public. The impact on my life of this pattern of illness and absence was obvious in ways easily imagined by the reader and which need not be belabored here. One that was not so obvious, perhaps, was that I had a tendency to socialize during the first few days or weeks back after being away for some time. I tended to talk in class a little more than the rest of the kids. This loquaciousness led me afoul of more than one teacher, but never to the extent that I was labeled a 'bad' or 'disruptive' child.

My conclusion that this tendency was less than obvious is based on the lack of understanding displayed by the teachers and my parents. I have a Grade 2 report card in which Miss Wall wrote at the end of the year's second unit, "Ignatius is not doing as well as he could. He tends to socialize too much." My grades were mostly B's, a few A's, and a C.

The interesting thing is that the report card also recorded that I had missed 45 days of school! Really!? What exactly did she expect from me? I had been away far more than I had been in attendance. What kid at that age misses that much school and goes back committed to catching up on schoolwork rather than catching up with his friends?

As a result of this tendency to socialize, I wrote more than my share of lines. You remember lines. "All right, Ignatius. That's enough. For tomorrow you will write 100 times, 'I will not talk in class.' Now be quiet and get back to work."

By the time I got to Grade 6, Miss Mousseau's class, the maximum number for the worst offense had gone up to 500 lines. I wrote a lot of lines for Miss Mousseau. Yet, she and I got along very well. Perhaps because I was not the only one to whom she assigned lines. She even had a corner of a blackboard set aside and labeled *Chatterbox Corner*. Many times she didn't even make a point of singling the student out. She would just walk over and write the student's name and the assigned number of lines in the chatterbox corner.

My friends and I wrote so many lines that year that we formed a consortium. The first thing we did when we got home from school was tackle the lines that needed to be written that day. Those of us who had no lines to write, wrote lines for the others. We became quite adept at holding 3 pens so we could write 3 lines at a time. Some pages were pretty ugly, but we got them done.

The ultimate insult? Miss Mousseau barely glanced at those pages full of chicken scratch before tossing them in the garbage can she kept beside her desk.

Darts

IT WAS SATURDAY afternoon. David Gillis and I were at my house with time on our hands. Nothing to do but dream up new adventures. We decided to play darts in my dad's garage until something more interesting occurred to us. Before long we were bored with the ordinary game, so we decided to make things a little more challenging. Who could hit the dartboard from farthest away? On the surface, that may not sound like such a big deal, but consider that the dartboard was only 8 inches in diameter and mounted on the rear inside wall of the garage. I think you'll recognize that, once we had backed up far enough to be outside the garage, things got complicated.

If we were more than a couple of feet outside, the board became difficult to hit. Not because of the distance. The problem was the top of the door. If we threw with the usual arc, the dart stuck in the front of the garage above the door. If we threw low enough to make it under the lintel, the dart would embed low on the back wall—if it even made it that far. Only a really hard throw, with a flat trajectory, could hit the board. The farther we got from the garage, the flatter the trajectory had to be and the harder we had to throw.

Interest flagged and we gave up the game as our skinny ten-year-old arms got sore. David speculated about the difficulty of hitting a moving target and that led to the idea of playing *Cowboys and Indians* with darts.

"No question about whether or not you got shot, right?" he said.

"What do we use for protection?"

We decided that corrugated cardboard from cardboard boxes would do the trick. We took a run to the grocery store and were back in minutes with several boxes from the garbage shed. After cutting them into strips, we wrapped them in layers around our forearms, biceps, torsos, thighs and calves, and secured them with string. We looked like primitive B-movie cardboard robots.

And the game began. We separated, putting a house and a duplex between us, then tried to sneak up on each other. The object was to 'shoot' your opponent before he shot you. We had great fun sticking each other with the darts—for about five minutes. The second time I got the drop on David and hit him with a dart, it went into the back of his knee in the joint between calf and thigh cardboard coverings. The wound was shallow, but he bled like a stuck pig. So perhaps that wasn't a good idea.

We still liked the idea of darts, but these were obviously too big, too heavy. We decided what we needed was a dart with a point as small as a sewing needle. Okay, so why don't we get a sewing needle and make one? That was the easy part. Into my house, get a needle from mom's sewing basket and back outside in less than five minutes. We tried several variations, but the resulting darts were inaccurate, flew erratically and poorly. We were called to supper by our moms before we hit on a satisfactory design.

You know how, when you can't remember something, you put it out of your mind and do something else and the memory pops up unbidden at a most unexpected time? That's pretty much what happened except it wasn't a memory I was trying to find. I didn't think about it through supper and my subconscious worked on the problem. The solution was there when I went back out to play. I went to get David and pitched my idea, my younger sister, Christine, tagging along as she commonly did. Although she was four years younger than me, we had always had a special bond, so she was often a part of what I was doing.

David agreed my idea should work, so we got to it. Got your pencils and paper ready? Here's the secret to the ultimate homemade dart.

Take a small sewing needle with a small eye and thread about forty centimeters of sewing thread so it hangs in two twenty centimeter lengths. Take a wooden matchstick and put a dab of epoxy at one end. Press the eye end of the needle into the epoxy and wind the two lengths of thread, in opposite directions, around the matchstick through the epoxy. The tighter you wind the thread, the better the dart. Using a razor blade, slit the other end of the matchstick twice at right angles, about seven millimeters deep. Cut two strips of paper about seven millimeters wide and twenty-five long. Put a 3.5 millimeter slit in each strip at the halfway point. Interlock the slit of one piece of paper with the other at 90° and slip them into the slits in the matchsticks. Set the whole thing aside and let the epoxy dry well.

These darts flew much farther and more accurately than we had expected considering their flimsy construction. The three of us ran around darting each other with our prototypes, laughing and 'owing.' They pinched, but didn't do any real damage, so we thought we really had something. We no longer wanted to play *Cowboys and Indians* with them, though. We decided to take them to school!

Of course I didn't let Christine have any of her own. Being just a little over five, if she had been caught with them, we both would have been in serious trouble.

The darts were great for throwing at kids in the class when the teacher had her back turned. As I said, they pinched, making the kid jump and, sometimes, let out a yelp, which he then had to explain to the teacher. Particularly funny was watching one of our friends standing in the aisle, making some phony excuse for his outburst, the dart still embedded in his back where almost everybody but the teacher could see it.

A bunch of our friends wanted to know how to make the darts, so we showed them. Then the technology spread to other classes. The whole enterprise, start to finish, lasted just over a week. Someone took the concept too far and made a dart using a large darning needle, resulting in a much more dangerous weapon. He missed his intended target and the dart embedded itself in the ankle of a girl in the next row. Not only excruciatingly painful because it hit the bone, the size of the needle meant a large hole and profuse bleeding.

An announcement the next day said anyone caught with a homemade dart would be strapped and expelled for a month. All our beautiful handiwork went into the garbage bin outside the janitor's room. Fun while it lasted.

The Fence

THE SCHOOLYARD at Levack Public, like so many other schools, was enclosed by a chain-link fence. Everyone is familiar with this type of fence: the strands of wire weave together to produce diamond-shaped gaps and pairs of wires are twisted together at the top. The chain-link is supported by metal poles that are actually pipes embedded in concrete piers with horizontal cross-bars at the top and braced by similar pipes set at an angle. On ours, every three or four sections, a horizontal pipe extended from one pole to the next halfway up the fence. Climbing the fence was strictly forbidden.

I got the bright idea one spring morning at recess to climb the fence and walk along one of the those horizontal braces. I would have been in Grade 6 at the time.

Getting up the fence was no problem. We had plenty of practice after hours when school was out. My little feet easily wedged partway into the diamond-shaped gaps. Once I got to the cross pipe, things got a little trickier. The pipe, being round, was slippery under my school shoes with the smooth leather soles. To stabilize myself, I put my left arm over the top of the fence and, holding on to the other side, began to work my way across the pipe. I had to be careful not to scratch my arm on the twisted pairs of wires sticking up along the top. My friends cheered me on and encouraged me to hurry, before a teacher saw me and I got into trouble.

Hurrying and distracted, about three-quarters of the way across, my foot slipped off the pipe and I was hanging by my left arm. One of the pairs of twisted wires had pierced right through the muscle of my left biceps. I dangled for a moment, then reached up with my right arm, grabbed the horizontal top pipe and pulled myself up high enough to lift my left arm off the barb. Then my strength gave out and I dropped to the gravel.

Once again, I ruined a set of clothing with my blood. I spent the rest of the morning at the clinic getting stitches on the inside of my arm; the exit wounds did not require stitching. My mother, none too happy, met me at the clinic. I had just enough time to get home, change clothes, gobble lunch and be informed that I was grounded for a week before heading back to school.

I was greeted by instructions to see the principal, who informed me that picking up debris in the schoolyard was my responsibility for the next month. As souvenirs of the event, I have an attractive anchor-shaped scar on the inside of the biceps and two little round scars on the outside where the wires exited.

Toboggan

HAVE YOU EVER BEEN having so much fun that you were loathe to stop for anything, even to answer the call of nature? This day, the fun was tobogganing.

Douglas lived four streets farther up First Avenue, past where it turned north toward the high school. Right outside his yard was a wonderful tobogganing hill. He invited me and a couple of other boys from our Grade 6 class over for the afternoon and my mom said, "Fine, just be home before dark," which would have been about 4 p.m.

Off I went, pulling my toboggan, dressed in snow pants over my long underwear, boots, flannel shirt, parka-style jacket and peaked winter hat with ear flaps. It was cold, but not as cold as that description makes it sound. I just had trouble staying warm.

The snow and the temperature were perfect. We had a blast! Enough so that when I started to feel the need to urinate, I decided to hold it. I was not walking all the way home to go to the bathroom and I *certainly* wasn't going to ask Douglas' mom if I could use their washroom. Over the next hour, up and down the hill, the pressure continued to build to the point of being painful. Finally I admitted to myself that, although it was still early, I had to go home and go to the bathroom. I knew my mom wouldn't let me come back because it would be near dark by then. So, one more run and I would go home.

That trip downhill, I intentionally went over a bump we liked, with an unintended result. My bladder let go, flooding my left leg with warmth. What a relief, yet how uncomfortable! The upside, in my young logic, was that I no longer needed to go home. We slid for another half-hour and I made it home with the last rays of the sun.

My mother expressed surprise that I stayed out so long, as I generally had trouble with cold air.

"You must've been having fun. Now, downstairs with you and get out of those wet clothes."

In those days, in Levack at least, only the children of money had nylon snow apparel. The rest of us got wet when we played in the snow more than a few minutes.

Downstairs I went, discovering I had difficulty bending my left leg and it ached dully. Getting undressed, the cause was evident. The urine had frozen, stiffening my long underwear and making it hard to bend my leg. The stiff cloth had chafed my skin red, accounting for the ache. I hung everything on the line that was strung across the basement for that purpose, hoping mom wouldn't notice the large yellow stain on my underwear. I dressed in the change of clothes she had tossed down and went up to help set the table for supper.

Thinking back, I'd be surprised if she didn't notice the stain. And she certainly commented on the redness of my leg later that night at bedtime. Perhaps she recognized that I'd had a great day and decided to let it slide.

My New Bow

MY TENTH BIRTHDAY, March 30, 1960. I went home for lunch, one of the perks of living two streets from the school. My parents decided to give me their gifts during lunch because dad was working afternoon shift at three and wouldn't be home until after midnight. I remember only one gift. My second bow and arrows.

This one wasn't a toy. It was a fiberglass longbow just under two meters long and the arrows had real fletching and real target points. I was in heaven. Dad stressed that I had to wait until the snow was gone, or just about, before I could use it. That was okay by me.

After lunch, my sisters left to go back to school and I waited for David Gillis to come and meet me, as prearranged. Mom and dad had shopping to do before he went to work, so they left me to lock up a minute or two later, when I left.

David arrived sporting a new hat, one of the wedge-shaped felt jobs so popular at the time. No occasion, just a new chapeau. I just *had* to show him my new bow.

"Are you any good with a bow?"

I couldn't let that slide, having bragged about my earlier toy bow.

"Of course, I am."

"Show me. Hit something with it."

I strung the bow as I'd been taught and we stepped out on the porch into the cold air. Looking around quickly, we couldn't find an appropriate target. We would soon be late for school, so David pulled off his new hat and tossed it about five meters out onto the snow bank.

"Bet you can't hit that."

Thinking he was probably right, I nocked an arrow, drew and sent it right through the hat. We both gaped. He looked back and forth from me to the hat a couple of times, then said, "Naw. Beginner's luck. You couldn't do it again in a million years."

Of course, I did just that. I was nearly giddy, not because I thought I was so good, but because of the adrenaline rush of performing in front of a friend and realizing we were in trouble for ruining his new hat.

I put the bow away, locked up and we went to school with little time to spare. The consequences of his arrival at home with two arrow holes in his new hat could not have been too dire because nothing is stored in my memory under that directory. I *do* remember feeling like Robin Hood for the rest of the day.

The Cave

GROWING UP in a small town in the fifties was great for pre-teens. On the rare occasions that we thought about it, we didn't understand why so many of the teenagers were dissatisfied. I moved away before my teenage years, so I didn't experience the change of focus that, I realized later, was the cause. When kids hit their teen years, interests turned to dating, movies, pool halls, shopping, cars—all extremely limited in a small town.

At ten years old, my friends and I had no such problems. We could always find something interesting to do. Sure, days occurred when we were listless, bored. I remember my mom saying, "Okay. Stop moping around the house. Go outside and play."

"But there's nothing to do. We're bored."

"So, go be bored outside," and she shooed us out. We'd sit on the steps of the porch and mope, bored. For maybe five minutes. Then someone would make a suggestion and we'd be off. Ironically, when mom called us in for lunch, we didn't want to interrupt what we were doing to go in, sit down and eat. Having too much fun!

A favorite pastime, once we became old enough to gain permission, was exploring the forests around the town of Levack. We came to know the area pretty well and devised all sorts of games to suit the local terrain.

One of our favorite places we called *The Cave*. It wasn't a cave, in fact, but a shallow, wide crevice scooped out of the rock by glaciers and capped by a huge glacial erratic, a boulder dropped by a receding glacier. The Cave was a kilometer out of town, in the bush about thirty meters from the Inco railway line. The entrance was so narrow that, small as we were, even we had to squeeze through the opening. Inside, the space widened so that four or five of us could sit on the floor with a few inches between our heads and the roof.

I'll admit I couldn't stay in The Cave for more than about half an hour. The place made me claustrophobic. The roundness of the ceiling boulder made me feel like it was rolling down on me. And I imagined the rock shifting, closing the narrow entrance and trapping us inside. But it served well, for short intervals, as our private hideaway.

In a mining town like Levack, ore trains are commonplace, passing through town several times a day on a reasonably predictable schedule. Having been raised there, we grew up comfortable around trains. So Brucie Brunelle's suggestion that we hop the ore train and ride out to The Cave instead of walking didn't seem the least unusual.

Logistics were perfect. The train slowed going through town and exited on a long curve, only picking up speed when it hit a straighter stretch. We could hop on between the downtown and the curve, while it was going slowly. We used the curve to our vantage. When part of the train was into the bend, the engineer couldn't see the rear side of the train facing the outside of the curve. That's where we would hop on.

The trick was hopping off. When the roadbed straightened out, the train accelerated for a short distance, still not going so fast that we couldn't jump off. A little farther on, a trestle crossed a creek and The Cave was just on the other side. The train really sped up after the creek and we couldn't jump off without serious risk. So, we had to hop off before the trestle.

That section of the track ran parallel to the Onaping River. At the trestle, only about fifteen meters separated the two. The creek itself was relatively fast flowing down a steep grade and plummeted two and a half meters into the river.

We got in the habit, usually on Saturday afternoons, of packing a lunch, hopping a train and spending a couple of hours at The Cave and playing in the bush. Nothing was ever said, so I don't know whether the parents ever found out.

We ran into a snag getting ready one Saturday. Everyone that has a younger sibling usually runs into this problem sooner or later. Brucie Brunelle, Ricky Cormier and I, lunches in hand (knapsacks or backpacks were nowhere near as easy to come by in those days), arrived to pick up the last member of our troop, David Gillis, to find him arguing with his younger brother (name lost in the mists of my memory). He was only a little more than a year younger, probably the biggest part of the problem. He wanted to come with us. David didn't want him to come.

After more heated discussion, Ricky said, "Let's just go. He'll never keep up. And even if he does, he's too chicken to hop the train and he doesn't know where we're going. We'll lose him at the train."

Good plan. Off we went and, indeed, David's brother lagged behind. But he kept coming. When we got to the tracks, we had about twenty minutes to wait, lots of time for the squirt to catch up. We could have walked to The Cave in that time, but that wouldn't have been any fun. Besides, we didn't want his brother to know where it was.

David said to him, knowing full well he was dangling a carrot stick his brother couldn't reach, "Okay. If you can get on the train yourself, you can be one of us."

Damned if he didn't do it. And he wasn't the last on, either. The train came by, we lined up and grabbed the ladders on the last three cars. Brucie was closest to him and I heard him yelling, "You have to jump off before the trestle. After that, the train goes too fast."

The kid nodded, not looking too sure of himself. Well in advance of the trestle, we jumped off to set the example, but he was too scared. Damn! So we were running after the train, which was pulling away from us, yelling at him, "Jump! You have to jump before the trestle!"

And he did. We could almost see him screwing up his courage, then he jumped—a full four meters or so before the trestle. Now, I know I don't have to explain momentum to you. Suffice it to say that, with his momentum, by the time he hit the ground, the ground wasn't there and he went straight into the creek—and over the falls into the river.

As it turned out, he probably was never in any real danger. He was quite a good swimmer. But Brucie and I wasted no time going in after him. He was already above the surface, sputtering but none the worse for wear, when we got to him. We spent an hour on the rocks in the sun, eating our lunches, the three of us drying out.

In the irony of these situations, the four of us decided he'd earned the right to be part of the group, especially because he didn't tattle on us. But he decided he really wasn't all that interested.

The Red and White

AT THE HEIGHT of my mother's illness, in the summer of 1961, I was given a part-time job at the Red & White Grocery Store downtown. The owners, brothers Aldo and Evo Piccolo, were both friends of my parents; Aldo and my mother were particularly good friends. The job was charity, really, a way of keeping me occupied for a while away from the stress of home. And for a few hours, my father didn't need to be concerned where I was or what I was doing.

I worked all day Saturday and from 1 to 3 p.m. every afternoon, except Sunday of course. On Saturday I would start at 9 a.m. and work until 4 p.m. with a half-hour lunch supplied by the Piccolos. Of course, I got all the crap jobs, but I didn't mind. I was earning a little spending money and, at my young age, having a job was a feather in my cap. Friends who came to the store with their parents looked at me with envy and called me a 'lucky stiff.' So, I happily swept up messes made by customers; cleaned up broken jars of pickles and bottles of milk dropped by our patrons; separated rotting produce from the untainted; removed the damaged outer lettuce leaves in crates and crates of heads of lettuce; cleaned and reorganized the stock room. I also did a lot of the other common jobs like restocking shelves.

The worst job I can remember was cleaning the concrete garbage shed. Over time, bags and boxes of garbage would break, spilling meat and produce on the concrete floor. The garbage men would leave the spilled debris, as they do today. The rotting material created quite a stench, enough to make you gag. Worst of all was the grossly rotten meat infested with squirming white maggots. Working in there made it difficult to keep my lunch down, so I tried to do it before lunch. When I was done and the shed was spotless, however, I remember being especially proud of my efforts. The shed didn't stay in that condition for long, though.

My weekday afternoons were quite different. My sole responsibility was to hawk fresh fruit. The two teenage boys who worked at the store regularly, both sons of the owners, would set the baskets out on the sidewalk under the awning in front of the store. Rain or shine, I would tend these fruit and sing their praises at the top of my lungs. Pacing back and forth in front of the array, I would yell their descriptions and prices.

"Free-stone peaches, $.39 a basket!"

I think that specific phrase has stuck with me because I recall having to ask what free-stone peaches were. I figured the stone came at no charge with *all* peaches. Aldo explained that the fleshy part of most peaches tended to adhere to the stone, or pit, making it very difficult to get all the flesh off the stone. Free-stone peaches were bred to release the stone cleanly; they were easier to eat raw and much more convenient for people, like my mom, who made preserves for the winter.

"Free-stone peaches, $.39 a basket!"

The two boys liked the idea of having me around. They had no time for me, personally, being five or six years younger, but my presence meant they were relieved of the menial jobs. They readily gave me advice on how to do the jobs, happy that they didn't have to do the jobs themselves.

Two Saturdays in a row, the owners decided to do some maintenance and cleanup while they had the extra help. I was asked to work my normal shift, then stay to begin stripping the floors, preparatory to resurfacing. They fed me supper and we all worked until 8 p.m., two hours after closing.

The second Saturday, the boys decided they'd have some fun with the little kid. They informed me that I was being cheated. The law required that any hours worked beyond the regular eight were to be paid at a rate of time-and-a-half. Next cheque, I was going to have six hours for which I should be paid 50% more than my regular wages. I do not remember how much I was being paid. The boys emphasized that *they* got time-and-a-half. They bugged me about it all day, encouraging me to bring it up with the owner. I was entitled to it!

Just after closing, I approached Aldo timidly and asked if I could speak to him.

"Sure, son, what do you need?"

"I've been talking to your son and he tells me that he gets paid time-and-a-half for the overtime shifts and that I'm supposed to get it as well. He said the law says I'm entitled to it."

"Oh, he did, did he?" Aldo said, looking up from me and scanning the store. He yelled for the boys, who immediately came out of the stock room, from which they obviously had been watching the proceedings. When they reached us, Aldo went on, "The boys are absolutely right. And it is commendable that they are looking out for your interests."

The boys began to smile.

"So I know they won't have any objection to me paying you the time-and-a-half out of their wages." He looked at us all, smiled and walked to his office. Smiles frozen, the boys' faces reflected bewilderment at what had just happened.

Aldo was as good as his word. Years later, I realized he didn't have to pay me overtime. I was short-term, casual labor and never reached the maximum 40 hours for a week, so I was ineligible. And neither were the other boys. They had lied to me. They were not being paid time-and-a-half either and were using me to try to get Aldo to pay them overtime. The boys didn't give me any more financial advice and went back to treating me like the kid I was.

The last gift I ever bought my mother, was purchased with money earned at the Red & White. With the lack of taste and narrow perspective of an eleven-year-old, the gift I chose was pretty tacky. A cheap, light wooden tray about 8 by 12 inches, it had six matching beverage coasters. The tray and the coasters had a series of silly, pseudo-humorous sayings of the type, "The opinions expressed by the husband are not necessarily those of the management." My mother kindly pretended to really like it; said she couldn't think of a better gift.

The Sexes

THE NADEAUS LIVED two doors down from us on Poplar Street. They had three girls: Louisette, the same age as my older sister, Margaret; Beatrice, about my age; and Dorothy, a little more than a year younger than me. Dorothy was a real cutie and, near the end of our residence on the street, when I was about 8, we had begun to play together. We didn't get a chance to play often because we had to do it on the sly. She wasn't allowed out of her yard and her mother wouldn't tolerate other kids in the yard.

Mrs. Nadeau, I learned much later, had emotional problems. She would have short periods when she was 'normal' and receptive to human interaction. Most of the time, she was incommunicative and antisocial. She seemed to be in a perpetual bad mood and, in particular, seemed to hate kids. She screamed at any child that came anywhere near their yard. The local children, me included, not understanding the true situation, avoided going near the place and developed the myth that she was, in reality, an evil old witch. Legend had it that, should she catch a child in her yard, she would tie the child into a baby's highchair and make her/him drink milk from a baby bottle through a nipple. A real indignity bordering on torture for an 8-year-old!

So Dorothy and I occasionally would contrive to get me, unnoticed, into their garage where we'd play for a couple of hours. Rainy days were best. We would play with building blocks or her Mechano construction set; we'd play card games like *War* or *Steal the Deck*; sometimes we would play house with her dolls.

Of course, when we played house, I was the dad, she was the mom and the dolls were the kids. The scenarios were based on imitations of the activities of our parents. Thus, in due course, one scenario involved putting the kids to bed, then retiring to our own make-believe bed to sleep. So my first kiss with a girl not related to me was a 'good night' kiss from Dorothy Nadeau in her family's garage. I remember thinking that it wasn't as icky as I had imagined, but didn't strike me as anything I wanted to repeat.

§

AFTER OUR RELOCATION to First Avenue, I developed a close relationship with another girl a year and a half younger than me. The O'Connors lived almost directly across the street from us in one of the houses the backyard of which butted against the baseball field. The oldest son, Patrick, was my age and, although we didn't chum around, we often played baseball together. You'll recall he was the fellow that bashed my forehead with a baseball bat.

Pat's younger sister, Joanie, was a tomboy and we hit it off right away. She wasn't part of my circle of friends only because the other boys didn't want a 'dumb girl' hanging around. But we enjoyed each other's company and, for about a year and a half, we regularly did guy things—hiking in the bush, walking the railroad tracks balancing on the rail, putting a patch on a bicycle inner tube or climbing trees.

Joanie was an attractive girl of the fresh, girl-next-door type, but I don't remember ever thinking of her as a girl first, then a friend. She was just my friend, Joanie. That, however, didn't stop other people's imaginations. My Uncle Rene's, for example.

One afternoon after school, during Uncle Rene's short stint as our caretaker after mom died, Joanie and I went upstairs to my bedroom to play with my collection of plastic cars—prizes that came in cereal boxes. Uncle Rene, busy doing something, didn't notice us come in the house. By the time he happened by my room, we had tired of the cars and were laying on my bed, going through an oversized atlas my dad had passed down to me. Well! By his reaction, you'd have thought he had caught us in the middle of carnal relations. I can't be sure he really felt as outraged as he acted or whether he was just concerned about my dad's reaction. Joanie was immediately sent home and I was confined to my room to await dad's arrival from work. His reaction was somewhat more subdued, but in the same vein as that of Uncle Rene.

Dad tried to explain to me that a boy should never be alone with a girl in his bedroom. Boys were given to almost irresistible sexual urges and the bedroom was far too suggestive an environment. And imagine how shocked Joanie's parents would be if they ever found out! They would certainly forbid my ever playing with her again and might even stop being friendly with dad because he obviously was an immoral parent.

From that point on, I tried to be more aware of the sensibilities of the adults around me, even though those sensibilities seemed ridiculous. I wasn't entirely successful. My intentions being open and honest, I didn't always remember how others might interpret them. Years later, when I was in Grade 13, I had two serious lapses in the space of a couple of months. Both times I received an extended version of the lecture, updated to take in my more advanced age and its implications. My parents went on and on about how grievous a lapse in judgment I had exhibited and how they trusted me, but others would assume I had ulterior motives.

The infractions? I got 'caught' in my bedroom showing and discussing my fossils with a female friend, a Grade 9 student from up the street. Another time, I had been discussing music with the girl next door (my age, for a change) and we had gone downstairs to my room so I could play her *No Time* by the Guess Who. This incident was particularly bad as she had been sunning in her backyard and was in her bikini! What can I say? Stud muffin, Iggy!

§

I CAN'T SAY THE FAYS, my dad's family, were at all close. To say that the family was dysfunctional would be belaboring the obvious because I don't think I've ever encountered at family that wasn't, to some extent, dysfunctional. The Fays had more than their share of sibling rivalries, jealousies, insecurities and more serious psycho-emotional problems. These were exacerbated by the fact that six of dad's eight siblings were alcoholics, as had been their father. Despite their problems, however, the family spent a lot of time together. I don't mean just holidays like Christmas and Thanksgiving. They did that too, but they regularly got together for days at the beach, hockey playoff games, that sort of thing.

One of the most popular venues for family get-togethers was Aunty Gertie's camp on the Vermilion River. At least a couple of times a summer, everyone would congregate there for the weekend, to swim, play games, sing and drink. At night, every inch of the floor space was occupied by a sleeping body. Sadly, as with so many aspects of our earlier life, dad cut off our participation in these events when my mother died.

Some of my earliest lessons in sex education occurred at that camp, most in the summer of 1960. It started when Henry and I overheard my older sister and some of my female cousins whispering about something that they refused to share with us. "This is none of you boys' business," was the response. So, of course, now we had to know.

We began sneaking around, hiding, trying to listen in. We were only partially successful. They kept repeating one word as if it was new to them and they were trying to get the pronunciation right—menstruation. But we were unable to determine the word's significance.

After a couple more days of intrigue, we went to ask Grandma Fay, Henry's mom. She reacted as if we had cursed a blue streak. She pulled us over to the kitchen table, sat us down and, almost whispering, said, "I should wash your mouth out with soap! Don't ever let me hear you using that word again. It has nothing to do with boys and good boys don't use it or concern themselves with it. You should be ashamed of yourselves."

How ironic, this speech occurring as it did in the first year of the decade that would blow the lid off Western sexuality.

Aunty Gertie, having heard her mother's lecture, intercepted Henry and me as we left the kitchen. She was always a straight shooter with me and she saw no reason why we should be left ignorant so our imaginations could build implausible scenarios. She explained menstruation, then informed us it was such a hot topic at the moment because her two oldest, the twins, had just started and my older sister, Margaret, was expected to start anytime. Our reaction? "Is that all? What's the big deal?" And we went off to find something interesting to do.

The focus on sex issues led some of the older kids to contemplate other aspects of the topic. Just up the road from the camp was a bird sanctuary where all visitors were welcome. On one of our frequent trips to feed the ducks, Henry and I were accompanied by my cousins, his nieces, Pauline (Polly) and Helen (Bugsy). Henry and I were ten and the girls were eight or so. Sitting with our feet dangling in the water of one of the duck ponds, the conversation turned to kissing. We all admitted that our only experience with kissing was the chaste, family sort. I didn't consider my brief smack from Dorothy a few years earlier rated a mention. We decided we should practice on each other. We paired up, experimented extremely clumsily, then switched partners and experimented some more. Talk about clumsy! We knew the tongue was involved, but didn't know what to do with it. We didn't know how to hold each other, what to do with our hands. We compared notes and, to be honest, no one got passing marks. Then we switched partners again. No, not back to the original pairing. This time, it was boy with boy, girl with girl. Gross! Not because of the same sex thing, but because Henry slobbered and his nose tended to run when he kissed. Yuck! None of us were embarrassed, but we agreed heterosexual kissing was preferable.

Another irony presents itself here. Henry would grow up to be extremely homophobic. The whole concept was repulsive to him and he became outraged if, say in a bar, a homosexual even talked to him, let alone came on to him. Henry was also a belligerent drunk, picking fights when inebriated. The worst beating he ever got was from a homosexual who had paid a little too much attention to him in a bar and with whom he picked a fight.

We had a few more practice sessions in the next week or so, but we soon became bored and moved on to other, more rewarding, pursuits—like investigating the two cottages under construction up the road.

Mixed Family

Points In Between

Frustration

My dad, by nature, was not a violent man. He was a lot of things that I consider negative—he was rigid; he was self-righteous; he was demanding; he was judgmental; he was officious; he was religious—but he was not violent. I do not recall a single instance, prior to my mother's death, when dad acted violently. Sure, he could get angry, yelling and carrying on, and he certainly had no problems punishing his children, but he never raised a violent hand to us. A well-deserved spanking on the buttocks was the worst we got.

He was, however, like the rest of us, capable of violence under the right conditions. The 'right conditions' vary with the individual, of course. For my dad, after mom died, extreme frustration and feelings of impotence, the inability to do something about what he viewed as a negative situation, could bring out intense anger. And, rarely, violence.

This happened twice in the ten months between mom's death and dad's remarriage. Drywall in the house on First Avenue bore the brunt of his frustration. The narrow strip of wall upstairs between the bathroom door and the closet, and the wall in the stairwell to the basement, each developed a fist-sized hole for the sin of being within dad's reach at the wrong moment. And both times, he hit the wall only once.

The remarriage was supposed to eliminate the sources of these colossal frustrations—the need of a mother for his kids, his need of a partner and a need for more manageable finances. To some extent it did, but the solution fell short. She wasn't the mother or the partner he had expected and wanted; and the larger, mixed family put even greater strains on financial resources. Plus, the situation and the interactions of personalities brought whole new frustrations with which he had to deal.

I was not surprised, shortly after we moved into the our stepmother's house on Redfern Street in Sudbury, when the drywall in the stairwell to the basement developed its own fist-shaped hole. Sadly, it didn't stop there. The fact that dad's violence escalated is testimony to the levels of frustration and impotence he was feeling. Predictably, although none of us saw it coming, the violence eventually was transferred to one of us.

The argument on that midwinter evening in early 1966 between dad and Isabelle, our stepmother, began like many of the others: in their bedroom and about money. As so often is the case, the coincidence of several events precipitated the dire outcome. They were arguing about some aspect of finances and dad was trying to convince mom her calculations were in error. She wouldn't listen, even though everyone knew dad was the math whiz and she was seriously math-challenged. The disagreement reached the point, as so often happened when mom got mad, when her ability to reason, to think logically, disappeared and she resorted to name-calling and belittling.

"You think you're so damned smart, you know everything. You didn't even finish high school. Who's the one with the education? Who earns more money? You're just a damned miner!"

When mom would no longer listen to reasoned argument, dad's level of frustration went through the roof. Rather than argue anymore, and mad as hell, he decided to get documentation to prove his point. The papers he needed were in the small cupboard above the fridge, so he came into the kitchen followed by mom. I was doing homework at the breakfast nook.

One of those complicating events occurred right then. Mom had a cherished cookie jar in the shape of a teddy bear that she insisted on keeping on top of the fridge. It had to be shifted out of the way to get into the cupboard. Yes, dad moved it over, but not far enough and he knocked it off the fridge with the door. The teddy bear divided itself into several pieces upon contact with the kitchen floor. And mom immediately flew into a rage, accusing him of doing it on purpose. Now there truly was no reasoning with her.

At that moment, the second complicating event occurred. My older sister, Margaret, came into the kitchen crying. She went to the garbage can and tossed a broken statue of the Virgin Mary into the bag. Dad turned on her and, in very angry tones, demanded, "What the hell's the matter with you?"

Before I give you her answer and his response, let me tell you what had happened downstairs. Margaret, Rosanna (just turned five), Gerarda and Christine shared a bedroom that dad had built in the basement. Margaret had a small plastic statue of Mary that she kept on the dresser towards the back. Because of the baseboard, the dresser didn't fit flush to the wall and tended to rock a little when drawers were opened or closed. More than once, the statue had fallen behind the dresser. That night, when Rosanna closed the top drawer after getting her pajamas, the dresser rocked and the Virgin went over. Unfortunately, it got caught between the wall and the dresser at the wrong angle and broke into three or four pieces. Margaret, who saw the whole thing, was devastated. She started to cry as she picked up the pieces and went upstairs.

In answer to the question, she said, "Rosanna broke my Mary." In his state of mind, dad jumped to all the wrong conclusions and headed downstairs. I quickly squirmed out of the nook and followed him. By the time I got downstairs, he had pulled a bewildered Rosanna out of the bedroom by her left arm into the open basement. He started to spank her on the bum, yelling about how many times he'd told us to leave other people's property alone, keep our fingers off what doesn't belong to us, yadda, yadda. Instead of slowing after a couple of swats, he just got angrier and started to hit her harder. The spanking turned into a beating, hitting her very hard anywhere his hand would land: rear, upper legs, sides, lower back. Even at that age, I could see he wasn't beating Rosanna—he was beating Isabelle.

I couldn't stand it. By now, Margaret was beside me and we made the same decision. I grabbed dad's arm and pulled while she pulled Rosanna out of his other hand. We stood between them and looked at dad, who was heaving for breath and becoming aware of his surroundings.

"What's the matter with you? Are you out of your mind? You will never do that again. If you try, you'll have to beat me and Margaret to a pulp first."

Completely subdued, he went upstairs without saying a thing. We watched him closely for months when he got angry, especially when the anger was aimed at mom. As far as I know, he never touched any of us in anger again.

The Lecture

The house into which we moved in 1962, when dad remarried, was owned by his new wife, Isabelle. The small single-floor three-bedroom bungalow at 1291 Redfern Street, in Sudbury, sat on the corner of Redfern and Kingsley Court. It was far too small to house the ten of us, even after dad built a bedroom and a rec-room in the basement, especially as we kids grew. In 1968, they purchased a brand-new two-story, four-bedroom house at 919 Grandview Blvd. The basement already had a finished rec-room, so first on the agenda was to build a bedroom for me next to the rec-room.

Off the rec-room was the cold storage, a room made of concrete blocks projecting outside the basement foundation under the front stoop. The temperature was consistently cool in the cold storage year-round. As the name implies, we stored anything that needed long-term moderate refrigeration: fresh vegetables, potatoes, pop, Isabelle's baking, leftovers, etc. My parents also stored treats that they bought on sale and doled out sparingly: chips, cheesies, gumdrops, jujubes, licorice allsorts, chocolate bars. The cold storage was not locked, but we had strict instructions not to touch without permission, on threat of punishment. That worked reasonably well for all except Gerarda.

By 1968, severe cracks have developed in the mixed 'family.' My older sister, Margaret, feeling unloved and unfairly treated, had already sought comfort in religion. Following Aunty Rita's example, she was studying to be a nun with the sisters of St. Joseph. Christine and I made ourselves scarce, staying away from the house as much as possible.

Christine was starting down the road leading to alcoholism and drug addiction that would take her years to kick. Rosanna was just beginning a rebelliousness that would lead her, too, into alcoholism.

And Gerarda? She became sullen, withdrawn. She became fixated on comfort foods, the only things that made her feel good. She got into the habit of coming downstairs in the middle of the night and sitting in the cold storage, in her pajamas, eating candy and sweets. And no form of punishment would deter her—not grounding, not added chores, not restricted access to t.v., not corporal punishment.

In a last-ditch effort, dad built a cabinet in the cold storage to house the treats and sweets. The door was secured with a padlock. No deterrent to Gerarda. Unable to unlock the padlock, she contrived to remove the hinges.

After this had happened a couple of times, dad decided to try another approach. He brought her downstairs to his work area in the basement to talk to her. His work area and the laundry area took up two-thirds of that part of the basement not included in the rec-room. The last third was my bedroom. I don't think he noticed that my door was slightly ajar and I was in my room.

He proceeded to give her the extended version of the 'evils of stealing' lecture. After all, he said, that was what she was doing—stealing. And taking without permission something that belongs to someone else was among the worst of sins. Theft was theft, didn't matter what was stolen. Not only did theft of small things, like candy, lead to larger items and, often, a life of crime, it was a sin that, if not atoned, would result in her being condemned to hell. Did she want that?

Throughout it all, Gerarda remained unresponsive. Her answers, when she answered at all, were restricted to yes/no. In the end, he let her go with the hope that he'd given her something to think about. He would pray for her because he abhorred the idea that her soul would be condemned to hell for the sake of a few licorice.

Poor dad. I actually felt sorry for him. In this whole 'mixed family' thing, he was trying his damnedest, but he was way out of his depth. He had gotten himself into a situation with which he could not cope. If he was aware of why his children were making bad choices, he didn't have the strength of character to do something about it. Instead, he opted to punish, brow-beat or intimidate into submission.

After Gerarda went upstairs, I let a minute or so pass, then said in a voice loud enough for him to hear, "You know, dad, one day you're going to give that lecture and one of the girls is going to throw it back in your face."

He came to my door, pushed it open and, scowling, said, "What do you mean by that?"

"C'mon, dad. We're not stupid. Do you think we don't know where you get the pads of yellow newsprint that we use to do our homework? Why they are always creased from being folded in half, lunch pail-size, and have greasy finger smudges on them?"

His jaw tightened and he was getting angry. I went on, "And what about all those almost-new pencils, also finger smudged, that seem to become available a day or two after we tell you we need them? Do you really think we don't know you lift that stuff from the level office at the mine and bring them home in your lunch pail?"

His whole body was rigid now, but he wasn't angry any longer. I think he was in shock. I don't think he had ever really thought about it as theft. The practice was so commonplace at the mine that he never questioned it. We didn't get any more yellow homework pads.

Movies

AS MIGHT BE EXPECTED, the move to Sudbury entailed a lot of changes in our lifestyle. We had been coached before the actual move about tolerance and accommodation of others, respecting their space and each pulling his/her own weight. We were assigned daily and weekly chores, in addition to keeping our personal space clean. Those of us who were older were given responsibility for beginning supper preparations after school, like peeling potatoes, taking meat out of the freezer, making salad, setting the table. When mom came through the door, all she had to do was finish the entrée and we were ready to eat.

The move had some unexpected minor consequences that nettled me. For instance, in Levack I had been old enough and trusted enough to walk downtown with friends and go to the movies unaccompanied. Not so in Sudbury. The theater was quite a bit farther away and I guess I was judged too young at twelve to be taught to take the bus. Or it would have taken too much of mom's or dad's time to teach me and the other kids. We couldn't go to the movies without being accompanied and our parents were too busy to take us. Too expensive anyway. I was fourteen before I was allowed to go unsupervised.

Let me qualify that: I was able to go unsupervised as long as all the kids went as a group to the same movie. My parents had to drive us to and from the movie theater; no way were they chauffeuring us to different movie houses. The upshot of this stipulation was that we rarely went because they seldom had time to drive us. When we *did* go, the choice of movie was put to a vote. I'm sure you can imagine that my one male vote carried little weight against the five female votes (the two youngest were not of movie-going age yet). For a few years I saw a lot of the *Beach Blanket Bingo* genre of movies.

Eventually I rebelled. Arguments that I should be allowed to go on my own with friends fell on deaf ears. So I tried another tactic—lying.

The next time we went to the movies, I arranged to meet Jim Turcott downtown at the theater to which dad was driving us. Dad let us off, checked the schedule at the ticket booth and told us he'd be back at 4 p.m. sharp. We were to be ready. Jim showed up just after dad pulled away. I left the girls to watch their chick flick and went two streets over with Jim to watch *Reptilicus*, a primitive science fiction movie.

We had a great time. I loved the cheesy special effects. And somehow the hot buttered popcorn was particularly tasty, flavored with that little extra apprehension, the fear of getting caught. I made it back to the other theater with about ten minutes to spare, enough time for the girls to fill me in on their movie. I had to be able to talk about the movie with the others on the way home.

My sisters thought this was great fun, putting one over on mom and dad. My stepsisters, however, tried to blackmail me for their silence. I turned the tables on them. They broke a lot of important rules when mom and dad were not home, did things for which they'd be severely punished if my parents ever found out. I threatened to expose them if they didn't keep silent about my little deception and they backed down. Always good to know where the bodies are buried!

I only used this subterfuge one other time. We were dropped at the Sudbury Arena, where we had tickets to take in the matinee performance of the Shriners' Circus. I slipped away and saw a newly released oater, *Shenandoah*. Everything went off without a hitch. But the number and detailed nature of the questions my dad asked me about the circus made my guilty mind wonder if he suspected something. Luckily I had been well briefed by my sisters.

I never asked my dad about it for fear of exposing transgressions that he didn't suspect, but I think my guilty conscience was right. Or it may have been coincidence. But just a few weeks after the circus, overhearing me talking to Christine about a science fiction movie I wanted to see, dad suggested I go with one of my friends. He offered the opinion that I probably was getting too old to be tagging along with my sisters to watch their romance movies. I couldn't have agreed more!

Point of Honor

YOU'VE HEARD THE term 'honor among thieves.' I think it probably could be expanded to encompass a broader scope, perhaps 'honor among miscreants.' I experienced this sense of loyalty or solidarity among transgressors first hand on the last day of school in Grade 8.

The four older Fay kids who had gone to English public school in Levack were enrolled in Saint Conrad's English Catholic school two streets away from our new home on Redfern Street. My youngest sister, Rosanna, and the three Lavergnes went to the French Saint Conrad in the other half of the same building.

The weather was warm, even for late June, and we really weren't doing anything except putting in time. The main Grade 8 teacher was the school principal, Mr. Sarmatiuk, whose office was situated right next door to the class. In order to perform his duties as principal, he needed some time away from class, so several times a week his class was given over to a part-time teacher, Mr. Gleason.

Talk about a study in opposites! Mr. Sarmatiuk was medium height, quite heavyset bordering on seriously overweight, stern, firm voiced and a disciplinarian. One got the impression he had no sense of humor at all. Mr. Gleason, on the other hand, was a beanpole, well over six feet tall, soft and gentle spoken, almost effeminate, with a wonderful sense of humor. And he was a pushover. The kids did, and got away with, things in his class for which they would have come close to crucifixion in Sarmatiuk's presence.

The morning of the last day, Mr. Gleason was in charge of the class and Mr. Sarmatiuk, unknown to us, was in his office next door. Mr. Gleason was doing his best to control a rambunctious class of kids who wanted only to be free of school and out in the sun. The first part of the day was occupied handing out report cards, handing in textbooks, cleaning out desks and handing out achievement awards. After recess, Mr. Gleason read a story, difficult to hear over the noise at times, then asked a series of questions about the story. The answers he wrote on the board.

While he was writing one of the answers, his back turned to the class, one of the boys threw a small piece of eraser across the room, where it lodged in the hair of one of the girls. Taking the cue, another boy tore a piece off his eraser and threw it at the first boy. By then, the girl had fished the first piece out of her hair and threw it back. Mr. Gleason turned just in time to see this last act. He scolded the girl for being unladylike and told her to sit down and behave. A couple of the boys stood and jeered at her for being unladylike. Frustrated, Mr. Gleason told them to take their seats and be quiet. He reminded the class that it was the last day of school and it would be a pity to be sent to Mr. Sarmatiuk's office on the last day.

Composing himself, he asked another question about the story and, after some spoon-feeding, got a reasonable answer from one of the girls. He turned to write the answer on the board and the air was filled with pieces of eraser, many of which hit the blackboard. Easily two thirds of the class was involved, me included. A few kids had the poor judgment to throw whole erasers. One of these larger missiles hit the door to Mr. Sarmatiuk's office. Mr. Gleason was trying to settle us down and erasers were still flying when the door opened. The room went silent.

Mr. Sarmatiuk, standing in the doorway, called out a bunch of names, all kids he'd caught in the act, and told those students to come into his office. Then he invited anyone else who had been throwing erasers to join them. No one moved. Not having seen us, he couldn't make accusations. He went in, closed the door and proceeded quite audibly to give those students the strap. Mr. Gleason sat at his desk, we at ours, and not a word was said. When the others returned to class, some in tears, we were dismissed for lunch.

I walked home for lunch, as usual. Mom and dad were at work, so my sisters and I made our own lunch and ate. I didn't say anything about what had happened, but I was abnormally subdued. I felt guilty that I hadn't had the guts to stand up, admit I'd been involved and take my punishment. The feeling increased when Ray Halleck, one of the kids who had been strapped, met me on the way to school and congratulated me on getting away with it. Real or imagined, I sensed an underlying note of sarcasm or disapproval.

When we got to the schoolyard, I was in no mood to play. I went straight into the school and knocked on the principal's door. Invited in, I entered and confessed my involvement. Mr. Sarmatiuk commended me on my honesty, belated though it was, but stressed that he still had to give me the strap. I said I understood. And he gave me five good ones on each hand. As I said, he was a big man and he was the type of disciplinarian who went up on tiptoes and came down with some weight behind the swing. It hurt like hell! I left his office, palms red and stinging, and went out into the sun feeling strangely good.

Lasalle Secondary

Mrs. Varpio

I THINK EVERY NORMAL child becomes infatuated with a teacher at least once during elementary or secondary school. I know my sister Christine, in Grade 6, fell head over heels for one of her young male supply teachers. Mine didn't happen until I was in Grade 9. And she wasn't even my teacher!

My first week at Lasalle Secondary School, I was walking down the second-floor hallway, the one with the blue students' lockers, toward the central staircase when I saw the sexiest woman I had ever seen. Man, what a babe! Looking back in my yearbooks now, I realize I can't have seen very many really attractive women in the flesh because she wasn't classically beautiful. But she had something. Perhaps it was her hips. They certainly were among her best assets.

Women generally have one of two hip shapes—apple- or pear-shaped. Apple-shaped hips are wider at the tops of the pelvis and taper downward in the buttocks, resulting in 'high' hips. Pear-shaped hips are narrow at the top of the pelvis and flare downwards, reaching their widest where they meet the thighs. These 'low' hips give rise to the classic hourglass figure. Marilyn Monroe had pear-shaped hips. Alice May Clarke had pear-shaped hips and she was mesmerizing when she walked.

I didn't know who she was when I first saw her, but I made a point of finding out. A.M. Clarke was an English teacher and unmarried. Unfortunately she was not *my* English teacher. And I was so impressed by my actual Grade 9 English teacher that I cannot remember her name or picture her face, and I am not interested enough to check the yearbook. I cannot even tell you that my English teacher was female, but odds are.

Whenever I was not in class, I kept my eyes peeled for Miss Clarke. My health betrayed me, though, becoming particularly lousy that year and I spent more than half the school year in the hospital. All that absenteeism put a serious crimp in my Miss Clarke ogling.

The summer between grades 9 and 10 seemed to drag on slowly whenever I thought of school and Alice May. Yes, I thought her as if we are on a first name basis. Now, I'm not going to try to tell you I mooned for her all summer. I was way too busy for that. But when I did think of school, which was often, I thought of her and became mush inside.

The first thing I did, literally, my first day of Grade 10 was check the list of faculty to find out which classroom she would be in. Horrors! Her name was not on the list. For a few seconds, there was a roaring in my ears. I was disoriented and could not have articulated intelligently if my life had hung in the balance. Then I methodically went through the list again—perhaps they had put her name alphabetically out of order. Nope. She wasn't there. I was devastated.

Truly dejected, I made my way to homeroom. According to my orientation handout, that year my homeroom would be in my English teacher's classroom, a new faculty member named Mrs. Varpio. When I arrived, a bunch of students were milling around, talking, getting either acquainted or reacquainted, but the teacher was not in attendance. Upon entering, I saw my friend Vytau Krucas and went to sit at a desk beside him. We began comparing our summers. I was in the middle of a description of the work my family had done on our camp, when I stopped in mid-sentence, mouth open. The teacher had just come in and I felt like I couldn't breathe for reasons completely unrelated to my asthma. It was Alice May! I was so happy—confused, but so happy! There was an error on the faculty list after all.

Well, not exactly. Actually, Miss Clarke had married Peter Varpio, a history teacher, over the summer. This was not good news, but at least I was going to be near her every day for homeroom and for English. In a perfect universe, she still would have been available, but I would take what I could get.

In a truly unexpected twist of fate, I was destined to have Mrs. Varpio for English for the next three years and she would have far greater impact on me than just being my first wet dream. She was an excellent teacher and her influence affects my life to this day.

And she wasn't just this schoolboy's wet *dream*. As I've indicated elsewhere, I was a slow developer due to illness, reaching puberty more than a year later, in Grade 11. That year, in one English class, while everyone was silently working on their descriptive paragraphs, I spent much of the time looking at Mrs. Varpio. In the quiet, warm room, I was surprised to find myself with what felt to me like a huge erection, one of my first. Trying to hide it, I crossed my legs. Wrong move! Or, maybe, right move. The pressure felt good and, while I still gazed at her, I had the second orgasm of my life. Very little ejaculate was produced, but the sensation was sublime. That was the only time it happened, although I found myself stiff in her presence at other times.

I have often wondered if Mrs. Varpio was aware of the impact, academically and otherwise, that she had on me. Did she know the special place she had in many boys' hearts? I know for a fact that I was not the only male student that appreciated those hips, although she had serious competition from the new female gym teacher, Miss Heaysman, with the magnificent boobs and the snug blouses!

§

ALICE MAY VARPIO was far and away the best teacher I ever had. She exerted a greater influence on the person I would become intellectually than anyone else in my life, before or since, including my parents. She encouraged and challenged my already deeply rooted love of reading. She exposed me to, and sparked within me an appreciation of, the infinite nuances of the English language. My fascination with word origins, proper pronunciation and usage, and grammatical construction had their origins in her lessons. Certainly not least of all the knowledge to which she introduced me was the importance of punctuation and the subtle shades of meaning achievable through its proper use. Further to all that, she imparted to me a love of education, a desire to know, to seek. I will be forever in her debt.

I am sure Mrs. Varpio had her faults, but they must have been in her private life. She was pretty damned close to perfect as a teacher. She was one of the few who could maintain control of her class. She took absolutely no crap. A dressing down from her was in such eloquent, yet embarrassing, terms that you avoided it at all costs. Those who didn't were the hard-core troublemakers and she dealt with them in a variety of demeaning ways, ultimately removing them from the class, if necessary. She did, however, have a sense of humor and allowed a certain amount of rambunctious acting out, but the line she drew was obvious to any who were paying attention. The students who got into trouble with her usually were the ones who didn't see or chose to ignore the line. They didn't know when to quit.

I did. For that reason, I got away with a fair amount in her class. That is not to say that she didn't have to rein me in occasionally. Easily my biggest offense throughout my grade and high school years was my tendency to talk in class. Not all the time and not disruptively, but I did talk a lot. I chalk it up to being so ill and missing so much school. When I *was* there, I had socializing that needed catching up. Perhaps, there is some truth in that. I actually had a math teacher in high school, Mr. Behnke, who called me 'loquacious Ignatius.'

I remember one afternoon when I had been particularly vocal in Mrs. Varpio's class. I was brought to an abrupt halt by her turning from the blackboard, withering me in my seat with her gaze and saying, "Ignatius Fay, you little piece of inconvenience. Shut up!"

Another time, her intercession was a little more elaborate. I sat in the second row from the door, right beside Jim Lanzo in the first row by the wall. Jim was a lineman for our Lasalle Lancers junior football team, and a good one. He had a little trouble with English at times, so I would give him a hand. It was not that his mental cleats were dull. English just wasn't a strength or an interest at that time in his life.

Jim was having trouble understanding the lesson Mrs. Varpio was teaching, so I was explaining it to him. Not in loud tones, but loud enough that Mrs. Varpio found it annoying and distracting. When she realized it wasn't going to stop of itself, she pulled the plug.

"All right. Enough. I'm going to have to separate you two."

To which Jim replied immediately, surprise and mild shock on his face. "You can't do that, miss."

"Oh, really," a little ice creeping into her voice. "And just why can't I?"

"Because we're a team, miss. He's the brains and I'm the brawn."

I think that little witticism caught both Mrs. Varpio and me more than a little off guard. I rushed to explain.

"We weren't just talking. I was explaining to Jim parts of your lesson that he was having trouble following."

"Well, that's quite commendable. I have no objection to you helping each other, but not when I'm talking. When I am teaching the lesson, you will be quiet. When I am finished and you are working on the assignment, feel free. But keep it down and keep it on-topic."

We were allowed to maintain our seating arrangements.

§

MRS. VARPIO BELIEVED that, to be effective, a teacher had to be approachable and open, at the same time commanding the respect due the position. A teacher should be neither an informal friend nor an aloof tyrant. Most of the time, she maintained the balance in numerous subtle ways, but occasionally a situation demanded something more direct. Mrs. Varpio and I experienced one of those more overt moments on the last day of school, Grade 12.

At Lasalle and, I take it, a lot of other high schools, classes were traditionally let out early on the last day so the students could clean out their lockers. The janitors placed large garbage pails down the centers of the halls, but little of the debris ended up in them. The students reveled in just heaving everything onto the floor—paper, notebooks, pens, rulers, bags with half eaten lunches, empty bags, whatever was in their lockers that they no longer wanted. A certain amount of trading of articles occurred and the hall was full of milling, talking teens. So much so that it was difficult to negotiate a path through the crowd.

Mrs. Varpio and I were on our way back to her classroom from somewhere I don't recall. She was ahead of me. Whenever we got to a knot of people, she'd pause and place her hand on the lower back of a student. Most, feeling the light pressure, would automatically move out of the way. Occasionally she had to add a soft, "Excuse me."

We came up to a tight knot with Denis Tarnopolsky and two other football stars entertaining seven or eight young ladies. A big linebacker, Denis was the tallest person in the hallway, head and shoulders above Mrs. Varpio and me. Denis had his back to us as we approached. Mrs. Varpio extended her hand to touch his back and said, "Excuse me."

"Why, did you fart?" was the smart-ass comment for the edification of his adoring public, made as he turned to look. Her open palm made full contact with his cheek, instantly leaving a red print, before he was fully aware of who was behind it.

"Keep a civil tongue, young man. And look before you speak," she said as she passed. Hers was the classroom two doors farther down the hall and, as we closed the door behind us, we both burst out laughing.

Variety Night

EVERY YEAR IN the spring, the students of Lasalle traditionally put on a variety night. The students, under the supervision of members of the faculty, would write the scripts for the skits, choose the music and songs for the musical portions, do the acting, directing and singing, and help prepare costumes. This last task was possible only through liberal help from moms, faculty and the Home Economics class who were skilled at sewing. The final product was presented to the public in two performances, one on Friday and one on Saturday evenings. A nominal fee was charged to defray costs.

I can't explain exactly why, but student participation and enthusiasm deteriorated steadily through my first four years at Lasalle. By Grade 12, the variety night was entirely written and organized by faculty. The performers were still students, but they had to be coerced and became more and more difficult to recruit.

In January 1968, the usual time to start preparation for variety night, an announcement was made over the PA one morning. If the student body was not interested in being involved, there would be no variety night. Faculty was reverting to a supervisory role, so student volunteers were needed in all capacities. We were given a week and a half, until the end of the school day the next Friday. If enough students hadn't volunteered by then, variety night would be canceled.

In Grade 13 my English teacher was Mr. Powell. The week of the ultimatum, however, he was away from the school. I don't recall the reason. Mrs. Varpio was taking some of his classes and mine happened to be one of them. On the afternoon of the announcement, as I was leaving English class, Mrs. Varpio asked me to stay for a few minutes. When we were alone, she expressed sadness at the idea that variety night might be lost. She was always heavily involved. She talked about how it was a great opportunity for the students to stretch themselves, to develop and explore skills they might not know they had, to meet new people—all in all, a character building and rounding experience.

I had to agree with her and said so. She went on to say that they already had a few volunteers, but they were all Grade 9 and Grade 10 students. To make it work, the experience and leadership of the upper grades were needed.

"Iggy, with your imagination and sense of humor, your ability to express yourself, your gregariousness, you would be perfect to lead the team. Everybody likes you. You get along with everyone and people usually hear you out when you speak. I can see you being instrumental in writing, directing and coordinating this year's show. How about it?"

"Sorry, Mrs. Varpio, I'm not interested."

"I'm sorry to hear that. Would you tell me why?"

"I can't explain it, but it just isn't my thing." I couldn't admit to her that I didn't share her confidence and was afraid to fall flat on my face.

She spent a few more minutes trying to change my mind, then let me go, again expressing regrets.

But she didn't give up. For the next week or so, every time I looked up from my desk during work period in English, she was looking at me, smiling. She would nod her head 'yes,' I'd smile and shake my head 'no.'

On the Friday, as I left her class she asked if I would reconsider. "You have to do it today. This is it. Not just the last chance to save variety night this year, but your last chance. Great 13. You know you have to do it. You can't let yourself miss this opportunity. I know, if you don't do it, you'll always wonder."

That close to the deadline, an 'out' occurred to me. My closest friends at the time were Jim Turcott, Cora Falkenberg and Vytau Krucas. Jim and Vytau were in Grade 13 with me; Cora was in Grade 11 and Jim's girlfriend. All three were intelligent, creative and at the tops of their classes. As a matter of fact, Jim, Vytau and I had been jockeying to see who would have the highest mark in our classes for the last few years. We had discussed the variety night and decided it wasn't worth the trouble.

"I'll tell you what. If you can convince Jim, Cora and Vytau to volunteer, then I'm in."

"I have already spoken to them and they all said if I could get you to do it, they would do it." She had me!

Never one to shirk, now that I was committed, I decided to give it my best shot. Jim and I wrote the scripts for all the skits, with liberal editorial suggestions from the other two. Cora recruited Alana Hortness, an exceptional art student, to design the costumes. What a terrific job. She produced truly professional looking full-color mock-ups that the costume makers used. Vytau coordinated the technical crew and directed with Jim and me.

Cora was attractive, tall and slender. Dressed, as she so often was, in a miniskirt, at first glance she seemed to be all legs. And what legs!

She lived along the route that I walked to school, but I never saw her when I walked because I left for school so early. Occasionally, in winter, the cold or some other complication necessitated that I leave later with my stepmother who dropped me off at Lasalle on her way to work. I can still see the smile on her face as we'd come over the hill and find Cora walking to school. She'd say, "What do you think, Iggy? Should we give her a ride?" A rhetorical question if ever there was one! She didn't even wait for an answer, pulling over and asking Cora if she wanted a lift. I would get out of the passenger seat, pull the back of the seat ahead and ogle those delicious legs as she contorted herself into the back seat. She was always grateful for the ride. Not as grateful as I. What a way to start the day!

Once the fact that we were involved in variety night became general knowledge, a number of other talented people decided to participate. The production quickly gathered momentum. In the end, we had more help and more actors than we needed, but we tried to use everybody. We had students happy just to run errands, to be part of the makeup crew, to move sets. The pit band, led by history teacher Mr. Kurlyiw, swelled from a bare-bones combo to an ensemble edging towards a small orchestra. They did a superlative rendition of *The Peanut Vendor*.

I even took an acting part. I had written the basis for a skit about Stone Age man. When I pitched the idea, I made the mistake of acting out my interpretation of the lead for the others. All I did was act as much like an ape as I could. They loved it and insisted I had to do it. And I'm glad I did. For a number of years later, I was stopped in the street by people who had seen the show and wanted to tell me how much they enjoyed my apeman bit. I even had two youngsters ask for my autograph!

The show was a huge hit. We received all sorts of accolades and many people felt it was the best in their recollection. And more than a few were surprised that the teachers had not been directly involved with the production itself. I don't want to minimize the value of their input, though. Without their assistance and advice in makeup, lighting, costume design—almost all aspects of the production, really—the variety night would have fallen well short of the quality it achieved.

A couple of interesting modifications were made to my role between the Friday and Saturday shows, both at the suggestion of Mrs. Varpio. She took me aside after the show Friday and offered the opinion that I might want to wear something under my loincloth-like apparel. That's me—all for authenticity!

"I'm pretty sure the audience couldn't see anything, but the girls in the orchestra pit are getting far more entertainment than they expected when they joined the band."

Saturday night I wore underwear.

Just before I went on, she came to me with a personal request.

"You do such a marvelous job as an ape. Just hilarious. I'd like to see you eat this on stage," and she whipped out a banana! Just outrageous enough to intrigue me.

The banana fit right in because the ape men had a meal during part of the skit. Sitting center-stage, I made a production of trying to figure out how to get at the fruit inside, as if I'd never seen one before. After puzzling over it for a bit, in mock frustration I decided to just squeeze one end! I squeezed a little harder than intended and the damned banana squirted out the opposite end into the air. In a display of reflexes I don't usually have, I snatched it in midair and jammed it into my mouth, smearing a goodly portion around my lower face in the process. The biggest laugh of the night.

I learned a lot about myself doing that variety tonight. That whole experience is, without rival, the single best memory of my high school days. Thank you, Mrs. Varpio.

The Dark Side

ALONE OF ALL the memories recounted in this volume, this entry is the most difficult to write. The difficulty lies not in the technical considerations of wording, organization, etc. Neither in the vagaries of memory. In fact, the topic is pretty straightforward. No, the issue here is pride, self respect. Although many of the incidents and personal decisions described in these pages may reveal lapses in judgment and poor decision-making, none evidence a desire to do something truly wrong, against the law. That changes here.

Let me begin by saying that I present no excuses to mitigate my responsibility. The brief explanation that follows is intended to illustrate my state of mind at the time, not to justify my actions.

Early in Grade 11, I took a brief walk on the dark side. The Reader's Digest version is that I was feeling sorry for myself: I was hard-done-by and unfairly underprivileged. The long version pulls together a number of factors. I had experienced serious health problems over the summer. That, coupled with being saddled with babysitting my younger sisters, meant my summer holidays disappeared largely unnoticed. The new 'family' now in its fourth year was decidedly imbalanced: the Fay kids were liars, were always the culprits and were never going to amount to anything; the Lavergne girls were never truly bad, were never in the wrong and were going to achieve great things. The message was the Fays couldn't do anything right and had better learn a work ethic if they wanted to survive, while the Lavergne's were special and the world would take care of them.

A minor example: I was left in charge while my parents went to do groceries one evening with specific instructions that 11-year-old Charlene, a Lavergne about four years younger than me, was *not* to watch t.v. until she'd done her homework. I came into the den to find her watching t.v. and I knew she had not done her homework. I told her to turn the t.v. off and get at it. She said she'd do it later. I walked over to the t.v. and turned it off, saying that she had to do it now, mom's orders. She got up and turned the t.v. back on. I turned it off. She turned it on. I turned it off. This continued for a couple minutes until she got frustrated and stomped out of the room. And she didn't do her homework.

When mom arrived home, she was no sooner in the door when Charlene came running upstairs crying that I had been mean to her and wouldn't let her watch television. I was punished.

Two weeks later, grocery night again, same scenario except, when I found Charlene watching television instead of doing homework, I ignored it. When mom came home and found that Charlene was watching television without having done her homework, guess who was punished. Yep.

All right, not happy at home. At school, I was never in a position to accompany my friends if some cost was involved. I had no money. I couldn't even do things with them that required a bicycle because I didn't have one and had no money to buy one. For reasons chronicled elsewhere in these pages, my parents weren't going to buy me one, either.

As I said, all of the above does not excuse my decision to become a custom order thief and supply kids at school with stuff they wanted at five-finger-discount prices. The irony didn't escape me years later when I met Skilling at Cortina.

So, for about six months, I stole from Woolco. Why that store? Well, before I started, I canvassed to see which stores had the laxest security. Their system really stank. Anything you brought into the store had to have a store tag affixed to it indicating it belong to you. Usually, all they did was staple a small Woolco bag over the opening of the bag you were carrying. If you are carrying something like a shovel, the bag was wrapped around the handle and stapled in place. Theoretically, cashiers were supposed to check to see if you had tampered with the tag, suggesting you may have added something to the bag while in the store. But they never did; they were too busy.

All I had to do was obtain a small stapler, a bag from any other retail store and a small Woolco bag from the garbage bin outside the store. I was surprised at how many people took their small merchandise out of the bag and threw the bag away immediately upon leaving the store. I would go into the store, choose my items, put them in the bag, staple the Woolco bag in place, buy a pack of gum at the cashier and walk out.

My 'clients' had surprisingly little imagination. The bulk of requests were for cartons of cigarettes, which were not guarded the way they are today. For some it was wallets and jewelry, cosmetics for the girls. Over a number of weeks, I acquired the entire *James Bond* library, in pocketbook format, for one guy. My most interesting theft, though no more difficult, was a canoe paddle. The boy went in, chose the one he wanted and gave me the details. I picked it up, stapled the Woolco bag around it and left. COD.

The dark cloud over me, thankfully, moved on in short order. I was standing with another pocketbook in my hand one day, to be included in the day's booty, when it struck me:

"What are you doing? This doesn't belong to you. What you are doing is wrong and you know it. You have no right to this book unless you pay for it."

I left the half-full bag on the shelf and exited the store.

Now my conscience started to work. Being sorry wasn't enough. The only way to atone was to repay the money. I calculated I had stolen about $185 worth of merchandise in the last few months. Some big-time crook, eh? But it was a lot of money in 1966. I may have been a little conservative in my estimate, but I included everything I could remember. I hadn't been keeping ledgers, after all.

Naturally, I had spent most of my 'fees.' I had a little over $15 stashed away. I sold a bunch of comics and pocketbooks I'd taken for myself and put that cash in the pot. It was midwinter by then, so I started shoveling driveways—lots of takers because I did a *very* good job. My parents were cautiously supportive, wondering why I decided to take on that particular job considering my problems breathing in the cold. I never told them anything about this period of my life.

When summer came, I mowed lawns, despite being allergic to cut grass. I took a lot of medication! Sometime about then, I wondered why I hadn't thought of this sort of solution to my financial woes as an alternative to theft.

One day in the fall, on the way home from school, I stopped at Woolco and asked to see the manager. He met me at the Customer Service Counter. I asked to go to his office, where I explained the situation, then handed over the money with sincere apologies. He thanked me, but said he couldn't commend me for correcting a situation I should not have created in the first place. "See to it you don't do it again, young man."

I said I wouldn't and I left. I am not naive—the Woolco Corporation probably never saw that money. But that's his moral baggage, isn't it?

For Want of a Nail

THE FIRST TIME I spent the weekend alone at my parents' camp on Windy Lake wasn't my idea and wasn't a holiday. I was 15 and being put to work. My parents were always so busy, had so many projects on the go at home and at the camp, they just didn't have enough time. And my stepmother kept finding new things to add to the list.

We had an old 16-foot plywood boat that we used for hauling construction materials and equipment rather than risk damaging the newer aluminum boat. During some heavy weather the previous summer, the plywood boat had broken free of its moorings and rubbed against the shoreline boulders, wearing a large hole in the hull. I had helped dad fiberglass that same boat a few years earlier when we purchased it for a song and were building the camp. But the rocks had done a real number on the fiberglass finish. Dad had been planning to patch the hole and put new fiberglass over the entire hull, but never seemed to get around to it.

One day in the basement at home, he asked me if I thought I could do the job myself. I said sure; the only ticklish part was keeping the resin at the right temperature.

"Good. You're going to camp this weekend to do it. With no one there to distract you, you should have no trouble getting it all done in the two days. You're old enough to stay there alone and I've taught you safe handling of everything. And that'll be one less chore I have to make time for."

Okay by me. To be trusted alone at the camp for the weekend was an acknowledgment of maturity that my dad would never verbalize—a rite of passage, if you will.

Late Friday afternoon, as soon as he got home from work at 3:30, he drove me to the landing at Windy Lake where we moored our boat. The landing was only thirty-five minutes away, so I was at camp by 5:00 p.m. Having lots of daylight, I decided to get right to the boat. By the time I quit at 9:00, I had the hole patched and the entire hull sanded. It was ready for fiberglass. The plan for Saturday was to start from the keel and work to the gunwale on one side, then switch to the other side and do the same thing. An overlapping strip down the keel itself would seal the two.

I went into the camp, made myself some fried Klik sandwiches with sandwich spread, read a bit and went to bed. But not to sleep.

I honestly don't think I was scared. Being alone in the bush for the first time, however, had all my senses sharpened and my nerves tingling, extending well outside my body. I heard every noise, I felt every change in air pressure as the wind shifted. For the first time I was aware of how *alive* the bush was around the camp, subtle rustles and movements that were overwhelmed by the cacophony of human activity when the rest of the family was there. Once I got used to it, I ended up lying on the dock, lost in the myriad stars of the Milky Way. The ghost shadows of pines only slightly less black than the sky waved gently, hiding and then revealing patches of stars.

The next morning, up early, I got to it. I worked from 7:30 to 10:30, then had a little breakfast. The day was sunny and warm so the resin was no problem. By one o'clock I was finished one side. If this kept up, I'd have almost the whole day Sunday to sit around and enjoy the sun.

I got a surprise at about 1:30 p.m. A big old wooden boat with a permanent roof enclosure came into the bay and pulled up to our dock. Ricky Cormier and Brucie Brunelle, two of my best friends from my Levack days, hopped out and tied up. I was so happy to see them! We hadn't seen each other since I had moved away three years earlier, but there was no sense of the passage of time. We fell into conversation like I'd seen them last week.

Ricky's dad recently had bought a camp at the west end of the lake and the boat had come as part of the deal. They had only been allowed out on the lake alone with the boat once before. Mr. Cormier was working and he'd be at the dock to pick them up at 6 o'clock. We had the whole afternoon.

First we went up the lake to check out Ricky's camp. And then over to Tower Bay for some cliff jumping. The bay has a wonderful cliff about 12 meters tall, perfect for jumping. I'd like to say we dove, but none of us had the guts. After that, we cruised the lake for a while, until the beating of the sun urged us back into the water. This time, we just stopped in the middle of the lake and dove off the side of the drifting boat.

They dropped me off at 5:30, all of us expressing how great it would be if they could stay with me overnight. "It's okay with me. Will your dads let you guys?"

They both agreed they wouldn't be allowed. Then Brucie got his 'bright' idea and Ricky and I, wanting so badly for it to work, shut off our common sense.

"Hey! Why don't we pull the cotter pin out of the propeller shaft? We'd be stuck here, not our fault. We can say it just snapped off. It'll soon be dark, so they won't be able to look for us until the morning. They can tow the boat back and get a new pin. Can't be that expensive."

Somehow we thought that was a great plan. We ignored the fact that I had a boat and could take them to the dock. And if they'd truly snapped the cotter pin, they'd have lost the propeller as well! I have no idea why we thought the parents would be so unconcerned that they would wait for the next day to come looking. Plus we missed the obvious solution.

We made something to eat and swapped stories about our lives since I left Levack. At about 10 p.m., we heard a boat approaching in the dark. The motor wasn't working very hard, so it was moving slowly. We went out to the dock and saw its lights off to the west, the direction of Ricky's camp. Mr. Cormier and Mr. Brunelle had rented a boat and gone to check the Cormier camp for the boys. Now, they were following the shoreline slowly, shining a large flashlight into the shallows and out over the water, looking for the boat or evidence of it.

When they got a little closer and the light hit the dock, they sped up and came directly over. As soon as they docked, the story gushed out of the boys' mouths. Through the whole explanation, Mr. Brunelle didn't say a thing and his face retained an unpleasant scowl. Brucie was in for it when he got home! Mr. Cormier said to Ricky sternly, "You know damned well a cotter pin is nothing but a glorified bent nail."

Looking at me with a knowing half-smile, he said, "Iggy, would you get me an ardox nail, please?"

When I gave it to him, he used pliers from the toolbox on his boat and had the propeller secured in minutes. Before he left, Mr. Cormier said to pass on his hello to my dad, then both boats chugged off into the dark. The boys didn't even get to say goodbye.

I spent a little time regretting the stupidity of our ploy and a little more wondering if Mr. Cormier would tell my dad. They still saw each other at the mine. Then, having had a full day, I went to bed. No problem sleeping that night.

Sunday morning, I realized I was lucky they hadn't stayed. I had forgotten all about the boat! But the weather held and I worked like a slave all day with only a short break at 12:30 for the only real meal I'd eat until I got home. I finished at 4 p.m. and got to the landing ten minutes short of the prearranged time of 5 p.m.

Contrary to his earlier comment, Dad expressed surprise that I had been able to get the whole boat done, but said nothing else about it. The next weekend, when the family went to the camp, he took ten minutes to look the boat over closely, then said to me, "Let's get this thing turned over and into the water." My weekend and my work wasn't mentioned again.

Odds and Ends

JIM LANZO, THE BRAWN to my brains described earlier, took his role seriously. He was a classmate of mine in Grade 10 and a member of the Junior football team. Several others on the team, including the quarterback, the two best running backs and a couple of linemen also were either my classmates or in one of the other classes of the same grade. Through grades 12 and 13, I actually tutored three of these players in Math and English. That was so funny. Each was grateful for the help, but adamant that I was not to tell anybody I was helping them, *especially* other members of the team.

Like many such organizations, the football team was cliquish. They expected a certain level of respect and consideration from other members of the team. A member never did anything to embarrass another member or the team as a whole. If sides needed to be taken, the member was expected to side with the team. You know—a macho brotherhood.

In Grade 11, I was still only four-foot-eleven, no hair anywhere but on my head, and a geek in that I got good grades, was interested in school and carried all my books in a big briefcase along with a large aluminum lunch pail. Never a last-minute person, I generally was one of the first two or three students on our floor to arrive in the morning, getting there about 8 a.m.

On that particular morning, I was running late, having stayed to help my step-mom get her car started. Her door locks had frozen and, once we finally got them open, the battery turned out to be dead. I helped a neighbor give her a boost, then she dropped me at school.

Walking down the well-populated second floor hallway at 8:45, I passed a group of people without focusing on who they were; I had to get to my locker. The group turned out to be four senior football players preening and strutting for the girls. If memory serves me, they were Ron Syrnyk, Denis Tarnopolsky, Art Antonioni and Oliver Corneau As I passed, one of the players snatched my lunch pail out of my hands and tossed it to one of the other players. Instantly, a game of *keep the lunch pail from the geek* ensued. For a minute or two, I chased the pail, always one step behind it, of course. I was reaching for the pail as it flew over my head from one jock to the other, when one of them tripped me and I went sprawling. Big laughs from the girls. As I was about to get up, reaching for the pail held enticingly toward me by the jock holding it, a foot pushed my butt and I went down again.

Just about then, Jim passed on his way to homeroom. He didn't slow his pace, he didn't look at me or the members of his team and he spoke just loud enough for me and the jocks to hear.

"Hurt him and you answer to me." And he was gone.

And the game was over. They had never intended to hurt me, of course, but a line had been drawn. The football team never hassled me again the rest of high school.

§

AS I HAVE SAID elsewhere in these anecdotes, I was (and still am) a stickler for realism when it came to games or jokes. I figured, if you were going to do it, do it right! More often than not, that touch of realism came at a cost.

Vytau Krucas and I became good friends in Grade 10 and for the last three years of high school, we contrived to have our lockers next to each other. We both were outgoing and friendly, loved jokes of all kinds and, to be bluntly honest, liked being the center of attention. We were generally the first on our floor to arrive in the morning, Vytau a minute or two ahead of me, usually.

As people arrived, many dropped by our lockers to chat, as we all socialized before having to settle down for the day. We always had a joke for the visitors and this pattern developed into *Joke of the Day*. Through the last two years at Lasalle, we had a loyal following who stopped by, each in their turn as they arrived, to have their morning brightened a little by our new joke of the day. We loved the attention and had some good laughs. We went through a lot of jokes, though, and it became somewhat of a pressure to keep coming up with new material.

And it wasn't just regular, verbal jokes. I could recite Bill Cosby word for word and Vytau was quite adept at impersonations. He did a great John Wayne, whom we both loved. His John Diefenbaker and JFK were riots.

One winter morning, I arrived a little late because of the strong wind. I had quite a lot of trouble breathing when it was windy, especially facing the wind, as I was that day on the way to school. I had to take frequent rests, turned away from the wind to catch my breath. As I came out of the stairwell at the end of the hallway and stepped around the corner into the hall, I took in two images—about 30 people distributed in small groups along the hallway and Vytau turning from his locker and dropping into gunfighter stance. In his best John Wayne, "Reach fer yer iron, pilgrim, or die where ya stand!"

I took a couple more steps down the hall, trying to come up with an appropriate response, but before I could, he 'drew' and 'shot' me twice. I went down like someone had cut my legs off, arms and legs splayed, briefcase tumbling into the lockers, my lunch pail skittering down the hall.

And I lay there facedown. Unmoving. The noise of me falling and of the aluminum lunch pail bouncing along the terrazzo flooring drew the attention of anyone who had not seen me fall. The quiet was so complete that you could hear the coffee gurgling out of my broken thermos and spreading on the terrazzo.

And I didn't move. Vytau was milking it. "That'll larn them Clancy Brothers to try bustin' up my town." And a few titters of laughter started.

And I didn't move. The tittering stopped. A girl's voice said, "Oh, my god. I think he really hurt himself."

A couple of the closer students rushed over to me and another voice, this one male, said, "I'll go get the nurse," and running footsteps started down the hall.

And I didn't move. Only when they rolled me over to find me smiling at them did the tension that had been building ease.

"Shit, Iggy, that's not funny! We thought you were really hurt."

Vytau and I began to laugh and, in seconds, most of the students joined us. Then I had to hurry to clean up the spilled coffee and get to homeroom. I wasn't looking forward to soggy, coffee-flavored bologna sandwiches at lunch!

That was the last of the long thermoses with the glass interior bottle for me. My mother was tired of me breaking the damned things, so she bought me one of the stubby, all-plastic versions. It didn't keep coffee hot anywhere near as long and everything tasted slightly of plastic, but it *was* a hell of a lot more durable!

§

REMEMBER THAT high school prank of putting a thumb tack on someone's seat and sitting back to enjoy the fun? And if you did it too often, everyone began checking their seats before sitting, so you had to lay off for a while, until people had been lulled into inattention again? I was a little slow on the uptake and for a while, my butt felt like a pin cushion. In fact, one time I sat on a tack, leapt up with a yeow and scanned nearby faces for a clue as to the culprit. Everyone laughed and professed innocence. I sat back down only to jerk right back up with another, louder yeow! Don Bouffard, the original perpetrator, had put another tack on my seat while I was looking around.

I developed a variation on the theme that was harder to defend against. It required a little more obvious personal involvement, so you couldn't feign innocence, but it achieved much more dramatic results. Best of all: the bulk of the pain experienced by the victim was self-inflicted!

The best time was in homeroom a few minutes before the morning announcements. The place usually was half full of chatting teens and quickly filling. Most were seated, turned to talk to people across the aisle or at the desk behind them, their legs jutting into the aisle.

I would come in with an ordinary straight pin held between thumb and forefinger where it wasn't visible. Picking a target, I would make my way up the aisle, weaving through the legs. As I passed my victim, whose attention was usually occupied in conversation, I would jab the pin into the middle of the thigh muscle—and let it go.

Yes, I would leave the pin sticking in the thigh! Almost invariably, the person would do two things by reflex, in addition to yelping: grab for the sore spot and straighten the leg. As the leg straightened, the muscle tightened around the pin and the grabbing hand pushed it farther in. The tight muscle resisted, making the process more painful.

The pièce de résistance is that the person now had to remove the pin himself. Of course, I could only play this prank on friends, who would swear to get me back. Someone with whom I was not a friend or with whom I didn't get along would have reported me to the teacher. In no time at all, most people quickly swung their legs under their desks at my approach and I had to abandon this particular practical joke.

Yvette

YVETTE LAJEUNESSE was my Sugar Mama in high school. In the last three years, anyway. We were in the same grade, although I have no recollection of her in Grade 9. We got to know each other quite well in Grade 11 because we spent a lot of time together. We both were exempt from gym class.

My asthma had kept me in hospital and away from school for more than half of Grade 9 (perhaps *that's* why I don't remember her) and my doctor recommended I be excused from physical exertion. Yvette was asthmatic as well, although much less severely. She was exempt in Grade 11 because she had seriously injured her neck, came very close to breaking it, and wore a neck brace for much of the year. Even after the brace was removed, they recommended she not engage in gym until she had strengthened it with special exercises.

During gym period, those of us who were exempt had to report to the cafeteria, where we could do pretty much as we pleased. Most of the time, there were just the two of us. We talked a lot and did our homework together.

Along one wall of the cafeteria was a row of vending machines: one for different types of milk, one for pastries and chocolate bars, one for frozen treats. We were not allowed to partake outside of lunch periods. Made no difference to me as I seldom had any money. During the first term, my illicit activities (see *The Dark Side* earlier) supplied me with treat money, but now that had ended and I was saving to return the ill-gotten gains. I was back to relying on my fifty cents per week allowance, which didn't go very far and seldom made it to school. Even toward the end of high school, when my allowance rose to a whole dollar, I was challenged in the area of spending money. Yvette, by contrast, seemed to have unlimited resources.

We did not sit together at lunch. She sat with girlfriends and I sat with the guys, several tables apart. One lunch period in the second term, having become comfortable in our relationship, I decided to ask her for a loan to buy an ice cream sandwich. She seemed surprised that I would approach her where others would witness the contact, but she received the request with a smile and readily handed over the dime.

The second time, three or four days later, it was a vanilla half-moon pastry. I hadn't repaid the first dime, so I was a little hesitant to ask.

"Yvette, uh, I know I haven't paid you the ten cents I owe you yet, but would you lend me another dime and I'll pay you the whole twenty cents next week?"

"That's okay, Iggy, I'm keeping track," she said, digging into the change purse she kept in her pencil case. "There's no hurry. Pay me when you can," and she gave me the second dime.

The third time was the hardest. I put it off for several days because I didn't have what I owed her and was embarrassed to ask for more. During that interval, however, we had two of our usual periods in the cafeteria and she didn't act any differently than usual. I fully expected her to broach the subject, especially since we were alone. We both would have been embarrassed if we had to deal with the issue in front of others. But no. No mention. We talked and worked on homework as usual. When two such sessions had passed uneventfully, I screwed up my nerve and asked that day at lunch. The dessert I chose was those chocolate-covered pastry squares with the circle of caramel filling that came in a package of two.

> *I don't want the reader to get the impression that my family was so poor that my lunch was inadequate and I was undernourished. Money was always tight, but we never went hungry. I ate a surprising amount for my size. In my big aluminum lunch pail every day there were: a large thermos of coffee (two sugars and Coffeemate creamer), two sandwiches, assorted vegetables (celery and/or carrot sticks, a whole tomato, etc.) and two fruit. In fact, I ate pretty much nonstop. My lung specialist explained in later years that most of my energy was being spent just in breathing. He also attributed the delay of puberty and the usual growth spurt associated with my age group to that same cause. In Grade 11, I was under five feet tall, very thin and underweight. I didn't hit puberty until late in Grade 12 and still had only three chest hairs when I married at age 23. Four years later, although still not bushy, it had become a small thatch and my wife took credit for putting hair on my chest.*

The asking became easier after that and Yvette never made me feel like I was being unreasonable or taking advantage of her. I was, of course, but she never let on. So, a pattern was established. Two or three times a week I'd cross the cafeteria and borrow a dime from Yvette—never more. The routine had become so inured by the middle of the fall semester of Grade 12 that I no longer asked. I would get up from my table and walk over to hers. While I was in transit, without interrupting her conversation, she'd go into her pencil case, retrieve a dime and put it on the table. We always smiled at each other and I'd say, "Thanks, lady." Some of her friends would give me a knowing smile, but none ever said anything. I wonder what they said about it in private.

All that time, I kept telling myself I'd pay her back someday, this was just a long-term loan. As Grade 13 drew to a close, I realized she had accepted that I would never repay her and she was okay with that. Somehow, that hurt my pride. Fine time for my conscience to kick in, eh?

That year I had scored a slave labor job washing dishes on Friday or Saturday nights at the Sorrento Hotel at a dollar an hour. I'd work my ass off from nine to midnight for three bucks!

I had also started babysitting and quickly outstripped my sisters in that capacity. In fact, they soon learned not to ask me to fill-in when they couldn't take a job because they'd never get it back. I didn't just sit on my butt when I was babysitting. I straightened up, folded clothes in the dryer, did the dishes. If the kids were up, I played with them rather than sit on the couch and read or watch t.v. And I didn't eat anything when I was there. So next time, when the client called, they asked for me. By the way, babysitting was twenty-five cents an hour!

With *all* my earnings, I had opened up a bank account. Sure, I could have bought my desserts with my own money by then, but the borrowing had become an easy reflex. I had accumulated about $35 in my account. I figured, by quick estimate, that I owed Yvette about $80. I had taken a job cruising timber for a forest management company for the coming summer, arranged by my geography teacher, Mr. Holmes, a family friend. I went to my boss-to-be, Mr. Austen, and negotiated an advance on my wages.

Monday lunch, the last week of school, I walked over to her table. I slid the dime, which she already had on the table for me, back toward her and asked if I could sit for a minute. Puzzled, she agreed and one of her friends slid over a little to make room.

"I know this has been a long time coming and I apologize. To be honest, I didn't keep track, but I figure I owe you about eighty bucks. I hope you'll take a cheque." I thought the cheque idea was a nice touch.

Her jaw dropped and she was momentarily at a loss for words.

"I, uh, I really, uh, really don't know what to say. Except, maybe, thank you. I really never expected you to pay it back."

"Yvette, honestly, that's at least partly why I had to. It rankled me that you thought I was irresponsible enough to ignore your kindness— and that I *was going to do exactly that*. I just didn't want you to remember me that way."

"Well, thank you, Iggy. Now there are absolutely no blemishes on our time together. So, do you need this dime, or what?"

Chris Cahill

YOU KNOW WHAT they say about good intentions and the road to hell. I learned the hard way that my good intentions would not always be enough to sustain me in difficult situations. And that's assuming I even recognized that the situation was becoming difficult.

The Grade 9 student with whom I was discussing fossils in my bedroom, described earlier, was Chris Cahill. She was a petite blonde with a boyish figure and a smile that involved her whole face. We had become acquainted when she volunteered to help out with variety night (see *Mrs. Varpio*). She was bright, outgoing and energetic, and we quickly became friends. I was pleasantly surprised to find she lived just up the street from me.

One of our shared interests was music. Her personal involvement outstripped mine in that she had been playing piano for years, but I was strictly a listener, despite a couple of failed attempts at learning guitar. I didn't have the manual dexterity, plus I found I'd rather devote the hours to listening rather than practicing. What I brought to the relationship was a much broader knowledge of different musical genres and of the musicians themselves.

A few weeks into our friendship, she asked if I wanted to come over on Saturday afternoon. We could listen to some records and she could play the piano for me. I agreed. Arriving shortly after lunch, I met her parents, very nice people who seemed genuinely pleased to meet me. They, apparently, had heard about me from Chris. The two of us retired to their den where we played records—some of hers, some of mine—then she entertained me on the piano. She really was very good. We had a great time.

After that day, we routinely got together every so often at her place on a Saturday afternoon. Sometimes I'd bring fossils, rocks and minerals, even books, to share with her. One of these sessions led to us being 'caught' alone in my bedroom. We had taken a quick run up the street to my place so I could show her something I had been describing.

She was always so eager and interested. And her parents always greeted me warmly. They seem very interested in what I wanted to do after high school and thanked me more than once for being willing to share so much time with someone younger. Her dad commented that she was becoming much more mature, something that had been lacking, probably the result of being an only child.

I want to assure you right here that I had no interest in Chris as a girlfriend or a sex partner. Yes, she was attractive, but what drew me to her was her personality and her interests. Besides, after my parents' lecture, I was quite conscious about propriety. *She was only in Grade 9!*

The year passed, variety night came and went. Since we lived so close to each other and both walked home from school, we often walked together, never short of conversation. When the school year ended, I went off to cruise timber for the summer, but got in contact with her as soon as I got back in the fall. Our visits were much less frequent due to my schedule at university, but we still spent time together semi-regularly. Then it was summer once more and I went off to cruise timber again. Upon returning in the fall, I went back to university and got a part-time job delivering at Cortina Pizza. I had even less free time, but I still managed to see Chris, now in Grade 11.

During one of our now infrequent visits, she told me she was involved with that year's variety night and that the group lacked guidance. Would I be willing to attend a few rehearsals and give them some pointers? Just about anyone else I would have told 'no,' but for her I'd make time. It took a little juggling, but I went to three rehearsals in the basement of St. Andrew the Apostle Church. They were all good kids, worked hard and took advice openly.

The last session was on a Sunday afternoon. My transportation was an old Rambler convertible, one of the spare delivery cars at Cortina. I was going to give Chris a ride home before heading to work. She suggested we go for a short ride; she had something she wanted to show me. Having a couple of hours before I had to be at Cortina, I agreed.

She had me drive north on Barrydowne, past Maley Drive, where Barrydowne became a wooded and sparsely populated gravel road in those days. A beautiful spring day, we had the top down, enjoying the wind and singing to the radio at the tops of our lungs. She asked me to pull over at a relatively secluded spot.

Shutting the car off, I turned to her and she was just sitting there, looking at me, smiling. "So, what did you want to show me?"

"Me."

"Huh?" I can be a little slow on the uptake.

"Me," she said again, as she began to unbutton her blouse. "I want you to kiss me. I want you to touch me. We have waited long enough."

I sat there dumbfounded and thinking, 'We? Oh, shit!'

She slid over next to me, her blouse hanging open, took my left hand and made to put it on her right breast. I finally came out of my stupor and, before contact was made, jerked my hand back.

"Chris! Do up your blouse. What are you thinking?"

"I thought you liked me, Iggy. We spend so much time together. I want to be your girlfriend."

Oh, man. How could I not have seen this coming? Where had my head been? "I do like you, a lot. But not as a girlfriend. I like being with you because you like so many things I like and you are so interesting. We're really good friends—but just friends."

She still hadn't moved to button her blouse or gone back to her side of the seat.

"Iggy, I'm not a young girl anymore. You don't have to be afraid to touch me. Look at me."

I didn't mean it the way it sounded, but I blurted, "I don't want to look at you. Cover yourself. I'm taking you home."

She hesitated, her eyes tearing. To be doing something, I reached forward and started the car. She moved back to her side, buttoning her blouse and crying freely. She didn't talk all the way home.

And she didn't talk to me again for nearly two years. She wouldn't take my calls and never returned them. The third or fourth time I called, her mom asked what had happened. I gave her the basics of the misunderstanding without the details and she expressed sorrow.

Apparently, she and her husband had been hoping our relationship would develop as Chris got older.

About a year later, her dad called to give me news because he thought I would want to know. Chris had quit school, taken a job at a travel agency and moved into an apartment. She spent all her money on outrageous clothes, alcohol and drugs. When her parents expressed concern and tried to give her advice, she cut off the relationship. To top things off, she had become quite promiscuous. Of course, I called her, but she hung up on me and promptly got an unlisted number.

Several months later, she called me at 2:30 in the morning, obviously high, wanting to talk to her friend, Iggy. Of course, I talked to her—until nearly 4:30—just trying to reconnect. I was afraid that if I said anything about her lifestyle, she would hang up on me again. She started calling me regularly in the middle of the night. She lost her job, was doing a lot of drugs and supporting herself on the money that men were paying her for sex.

When we'd been talking often enough that I felt comfortable, I broached the idea of rehab, cleaning up and getting a job. I tried to talk to her about the prostitution, but she was in denial and rationalizing her actions.

"I'm not a prostitute. I don't go to bed with just anyone. But when I do, he can damned well pay for it. Why shouldn't I use my body to earn money? That's all it's good for. Nobody's ever going to love me, especially now. You didn't want me, nobody wants me. My life sucks. The only time I can stand being with myself is when I'm stoned."

Finally, tired of me preaching and trying to get her into rehab, she stopped calling. She had never given me her number. I don't know what happened to her after that, aside from having heard she left town.

How much of what happened to Chris was my fault? Would things have turned out better for her if I had not befriended her? Could I have been more aware, more sensitive to her feelings and recognize a developing problem? If I'd been less blunt in the car, would things have gone differently? Or would she have been better off if I had just had sex with her? I don't know. And I've lived all these years wondering.

Summer Job

Points In Between

Junior Forest Rangers

I STARTED EARLY in my Grade 12 academic year trying to convince my parents to let me apply for a summer job as a Junior Forest Ranger. The only real requirement was that the student be 17, which I would be by summer, and that the application be submitted by March 1, 1967. I was stonewalled because of my health. My asthma was too difficult to manage, I had too many allergies, the work would be too hard.

Just after Christmas, I decided to try an end run around their defenses. A close friend of my parents, Mr. Holmes, was also a teacher at Lasalle and had taught me geography in Grade 10. We got along famously and are great friends to this day. In addition to teaching, he was a Registered Forester and worked on contract in forest management during summer months. I talked over the Junior Forest Ranger idea with him and he thought it would be very good for me. He volunteered to talk to my parents, who placed much store in his opinion.

Abruptly, applying to the Junior Forest Ranger program became their idea. I sent the forms in, which I had already prepared, before they could change their minds. I received acceptance in May. I would be assigned to Esker Lakes Provincial Park, not far from Kapuskasing in northern Ontario, for eight weeks in July and August. I would be paid $20 a day, 6 days a week. I didn't know it, but I had signed up for an eight-week crash course in maturity.

My parents drove me to the park early on the day because, later that same day, the family was leaving for Montréal and Expo 67. As they drove off, it struck me. For the first time in my life I was free from mom and dad's supervision—and their protection.

§

THE FIRST COUPLE of days were spent with orientation, becoming familiar with camp layout and routine, learning our responsibilities. We were 24 boys housed in two bunkhouses, a foreman and his assistant in a separate building, and a cook who had a room off the kitchen in the dining building. Esker Lakes Park was a small and expanding campground vacation area.

The boys would be split into several teams and rotate responsibilities on a weekly basis. On a given week, one team would be doing maintenance on existing campsites: clearing brush, repairing fire pits, etc. Another team would be clearing areas and defining new campsites. Other boys would be assigned to making new picnic tables for the new sites, while still others cleaned and maintained public washrooms. The least coveted job was working on the garbage truck, which usually required only two boys. Finally, two boys were assigned to help the cook, the plum job after the first two weeks.

I had a tough time that first week. I had never been away from home before, let alone thrown in with a bunch of strangers. Some stability in my health had been achieved by sticking to a routine that went out the window when I got to Ranger camp. So, despite the fact that the boys were generally a good bunch and got along, I was terribly lonely. From day one, my thoughts were focused on how many days left until I could go home and how big a mistake this had been. I was so homesick that first week, I wrote daily letters to *every* member of my family, even those to whom I normally wouldn't have much to say. And not just notes—letters! Several pages each. I mailed them at the park concession stand each morning.

Naturally, if I were spending so much time writing in the evening, I wasn't getting to know the boys. Luckily for me, I spent all day working with them and relationships began to develop. By the second week, I was playing cards in the evening or talking music. That second week, I just wrote letters to Christine and my parents. From the third week, Christine got a weekly letter and the rest of my correspondence dried up. I had made friends, become comfortable with my new surroundings and stopped counting days. Truth be told, at the end of the eight weeks, I did not want to go home and would've signed on for an extension as Ranger if it had been offered.

§

UNEXPECTEDLY, I gained a certain reputation and respect among the boys in my bunkhouse that lasted all summer. We had a couple of musicians with us, each having brought their guitars. By the end of the summer, they had taught the basics to three other boys, sold their guitars and bought new ones in Kapuskasing. We would sit around in the evening, they'd play and sing; sometimes we'd all join in. We quickly ran through their short repertoire of songs several times.

Requests for new songs became frequent. Most of the time, the guitarists could work out the chords, but lyrics would have been a much bigger problem had I not been there. It quickly became evident that, although I didn't play an instrument and certainly couldn't sing, I had an extensive library of music lyrics in my head. I became the 'go to' guy for lyrics to songs and to arbitrate disputes about the correct words to songs. I enjoyed being recognized and appreciated for having a valued talent.

Then, irony of ironies, I developed notoriety as a singer! Me. My voice epitomizes that old saying 'couldn't carry a tune in a bucket' and 'key' refers only to something that fits into a lock. So, no, the quality of my voice was not the attention getter; it was my catalogue of old novelty tunes.

One night after lights out, we were singing in the dark, each boy in his turn singing a song he remembered from childhood. At my turn, I decided to sing an old novelty song I had learned from my dad. And they loved it. Over the course of a few nights, I was asked if I knew any others and, of course, I didn't disappoint them.

Some of my fondest memories of dad when I was a kid in Levack was his singing. There was always music in our house: the radio or, later, the phonograph that a priest gave dad—but more often than not, dad himself. He sang while he worked, sang to entertain us, sang at celebrations. He kept a scrapbook full of songs clipped from music magazines. The best Sunday afternoons were the ones when he pulled out the scrapbook and his harmonica, and sang for us while we sat on the living room floor. And we never found car rides long because we'd sing all those great novelty songs with dad. He was a stickler for lyrics, too. If you were to strip the wallboard off the rec-room that he built in the basement on Redfern Street, you would find handwritten lyrics to Marty Robbins' Devil Woman on the two-by-fours inside the wall. For about a week, every time he heard the song on the radio, he would stop and scratch more lyrics on the wood with his pencil.

Sadly, that changed after the remarriage. Isabelle had no use for music, saw it as using time that could have been better spent on other things. And, I think, she was more than a little jealous of the love and attention he had for it. In short order, her negative vibes and outright criticism had its effect and music became seriously diminished in the new home.

Of course I was asked where I got all the songs. When I told them, some of the boys were convinced I had been fooled and my dad had actually made up some of the silly lyrics. They weren't the last to think that. Some of dad's own children and grandchildren have needed convincing that these were real songs. Anyway, I became a teacher of sorts and several of the boys left that summer with unexpected repertoires.

While I'm on the topic of music, let me tell you about a truly fortuitous event. Although I took a lot of medication, I was only unable to work due to illness on a handful of days that summer. One of those days, a beautiful sunny day, I was alone in the bunkhouse propped on my bed having serious difficulty breathing. I was listening to one of the boys' radios. Early in the afternoon, the d.j. cut away live to Nathan Phillips Square in Toronto for an open-air concert. I heard Gordon Lightfoot sing, for the first time in public, the *Canadian Railroad Trilogy*, which he had been commissioned to write in honor of Canada's Centennial that year. Gordon Lightfoot was then and is now my favorite solo male musician.

§

THE COOK WE HAD was a grizzled old fart in his late fifties, unkempt, smelly and ill mannered. He had worked for years in diamond drilling camps, usually being let go eventually because of unreliability due to alcoholism. He took the job with us because it was all he could get and he was on probation. Grumpy and authoritarian with the boys assigned to help him, he didn't take requests for meals or desserts and allowed absolutely no snacking between meals. But he was a good cook. Unfortunately, he had sneaked some booze into camp with him and got stinking drunk every night the first week. He was even louder and coarser in that condition, verbally abusive to the boys and neglected his duties. The third time he was late with breakfast, middle of the second week, the foreman let him go.

One thing he *did* do right. He made the greatest coffee. I learned how he did it while I was on cooking duty. First, never scrub the coffee pot; rinse, but no soap, no scrubbing. Put the coffee in the bottom of the pot, no drip basket. Crack a large egg and put the whole thing on the grounds and add water. Boil for five minutes, then let the grounds settle. During the boiling, the egg white gets pulled out of the egg and mixed with the coffee. The result is a rich, thick, tasty cup of coffee—almost a meal in itself!

He was replaced by Mary, a gentle, kindly, grandmotherly woman in her early sixties, also a veteran of field camps. She was the exact opposite. She enjoyed cooking what the boys wanted and handed out snacks between meals to any boy who happened by the cookhouse— and we all found excuses to do so. With the first cook, the kitchen helpers did only what was asked and never volunteered. The boys loved kitchen duty under Mary and went out of their way to be helpful, often offering to do extra beyond the strict interpretation of their duties. And she was a *great* cook.

§

A SERIES OF DOUBLE-seater outhouses stood out back a short distance from the bunkhouses. One of our projects that summer was to dig a hole and build another outhouse because one of the others was rapidly approaching the day that it would need to be removed from service and filled in. A crew had spent a couple of days digging the hole to specifications and were ready to start building. The old weather-beaten structure would provide kindling for the kitchen.

On the way to the wash house before breakfast, one of the boys glanced into the eight-foot hole and saw a skunk at the bottom. It must have fallen into the hole sometime during the night. Half the boys in the camp were soon milling around, looking at the skunk, wondering what to do. We couldn't just leave it down there in the hole. It would die and before it did, anyone working on the outhouse would be doused in unwanted perfume. A couple of the boys took off to get the foreman.

They had no sooner gone than one of the boys said he had an idea and walked to the edge of the pit. Somehow I sensed what he was going to do and quickly move away from the hole, followed by two or three others. The boy jumped into the pit and, in one motion, grabbed the skunk by the tail and swung it in an arc. He let go at the top of the arc and the skunk came spinning out of the hole, spraying in all directions. It hit the ground running and was gone. All except its scent, that is.

What a reek! About fourteen boys had to scrub thoroughly in the lake before being allowed to come to breakfast. And they were still pretty ripe! All but one spent the evening scrubbing smelly clothes. And that one? He just burned his stack!

§

IN THE EVENINGS, there was always at least one card game going on: hearts, cribbage, fish, concentration, poker, blackjack. Inevitably, some of the boys began playing for money. Of course, it was against the camp rules; since when did that matter? Those games were not for me, as I took my dad's philosophy seriously: don't gamble with money you can't afford to lose. I couldn't afford to lose any money. I *did* play a lot of hearts and crib for fun, though.

Some of the boys played only for money. Stakes were never high, but over eight weeks, small amounts can add up. We had two boys who went home broke at the end of the summer. They had lost all of their earnings playing cards. I wonder if they learned anything.

§

MOST RAINY DAYS we worked right through the rain because we had a lot of work to do in the short time that we were going to be there. Those of us that had rain gear usually got pretty wet anyway, between the rain and our own sweat. One particular day, rain fell in an almost continual downpour all day. We got back to the bunkhouses completely drenched. The temperature had dropped significantly during the day, so we were quite chilled. We lit a roaring fire in the stove and arranged our socks and boots in concentric circles around the stove to dry.

Someone got the bright idea that, while we had the stove so nice and hot, we should dry some banana peels and smoke them. Rumor had it in the sixties that smoking dried banana peels could give you a mild high. A number of bananas were eaten and their peels put on the stove to dry. The stove was so hot, drying took only a matter of minutes. The peels were then shredded and rolled in rolling papers that one of the fellows had. There were only four or five guys willing to try, but the rest of us were eager to see what happened. In the end, nothing much except that a couple of the smokers got pretty nauseated and pale.

We were paying so much attention to these guys with their phony cigarettes that we failed to watch our clothes around the stove. We had stoked the stove so full that, once all the wood was ignited and burning well, the temperature soared. In the middle of the banana peel smoking, another smell pervaded the bunkhouse, drawing us to the stove. All the socks and boots in the center two rings around the stove had burnt even though they had not been in contact with the fire. The socks had blackened and turned to ash, the boots had shriveled up. I lost a very good pair of wool socks that afternoon, but I have to tell you, the bunkhouse was nice and toasty for a couple of hours.

§

I CAME AWAY FROM Junior Forest Rangers feeling pretty good about myself. I had learned I could handle my own health issues; I could do physical work as long as I paced myself; I could adapt to new situations and function well. I had been told for so long all the things I couldn't do that I had begun to believe they were true. Junior Forest Rangers did wonders for my confidence. I felt good enough that I even decided to take the bus home rather than have my parents come to get me. The independence felt great.

The other thing I brought home was a foul mouth. Before that summer, I didn't curse. And I didn't start just to be one of the guys. But surrounded day after day by boys whose everyday language was peppered with coarse expletives, the habit slowly seeped into my speech. It was insidious. By the time I went home, I cursed like a sailor. Back in my normal environment, I became conscious of that habit in no time. Although I never cursed in the presence of girls even then, with the guys my language was terrible. In early October I was asking myself if I really wanted my vocabulary to be that foul the rest of my life. Deciding I didn't, I made a conscious effort to stop. Every time I opened my mouth, I tried to focus on what I was saying, control the subconscious tendencies. When I lapsed, I had to concentrate on the mistake and repeat to myself why it was not the type of language I condoned. The process was very difficult and I wasn't lapse-free until early in the new year.

Cruising Timber

I WORKED FOR two summers cruising timber under Sydney Holmes for a forestry management company based in Sudbury. The company had a long-term contract to manage forest resources throughout northern Ontario on behalf of the Provincial Government. At the time, Mr. Holmes was responsible for the townships around and immediately north of the little town of Foleyet.

Among their several areas of concern, the company oversaw commercial logging practices in the forested areas under their supervision. As pertains to logging, the company had essentially two mandates: to assess the timber resources in a given area, i.e. how many trees, of what type, of what sizes; to oversee the cutting itself and make sure the logger removed all required trees and did the requisite replanting before moving to the next site.

The assessment was completed before a logging company was awarded the license to cut in the area. Government regulations required that the logger *clear-cut*, harvest all trees greater than three inches in diameter. The big money was in larger trees, however, and many companies tried to cheat, taking only the larger trees and moving on. In instances when a logger was found in breach of contract, the overseer would require that the logger to return to an area and complete the contractual responsibilities. If the logger did not comply, the overseer had the authority to yank the license and close the operation down.

§

THE FIRST SUMMER, 1968, we spent fulfilling the first of these mandates—the assessment phase for our area. I acted as field assistant to Mr. Holmes, working out of Foleyet, and as map-maker in the office in Sudbury. The field work primarily involved a detailed survey of timber resources in the area and lasted half the summer. The second half I spent in the office in Sudbury transferring our data to base maps of the area, then coloring them. The result was a series of township maps showing the distribution, by type and size, of the timber resources.

That summer was relatively uneventful, although the first day in the field suggested it might be otherwise. I had never been in a canoe and many of our survey areas could only be accessed from the water. So I had to learn. The afternoon of our arrival, we threw our belongings into our quarters, an old medical clinic now unused, and took the canoe to the Ivanhoe River just outside of town.

"No time like the present for your first lesson," said Mr. Holmes. "The sooner you get comfortable in a canoe, the better."

He talked me through how to get in and out of the canoe, gave me some pointers on keeping my mass centered and how to manipulate the paddle without shifting my center of mass, then held the canoe while I got in the front. When I was settled, he got in the back. We were out for about three-quarters of an hour. We had a few shaky moments when I shifted my weight unnecessarily or, worse, unexpectedly, but it was okay. He showed me several different paddle strokes and how to use them to control the canoe. All in all, I was feeling pretty good about the whole experience as we approached our starting point.

Seated as he was behind me out of my sight, I don't know what he did, but probably all he did was shift his weight suddenly. Whatever he did, the canoe suddenly pitched to the left and I reflexively compensated to the right. Perhaps I overcompensated or he shifted right as well purposely. I was underwater before I fully realized the canoe was going over. I was a good swimmer, so I was never in any real danger and I was on the surface treading water in seconds. I felt water-logged with all my clothes weighing me down. Mr. Holmes and the overturned canoe were just a few feet away.

"You okay?" he asked. At my nod, he went on, "Good. Before we swim to shore, I want to show you how to right the canoe and get back in it while you are treading water. You won't always be this close to shore."

Getting the canoe upright was no real problem. I took a little longer getting back into the canoe. Although we didn't attempt it that day, I recognized that the feat would have been infinitely more difficult had I been alone and had to do it unassisted. When we were ashore, he apologized for putting us in the drink on purpose.

"I figured you should learn what it feels like and what to do about it as early as possible under controlled conditions, so that you know what to expect. And you had to learn to tread water fully clothed with your boots on. Now, if and when it happens again, it won't be as much of a surprise and you'll know what to do. You did very well, by the way."

Part of the day's lesson had been to emphasize the need to tie everything to the canoe before starting out. He had brought an aluminum clipboard with him specifically for that purpose. When we tipped the canoe, the clipboard went to the bottom of the river. The river was only a few feet deep right there, so I stripped and easily dove to retrieve it.

Mr. Holmes smiled and said, "Now, if we'd been in the middle of a lake when that happened, I'm sure you recognize that the clipboard and anything else not tied down would be at the bottom of the lake. A good way to lose valuable equipment, your best work boots or, heaven forbid, your lunch!"

§

THE NEXT SUMMER, 1969, brought a couple of changes. The focus shifted to the second of the two mandates and I took on more responsibility. I was assigned a logging area to oversee and given two field assistants of my own, Rick and Jim. Both were a couple of years younger than me.

The weather was particularly hot and sunny that year and we quickly realized that working in the heat of the day was unpleasant in the extreme. In addition to the heat, the black flies tried to eat us alive! Since we had the option of setting our own hours, we decided to get up at 3 a.m., have breakfast and head out to the logging area so that we arrived with the sun at just after 4 a.m. We would work straight through and be on the beach by 1:30 or 2:00 p.m.. If I had to deal with the officials of one of the logging companies, I could leave my assistants on the beach and see the loggers in the late afternoon. The system worked for everyone.

At 19, I found it heady stuff to be offered a position with such theoretical authority, comfortable in the fact that I'd never have to use it. Mr. Holmes and I hadn't had a single problem the year before. In '69, I was up to my neck at the end of the third week! My authority was challenged by the foreman of one of the logging companies and I had to do a little more maturing in a hurry.

The first two and half weeks, we spent cruising an area that had been logged during the previous season. The company had since moved on and was logging another area. Our assessment showed that they had taken only trees over six and a half inches, leaving literally a couple of thousand less-profitable trees. And they had only replanted half the number of trees they should have. My job required that I go to the foreman at their present logging site and have him halt operations and return to finish the clear-cut and replanting.

Okay. I could do that. Never occurred to me that he wouldn't comply. Nor that he would laugh right in my face! Like most of the companies, his field office was in a long trailer. When I got there, the door was open, so I called from the bottom of the three steps leading up to the door. In a gruff, no-nonsense tone, a voice told me to come on in. He was in his early forties, I'd say, maybe 5 foot 11, partly bald, built and dressed like the rest of his men—deerskin shirt, blue jeans, Greb Kodiaks, leather gloves in his back pocket.

He listened while I introduced myself and told him why I had dropped by. When he stopped laughing, he said he had a schedule to keep and had no time or patience for some kid that was still wet behind the ears. And he certainly didn't have time to move all his men and equipment back to the old site for the sake of a few unprofitable trees. He laughed again and suggested that I go back to counting trees and let the men get back to work. While we were talking, a couple of his men had come into the trailer and he turned to share the joke with them.

I could see he wasn't going to take seriously anything I had to say, so I decided not even to threaten him. I left the trailer to a chorus of chuckles. I got into my truck and drove straight to the RCMP office in Foleyet, the only police presence in the area. I presented my credentials and the documents that established my authority on behalf of the Government of the Province of Ontario. I explained the situation and the constable suggested I call the office of the forest management company to verify that I was making the right decision and that they would back me up. I refused. I remembered Mr. Holmes telling me I had to exert my authority, not let anyone give me the runaround.

"The moment you show any weakness, they'll try to walk all over you, especially because you are young. You know your job. Do it."

I told the RCMP officer he could call if he wanted, but I wouldn't. I added that I would also file a report that he ignored my credentials, refusing to take me seriously due to my age. He hesitated a beat or two, then agreed to accompany me.

Whew! My armpits were soaked! He followed me back to the logger's office trailer. The foreman was impatient and, ignoring me, asked the RCMP officer in an argumentative voice why he was there. The constable replied he was present to enforce the decision I was going to make, so the foreman should listen to me. The foreman turned to me, a scowl on his face.

I informed him I was shutting down his operation for ten days, at the end of which time they could either return to their previous contract area and fulfill their commitment or they could pack up because all licenses would be rescinded.

Suddenly solicitous, he said, "Now, hold on. No need to go that far. I was only joking with you earlier, having a little fun with you. I always intended to go back and clean up that last patch. So let's just call this a misunderstanding and we'll get ready to go back bright and early tomorrow."

"Sorry. There's no misunderstanding here—and no second option." Turning to the officer, I added, "In accordance with my authority, I'd like all their equipment under lock and key and everyone off the site by 5 p.m., not to be allowed to return until 6 a.m. Tuesday after next."

That's what happened. Man, it felt good. I made sure to act like this was just part of my job. When he started up again a week later, I dropped in to talk to him about which trees he had to go back to get. I acted as if the incident had never happened. Word gets around, though. I didn't have a problem with any of the loggers the rest of the summer.

§

THE VEHICLE AT MY disposal that summer was a beat-up, red, mid-fifties Ford pickup. It had a four-speed stick shift on the floor, wheezed and chugged, and had a tendency to pull to the right on braking, but it got us where we needed to be. It was fun to drive because it was so rusted and dented that I didn't have to be careful with it on the gravel roads. That it was in pretty rough shape turned out to be a bonus one afternoon.

All of the logging roads were gravel and most were narrow, allowing only one lane traffic. They were built by the logging companies to gain access to their licensed areas; no more time or money was spent on them than absolutely necessary. The logging trucks had right-of-way by virtue of their license and their size. Other vehicles had to make way; back up to a clearing or just push into the bush off the road to allow the logging trucks to pass. This could be hard on the paint job unless the vehicle was already heavily scratched.

Mid-afternoon, we were headed to our next cruising assignment. The road we were traveling was very narrow and we were booting it, anxious to get done and hit the beach. I was driving, as usual. We were rounding a long, blind left-hand curve with a wall of bush on the left and an eight-foot drop to a marsh, dry that time of year, on the right. Around the corner ahead, traveling easily as fast as we were, came a fully loaded log truck. By reflex, we both hit the brakes. My Ford pulled to right, slid off the embankment and down, landing on its right side.

Jim, who was sitting against the passenger door, had been riding with his right elbow out the open window, arm on the window frame. When we hit the ground, his arm was driven left by the impact with the ground. He punched Rick, sitting between us, in the face, resulting in a broken finger and an extremely bruised jaw.

Once I had established no one was seriously hurt, I climbed the embankment, followed by the other two. I approached the driver of the log truck and asked if he would give us a ride. I needed to find some way to retrieve the pickup.

"Nope, ain't necessary. I'll get it for you."

He got in the cab of his truck and flipped a couple of switches, then climbed onto the trailer piled with logs. Attached to the front of the trailer was the boom claw used to load and off-load the logs. He swung the boom out and dropped it over the embankment to grasp the pickup with the huge claw. The load of logs gave the truck plenty of counterweight and, in short order, the truck was on the road behind the logger and facing the proper direction.

We thanked the driver and were about to get in the pickup when he asked Jim if he could look at his damaged finger. Upon examination he determined that it was actually dislocated where the finger meets the palm as opposed to being broken. He said he could reset it very easily.

"This could hurt a bit, so I need you to describe to me what your girlfriend looks like in a bikini."

Jim blushed and started to object. Just as he opened his mouth, the truck driver yanked on the finger. A snapping sound and shock flashed across Jim's face, then a look of surprise. He looked at his hand and slowly flexed his fingers. "Still hurts a bit, but that's much better. Thanks."

"No problem. We get a lot of that type of injury in our line of work. Pays to know what to do; saves a lot of running back and forth to town. You guys take care."

The two trucks left in opposite directions. And you know, looking at the dented pickup, you couldn't tell the incident had ever happened!

Laurentian

Points In Between

Education Gap

MY YEARS AT Laurentian University fall into two periods: 1968–1971, at the end of which I was asked to withdraw by the administration; and 1975–1978, from which I graduated with a Bachelor of Science (Honors) and went on to study towards my doctorate at the University of Saskatchewan.

The early years were not the fiasco that the introduction might imply on first reading. Yes, they were a setback and a permanent blot on my record academically. On the other hand, in terms of life lessons, they were extremely educational.

My first year at the university was quite successful. I did well enough to be invited to pursue geology in the Department of Geology. That was my intention because a Bachelor of Science in geology and related sciences was the first step towards Ph.D. studies in paleontology, my ultimate goal.

In my second year, I majored in geology, but things did not go quite as planned. I got a little sidetracked. No, not a girl. A job.

The job came courtesy of my uncle, Henry. I know how that sounds, but it wasn't like that. Henry was three months younger than me. My dad was the oldest of eleven children, Henry the youngest. Every now and then, Henry would half-jokingly demand that I call him 'Uncle,' to which I would reply, 'the day you start calling me sir. Respect your elders, boy.' Being the same age, we spent a lot of time together growing up.

Henry, not in the least academically inclined, took an occupational program at high school and left before I did. He soon found a full-time job at a successful local pizzeria, Cortina. A few years later, when I was finishing my first year at university, my search for a summer job coincided with the expansion of the Cortina business to two locations. Eventually, there would be several others in Sudbury, plus a number in surrounding communities. Henry told me he could get me in as part-time delivery boy. I was not very keen on that idea, but he stressed that the bosses were good guys and all I had to do was impress them and, when an inside position became available, he'd make sure I got it. And he was good to his word. Turned out the bosses loved him, and with good reason. He worked hard, was dependable and excelled at every aspect of the business.

My experiences as a pizza person are documented in the *Cortina* section of this book. I mention it here only to explain the source of my debacle at Laurentian University.

Needing the money, I took as many shifts as possible. And the scheduling was perfect (?)—work as many shifts as I wanted over the summer and, when school started, attend classes during the day and work in the evening. No conflict, no problem, right? Wrong.

The pizzeria closed at one or two in the morning, depending on the day of the week, and most of the guys did something for a while after work. This suited me because I was never one to go home and jump directly into bed. I always needed some wind-down time. Plus, this was all new to me and, for a while, very enticing.

Being of generally poor health, this pace took its toll and I became rundown. I began sleeping late to recoup energy expended in late nights. That was okay for the summer, but once school started, I was in trouble.

I paid car fare to a friend, Bruce Gates, for a ride to Laurentian in the mornings. His first classes were at 8:30 a.m., but mine began at 9:30. So I developed the habit of going to the student lounge with Don Bouffard, a close high school friend in the same program as me, also riding with Bruce. At that time of the morning, the student lounge was almost empty, so I could commandeer an entire sofa and stretch out for an hour's nap. In no time at all, the routine became: arrive in the lounge at 8:30, stretch out, wake intermittently for a minute or two, rouse myself just in time to make an appearance in one of my lab classes, then go to work at four p.m.

Years later, after I had successfully returned to my studies, one of the professors, Dr. James, commented on how frustrated he and the other professors had felt to watch my earlier performance.

"It was hard to watch. You'd come into the lab late, spend half an hour explaining that week's assignment to Don Bouffard, then leave without doing the assignment yourself. Our hands were tied. We couldn't give you marks for work you didn't hand in. It was obvious that you knew the material, but we had no concrete way of verifying that. What a waste."

I became such a fixture in the lounge that other students made accommodations for my presence. When the place filled at lunch and periodically during the afternoon, most of the students who were lying down would sit up and make room. Not me. They let me sleep. Many times I'd wake briefly to find one or more students sitting on my couch with my legs across their laps, eating their lunches and watching t.v. Next time I stirred, they'd be gone.

One of those lunch hours, I woke to television history. That day, Sesame Street aired for the first time on local t.v. for an hour at noon. Within two or three days, word got around and even standing room could not be had in the lounge for that hour. Quite an interesting sight, actually. More than a hundred young adults pursuing post secondary education crammed into the lounge, eating their lunches and counting one to ten out loud with the on-screen muppet and laughing at the contrived way the chef always managed to drop the cake. They repeated *en masse* after Grover as he illustrated to the point of collapse the distinction between *near* and *far*. The popularity of the show among the students never lessened through both my stints at the university.

By the time the end of the year rolled around, I had not attended the minimum number of classes required and was not eligible to write the finals. No way I could pass without them. To make matters worse, I did the same thing the next year. After about six months on delivery at Cortina, I had moved inside to the preparation area and was working even more hours.

Spring, 1971, and again ineligible to write, I received a letter from the administration inviting me to withdraw and take some time to assess my priorities. I took half of their advice. I withdrew, but I did precious little self-examination. My level of maturity would change significantly over the next year, but for now I was having too much fun!

§

ONE MORNING, ensconced on my sofa with my back to the room, I was in the never-never land of pre-sleep. Don was reading on the next couch. On a nearby couch, facing us, sat a young lady who had begun making a regular morning appearance in the lounge. We didn't know her, but wanted to—good-looking, nice body, legs that went on forever. While I was dozing, Don decided to chat her up; I caught only bits of their conversation. Eventually, he introduced himself and asked her name. Her response, or what I thought she said, brought me to a sitting position, wide awake.

"Bruce?!" I asked, astonished.

She started laughing and said, "No. Grace!"

"I could've sworn you said Bruce."

In time, the three of us came to be good friends. We spent a lot of time together at and away from campus until I lost track of her about five years after she graduated. And all that time, Don and I always called her Bruce.

§

NOT TOO LONG after meeting her, Bruce introduced me to one of her friends. Mary Jane was also a student and, as I found out later, the daughter of a public health nurse who worked with my stepmother. She was pretty cute, so I asked her out. Big mistake.

Mary Jane was hesitant, expressed interest, but indicated she was seeing someone.

"Serious?"

"No. In fact, is not even exclusive, at this point. We're just dating."

"So what's the problem? We're just talking roller skating here. Nothing long-term or committed."

"True, but it just wouldn't feel right. I'd feel like I was cheating."

I worked on her every day for a week and she finally decided she would go roller skating with me Friday night. We really had a good time.

Are you ready? Now it starts.

Mary Jane, Bruce, Don and I, and a few of our classmates had begun eating lunch at the same table in the cafeteria of the science building. Monday morning, Mary Jane confides to the group that over the weekend she had broken up with her former boyfriend and that she and I were an item. Congratulations all around, while I struggled to hide my surprise.

I didn't disabuse her of the notion because I'd never had a real girlfriend and I figured, "What the hell? Could be fun."

That evening at supper, my mother commented that her coworker had been suitably impressed with me when I dropped Mary Jane at home after our date. We had chatted for a bit. More important were her comments about just how strongly taken with me Mary Jane was. I should've seen it coming.

Mary Jane and Bruce were odd girls out in our lunch group, actually. They were arts students and the rest of us were in the sciences. During our first conversation, I had learned that Mary Jane was taking psychology. Now, most of the professors and students of psychology that I had met to that point were whack-jobs themselves to greater or lesser degree; that opinion still stands today. I decided not to prejudge for the sake of our fledgling relationship. After all, she was just in second year—how tainted could she be?

Well, she was already too far gone to save. Almost every lunch, something came up that set off her compunction to analyze. If I bought a chocolate bar two days in a row, she tried to analyze the root cause of this fetish. She said straight out that someone could not just *like* chocolate. The liking was deeply rooted in one's psyche. Perhaps I was a late bed-wetter or insecure about my masculinity. My dislike of a particular professor probably reflected a repressed fear that I was homosexual. She was continually psychoanalyzing me—and the others, as well.

§

MARY JANE WAS QUITE opinionated, not necessarily a bad thing (I am, as well), but she jumped to conclusions; definitely a negative. One lunch hour, I was keeping an eye on the door because I had invited a new Asian student to join us. Our table was about two-thirds of the way towards the back of the cafeteria and I wanted to be sure he found us.

When he came in, he stood at the door, books and brown bag in hand, looking around the hall. I stood up, waved and called,

"Hey, Yu! Over here."

Before I regained my seat, she was all over me about insensitivity, racial intolerance, a false sense of white supremacy. Where did I get off just yelling at him 'Hey, you!' as if he were some second-class citizen who did not deserve respect? The least I could do was address him by name. I just let her go on and on, having had just about enough of her attitude.

When he arrived at our table, I stood.

"Everyone, I'd like you to meet you Yu-chen Wing, a new student in geology." I went on to introduce everyone else at the table.

Seated again, I was assailed once more by Mary Jane, in subdued tones this time. How could I have done that? I had obviously purposely set her up to humiliate herself. I was so insensitive. Blah, blah, blah. Our relationship was rapidly becoming tenuous.

§

THE END CAME ON a Monday, again at lunch in the cafeteria. I had been scheduled to work the day shift at Cortina on Saturday and with the rare Saturday evening off, Mary Jane and I were going to the Club Alouette to take in the long-standing Saturday night youth dance. I wasn't off until 6 p.m., but that was lots of time.

Just after five, a good friend named Maria came by, quite distraught, asking if we could talk. I really couldn't until six, but I figured I could give her a half an hour or so after work. She waited in obvious agitation.

When I got off, I brought a couple of cans of pop and sat down with her at one of the corner tables. It was an old story, just new to her. Through racking sobs, tear-streaked mascara and repeated nose-blowing, she told me she was pregnant. To further complicate matters, the father, Al, was black and she was as white as is possible. She had informed Al a few hours earlier and he had dropped her like a live rattlesnake. He had belittled her for being so careless, then laughed in her face when she suggested he pay for an abortion. The idea that he might want to get married brought the biggest laugh. He slammed the door on the way out.

The time was already ten to seven. I just couldn't leave her like that, so I called Mary Jane. I explained I had a friend in crisis, I had to break our date, I would explain tomorrow at lunch. She wasn't happy, but said she understood.

We were still talking at 8:30 when Bruce came in with a date to pick up an order. They were only at the counter a few minutes since their order was ready and waiting for them. She saw me, we exchanged smiles and waves while her date paid and they left.

I sat with my friend, drinking pop and talking, until after ten. I gave what advice and support I could and referred her to my stepmother at the Public Health Unit. I said I'd talk to my stepmother, give her the details and asked her to arrange for my friend to see a counselor to discuss her options. Then I drove her home, just a few blocks away.

Monday, lunch. I stepped into the full cafeteria a few minutes later than usual to be greeted by a female voice yelling obscenities and calling me every vile name in the book. She was standing at our usual table screaming across the rows of occupied tables, red-faced, body tense. I was such a lowlife, two-timing, lying, etc., etc.

Bruce had *mentioned* seeing me at Cortina the night before seated at a table in the corner with an attractive girl.

I came close to just turning and leaving. Instead, I went to the table, let her abuse me until she ran down, explained, told her I didn't want to see her again. And then I left.

New York, New York

I MADE MY SECOND attempt at getting through the second year of my BSc in the academic year 1970-1971. I fared even more poorly than the previous attempt, neglecting my studies in favor of work and play at Cortina. More than half my motivation for even enrolling was to avoid telling my parents, with whom I still lived, that I was dropping out. In the end, I was invited to withdrawal by the administration. It was, however, not a total write off. I achieved nothing academically, but I had a number of experiences that made micro-adjustments to the life path I was traveling. Most of these experiences were related, directly or indirectly, to a field trip to New York City led by Dr. Paul Copper.

Paul had already been Professor of Invertebrate Paleontology at Laurentian for a number of years, since the mid-sixties, and was well on his way to becoming one of the world's preeminent authorities on brachiopods in general and Atrypids in particular. He would be the first foreign scientist of any kind to be allowed into Red China to do research after they lifted the ban.

Paul could have scored a position just about anywhere he wanted, so why Laurentian? Because of its proximity to Manitoulin Island. The island has one of the best exposures of Ordovician/Silurian fossiliferous strata in the world. By teaching at Laurentian, he was only a couple of hours away by car. He could do fieldwork with little logistical planning or expense and could even do it over weekends. Despite numerous offers from institutions around the globe, he lived out his academic career at Laurentian University.

A few years after the trip, when I got it together and returned to my studies, he became my mentor. One of my few regrets is that my health pooped out before I could make him truly proud.

In February of 1971, Paul organized a field trip to New York for his second year paleontology students, ostensibly to see the American

Museum of Natural History. Although I did learn valuable things of an academic nature at the museum, other events were much more educational and fulfilling. A major one occurred the night before we left.

§

AT THE TIME, I was casually seeing a young lady with the unfortunate name of Maria Fish. Until recently, she had been with Al, the father of her illegitimate son and a good friend of Henry, my uncle. Al always treated Maria like dirt unless he wanted something. That she was his white trophy (he was black) and sex toy was obvious to everyone. He didn't assume any responsibility for his son, ran around on Maria and had at least one other illegitimate child to my knowledge. Maria began dropping by to talk to me when things between them were particularly bad and sought my advice when she decided she had to end the relationship. During the process, we were getting closer. A short time after she pushed him out of her life, we began dating informally.

Don Bouffard and I had been close friends since early high school and spent a lot of time together. That changed when I started working at Cortina. I had very little time off and he went to his university classes during the day, while I slept in the lounge. When I moved from delivery to working in the prep area at Cortina, Don began dropping by occasionally to visit during my breaks.

Don met Betty on one of these visits. We were eating pizza one evening when Maria and her best friend, Betty, came by to chat. Don was immediately taken by Betty, without question the more attractive of the two, although Maria held her own. Don assumed what he considered his 'smooth, lady-killer' persona. By the time I had to get back to work, Betty had agreed to a double date. Even then I recognized she was just being polite to me, Maria's 'boyfriend,' something Don wouldn't realize for quite some time.

Don had been playing the role of ladies' man around me for about two and a half years, ever since his first summer of fieldwork in geology. Writing to me that summer, he had recounted in detail how he had lost his virginity, how wonderful the sex was and how eager his partner was.

Don's need to lose his virginity was quite normal, in my experience. That was the focus of most teenage boys and still is, I guess. I was the oddball. For Don, losing his virginity before me was a matter of pride. It wasn't important to me. Sure, I looked forward to it, but sex just for the sake of sex had never interested me.

Several times over the next two years, Don bragged about his latest sex partner and described his smooth technique for getting women into the sack. We occasionally discussed my virginity and at least once he tried to give me advice on what to do to lose it.

The night before leaving to go to New York, I was working with Joe. The bus was scheduled to leave at 7 a.m., so the students had to be there no later than 6:30. Joe and I would get out of Cortina at 2:30 and had planned to go to my parents' house and listen to tunes until Don and his brother picked me up at 6:00. No hardship, as I seldom got home much before that time anyway.

Maria and Betty stopped in mid-evening for a bit. Hearing our plan for the wee hours, the ladies suggested they join us—Betty had long had a lust on for Joe, unbeknownst to him. Joe said he would get them home afterward, so we were good to go.

Everything just fell into place. First, my parents were away on a Caribbean cruise. Second, my room was in the basement next to the den, two floors below my sisters' bedrooms. We would have privacy as long as we kept the noise down. Third, I think the girls were working a conspiracy. I put some *Lovin' Spoonful* on my little stereo, got us some cans of pop and had hardly settled beside Maria when she suggested, in low tones, that we should give Joe and Betty some privacy. We retired to my room and the intimacy on both sides of the wall escalated.

Yep. 'It' happened for me that night. And how! My elbows and knees left sweat stains on the bedspread that my stepmother was never able to remove. And we kept at it until 5:45, stopping because I had to get ready to leave. I felt great! Exhausted after working all evening and 'working' all night, but great!

The four of us left together, the other three in Joe's car and me with the Bouffards. I can still see the huge grin on Joe's face as he backed out of the driveway. On the way to Laurentian, I was aware that Don was atypically quiet and withdrawn, but I was too tired to focus. I did have enough energy left to smile and say that, as of that night, I was a man!

Among the last to arrive, we wasted no time getting on the bus and settling into a pair of seats. I was asleep before the bus pulled out. The ride to New York City took thirteen hours and I awoke as we slowed to a stop at a toll booth just outside of the city. The operator asked our destination, out of curiosity. When we told him, he laughed and said, "Just be sure to stay away from the downtown section of Forty-Second Street."

Guess where our hotel was. In those days, Forty-Second Street where it traversed the downtown area was home to sleazy hotels, strip clubs and pawnshops, and populated by whores, pimps, junkies, strippers, con-men and thieves. This was going to be great!

Don was downright sullen and uncommunicative by this time—thoroughly pissed off, with me anyway. He wouldn't give me the time of day, let alone tell me what was going on with him, so I decided I wasn't going to let him spoil the trip. We were only going to be there for two nights, three days; I was going to make the most of it.

Only on the bus trip home, three days later, did Don open up and tell me what was bothering him. He told me it started when he saw Joe and me come out of the house with the two girls that morning. He was hurt and angry.

"Why didn't you call me? Tell Betty that Joe couldn't come and I'd be going instead? You know how much I like her."

"How the hell could I do that. Betty's had the hots for Joe for the longest time. How could I try to make her want to be with you instead? It was her choice, man, not mine."

"Yeah, well. *Then* you had the nerve to tell me you lost your cherry that night. To top it off, you had the audacity to be so tired from all the sex you'd had that you *slept* all the way to New York City."

Now I was really puzzled. After all the things he'd said in the past, shouldn't he be happy for me?

"Why was that a big deal? I'd have expected you to be happy for me. Sure, I have a lot of catching up to do to be your equal, but at least I'm in the game now."

Don got this look on his face that seemed to shift between embarrassment, indignation and frustration. He didn't say anything.

"What?" I said. "What's with you?"

"I'll kill you if you tell anybody. I lied. I'm still a virgin. Okay? Now you know. I've been lying all along, wanted to impress you. And now you go and lose it first!"

I started to laugh, which made matters worse, I suppose.

"I can't believe it. You know damn well that doesn't matter to me. Or you should. I don't give a rat's ass if you are a virgin or not."

Luckily our friendship was strong enough to weather this storm. We are still best of friends and this episode is now a source of nostalgic humor. Even my daughters think it is funny.

§

A BUNCH OF US decided we weren't going to use our rooms, not for sleeping anyway, while we were in the Big Apple. We'd use them as a base to clean up and store our extra clothes, but we were going to be in the city such a short time, we could sleep when we got home. Five of us decided to see the town together. I have to admit, I don't remember the names of the others. I was so seldom in class that I had not developed much of a relationship with any of them. Don may have been there, but I was ignoring him so thoroughly that he has no place in those memories.

We began by doing exactly what the toll attendant had cautioned us against. We spent the first evening taking in Forty-Second Street. For young, naive men from northern Ontario, to say it was an eye-opener would be a gross understatement. We gaped and we gawked. Every store, not just the big or pricey places, had some sort of anti-break-in metal grill or bar structure that was pulled across the store front at closing. And we saw people that, in our experience, only existed in movies. The entire street was a Hollywood cliché.

We saw vulgarly clad hookers with bodies that were dreams and legs a mile long, their hot pants so tight they looked painted on and we could see the details of their pubes outlined by the fabric. They wore all the colors of the rainbow and walked on platform shoes so tall you'd think they would be afraid of falling off them. These women actually bent over enticingly and solicited or were solicited through the open passenger windows of cars!

And the pimps in the broad hats, silk pants and fur half-jackets; more rings than they had fingers; driving pink or white or baby blue Cadillacs convertibles; walking with the attitude, "Who's the best lookin' dude on the block and why am I?"

The peep shows displayed more on their sidewalk advertising than was available in illicit magazines back in Sudbury. The massage parlors advertise absolutely no sexual contact, yet had two markedly different pricing structures depending on the level of 'personal attention' the client desired.

Forty-Second Street was my first exposure to openly, flamboyantly gay people. And I don't mean they were just really happy. Lesbians and homosexuals were on display walking hand-in-hand, necking against buildings, groping each other. Many of the pairs had definite role distinctions, dominant versus submissive. Both groups displayed a lot of leather and *avant garde* haircuts. When they met and stopped to talk, they did a lot of touching with their hands. They seem to have only two facial expressions—friendly smile or belligerent scowl.

These were not the first gays I'd seen; in fact, I had a couple of really good friends who were gay. But my friends didn't walk down the street broadcasting the fact. To my mind, the posturing of the gays on Forty-Second Street was more about defiance that it was pride.

We went into a number of sex boutiques out of curiosity more than anything else. I won't describe the paraphernalia on display, but I will say I had a hard time imagining how some of these implements would be put to use. A couple of the guys bought some fairly benign pieces for their shock value back home.

At one point, we were accosted by another cliché. A black youngster no more than ten or eleven years old ran up to the five of us as we strolled up the sidewalk. Stopping abruptly, he whipped his jacket open and pulled up a sleeve. "Wanna buy a watch?" he asked. The inside of his jacket and his arm displayed an array of timepieces. Not a Timex in sight, either. All golds and silvers and expensive looking. We gaped, caught flat-footed. Before we could react, he was gone. You had to act fast if you wanted a bargain in New York City.

A case of right-place-right-time, we ran into a young man in ordinary jeans and t-shirt (he was as out of place as we) scalping tickets to the hugely successful Broadway show, *Oh, Calcutta*. One of the group suggested he give us a package deal for five tickets, especially since we had come all the way from Canada, and he agreed. I got the impression this sort of request was not new to him and the discount was built into the pricing structure. Bonus to him if the discount was not requested. Off we went to see *Oh, Calcutta* and, among other things, watched Bill Macy, later of television's *Maude* fame, running around on stage nude. The show deserved all its accolades and we thoroughly enjoyed ourselves.

We got back to the hotel around 4 a.m. and dozed in the chairs in the lobby until breakfast. We went to our rooms to clean up, then met the rest of the group. On the agenda: American Museum of Natural History.

§

YOU WILL BE SADLY disappointed if you are expecting even a cursory description of the AMNH. Not happening. Too much to absorb in person, I could do nothing but injustice to that great institution with just a few paragraphs. And we focused on only the paleontological section!

I was repeatedly awed at every turn. Although the aspiration wouldn't surface for three or four years, I think my commitment to becoming a paleontologist recrystallized in my subconscious on that visit. Just the exhibits themselves, the vast array of fossils representing previously living organisms from an unimaginably distant past were overwhelming enough. But Dr. Copper had arranged for us to tour the collections, research and preparations areas as well. The mind boggled, then numbed in short order. We saw hundreds of specimens that the public never got to see because of space limitations or because the specimens were too valuable to risk. Then we were shown rows of cabinets with hundreds of drawers, each containing hundreds of fossils.

We watched as they painstakingly used the tiniest of instruments to extract delicate specimens from the rock in which they were embedded.

We met specialists who worked on microscopic fossils, and others who studied mammoths and dinosaurs. Some specialized in ancient plants and the origins of coal and oil.

Our little group of five, saturated but not sated, stayed later than most of the others. Our stomachs drew us away around 7 p.m. We found an automat and ate an inexpensive and tasteless supper, then took in the Empire State Building.

§

TRYING TO DECIDE what to do next, we found that most of us were out of cash. We all had travelers' cheques, but had neglected to keep an eye on finances. Banks were closed at 9 p.m., even in New York City. We canvassed around at shops, convenience stores, department stores, with no luck. Most would allow us to use the cheques if we bought something worth almost the entire amount of the cheque and they'd give us the change, but none would just cash them.

I suggested we go back to the hotel. Perhaps, being guests, we would have cheque-cashing privileges. Yes and no. The Canadian dollar at the time was worth $1.10 US. The night manager was willing to cash our cheques if we agreed to pay a 20% premium. Take it or leave it at 10 p.m. We took it.

After all the rigmarole, we were back on Forty-Second Street ready to tackle the city without any idea where to go, what to do. After a couple of unsatisfactory suggestions, one of the guys pointed up the street at a taxi and suggested we flag one down. Cabbies in the movies always seem to know where it's happening, so what the hell?

I had a good feeling the moment I heard this guy speak. So people from the Bronx actually talk like that. Too cool. We asked if he could take all five and show us some highlights for a while. We figured, split five ways, it wouldn't be too expensive. He nodded towards the interior of the cab and said it was okay with him as long as we didn't mind being a little crowded. We piled in, one in the front passenger seat.

Once we were moving, he said, "So, you're from Canada," a statement, not a question. I'm not going to try to imitate his accent in writing! He was very friendly, as interested in learning about us and our country as we were about New York. He wanted to know what it was like to live in a smaller city surrounded by lakes and forests, where we could be roughing it in a matter of minutes. He complained that the big city, with all the people, the crime, the dirt and smog, wore a person down. He had never been farther away than New Jersey.

"I love listening to you talk. You have such interesting accents," he said, smiling. I reflected to myself the truth of that statement. Down there, *we* were the ones with the accents.

By then we had driven a few blocks going nowhere in particular. He asked if we had any idea what we wanted to see. I offered, "We're not much into the touristy stuff. How about we leave it up to you? You show us your New York City."

He agreed. "How about a ride on the subway?"

"We did that this afternoon from the museum back to our hotel."

The cabbie sent back, "Ah, well, you haven't really experienced it, then. There's nothing like the NYC subway at night."

He said he'd let us off at a particular station. We were to take such and such a train to Grand Central Station, where he'd pick us up.

"You'll get there ahead of me, but don't worry. I'll get there as quick as traffic allows."

He was right. It certainly was different. The very lighting itself seemed strange after dark, even though the subway is always lit by the same lighting system. Must be psychological, the knowledge that it is dark outside. The subway station had an anemic pale yellow tint and everyone, no matter the complexion, took on a slight sickly pallor.

Earlier in the afternoon, even on cars that weren't full, riders seemed to have no compunctions about sitting near or next to strangers. At night, unless in a group, everyone consciously sat as far away from others as possible. And avoided eye contact.

Many of the young people our age were dressed in variations on the punk theme, a sinister air about them. Not that they did anything overt; just their dress and their in-your-face attitude was troubling.

Even the graffiti, fun and entertaining in the afternoon, was dark and threatening at night.

One high point was the middle-aged Negro man busking on the violin on the station platform. Man, could he play! We stayed around while he did a classical piece, then some bluegrass. He asked if we had any requests and I asked if he knew 'Summer Time' from *Porgy and Bess*. He didn't even answer, just fell right into it. Exquisite! We left him a couple of bucks apiece, for which he thanked us.

Grand Central Station was another of those 'you've got to experience it' places. All the major bus, rail and subway systems intersected in a huge, multilevel complex. You could get lost in there. Or, if you're into studying people, a lifetime of research could be conducted without leaving the building.

Either traffic had not been too bad or the time we spent listening to the busker slowed us enough, but the cabbie was waiting for us when we arrived. From there he took us to see Madison Square Gardens, the Statue of Liberty and the Brooklyn Bridge. Each was impressive in the daylight, but took on added allure at night. The lights, especially on the Brooklyn Bridge, added an almost fantasy dimension. But the dark also obscured the shabbiness of age and the dirt that marred the sites in daylight.

Then we were off to see Harlem. What a scene. I truly wasn't prepared for the reality. Large parts of Harlem, as documented by many visitors, really did look more like war zones than areas of one of the leading cities of the world, areas that had been neglected and allowed to deteriorate. The gutted buildings, the stripped cars right on the street, the people who obviously were *living* in some of those cars, the large number of black people just seeming to be hanging around with no purpose, all eyes watching our cab intently as we passed—everything radiated how unwelcome we were. I still shudder thinking of it. I would've hated to break down in that neighborhood.

He took us to Shea Stadium. Some winter production was being prepared, but I don't recall the details. We didn't go because it was the home of the New York Mets anyway. We wanted to see the venue where the Beatles had performed their famous first North American concert.

§

GETTING ON TOWARD 3 a.m., we asked if the cabbie knew a place where we could get something to eat at that time of night.

"What, in this town? Are you kidding? How much you wanna spend? How fancy?"

"We need it to be affordable and we're not looking for anything fancy. Just some place where we can sit quietly, have a good homemade hamburger or hot pork sandwich, maybe."

"Great. I got just the place. It's a little diner, three or four tables and a sit-down counter. Good food, decent prices, open 24 hours."

"Let's go."

A few minutes later, he pulled over to the curb. Just up ahead, a side street formed a 'T' with the avenue where we were parked. A line of three sawhorse-style barriers emblazoned NYC PW stretched across the entrance to the side street.

"This whole damn town is always under street repair. You gonna have to walk. It's just up that street. Mind if I come along and grab a cup of coffee?"

"Of course not. We'll even buy."

We climbed out, moved past the barriers and headed up the street. We had to skirt a large hole in the asphalt guarded by a backhoe. The side street was more dimly lit than the avenue behind us and we were joking about how screwed we'd be if we had to find our way back to the hotel quickly. None of us had really been paying attention to our route. I'll admit I was getting a little apprehensive. The area was dark enough that the possibility we had been set up to be mugged played at the back of my mind.

A few buildings ahead we could see a small 'Diner' sign and a larger, well-lit window. Just this side of the diner was a narrow alley, pitch black. As we came abreast of the alley, a stark white face appeared in the air about five feet off the ground. Instantly my heart came into my throat, I felt the head rush of adrenaline and my armpits started to pour sweat. I froze, but before I could utter a word, the rest of the little old lady stepped out of the alley into the dim light of the street. Did I feel foolish! She had scared the hell out of me!

Her face was white because of the amount of powder she was wearing. Her hair was incongruously blonde and well kept, but in a recognizably fifties style, held in place by a tiara. She wore a satin looking ankle-length gown that shimmered in the light and a furry white and gray half jacket. Her hands and wrists sparkled with jewelry. Her feet were encased in delicate, low-heeled satin pumps.

"Sorry, young man. Didn't mean to frighten you. Where are you headed at this time in the morning?"

"That's okay. Just caught me by surprise. We're going to get something to eat at the diner."

"Let's walk together; that's where I'm going. I come here every morning this time."

The others had moved on and were entering the diner when we turned to follow. The diner was nothing special aside from being scrupulously clean. The only person in the place was the cook behind the counter, a partly bald friendly looking guy in his fifties, I'd say. The counter had eight stools, so we took seven.

"A few more of you, and we'd have a full house. Good to see you this fine morning. Coffee and menus?" Some of us had pop.

During the course of our meal, the old lady kept up a string of friendly chatter that eventually led to her telling us why she came out to the diner at that time of night. She said she lived in a suite in a residential building a few streets over, that she owned the suite. She lived there with her daughter and her son-in-law.

"They keep me locked up, don't let me go anywhere. They obtained a court order that gives them the legal right."

She went on to explain she had been quite a respected Broadway dancer in the late forties to early sixties. She made a fair amount of money and took some good investment advice, so she was well-off.

"My daughter married a no-account lazy bum who never worked a day in his life. The two of them have been sponging off me since they got married. Then I became too old to dance; not infirm, mind you, just not as attractive as the new, young dancers and not quite as supple anymore.

My bastard of a son-in-law became nervous that I'd live long enough to use up all my investments.

"He convinced my daughter and together they contrived to make it look like I was losing my marbles. Then they got a shyster lawyer who obtained a court order making me their ward and putting them in control of my money.

"They keep a pretty good eye on me during the day, even have attendants to watch me, to keep me from going out when they're not home. They don't want me spending any of my money. But I have a key they don't know about. And when I realized what they were up to a few years ago, I moved a lot of my funds and put them somewhere safe. I don't tell anyone, not even you nice young people, where it is or who brings it to me when I need it.

"My little daily outing is to come here, have a coffee, sometimes a beer. Isn't that right, Lou?" She looked at the cook, he smiled at her, nodded and said, "Every night, like clockwork."

I didn't know what to make of her story. There was a tragedy here: either the one she described or the fact that I was gullible enough to believe her.

A little more small talk and we were ready to leave. I asked Lou for separate checks. As he began to prepare them, the old lady waved her hand at him, then looked at us, "I have had such a pleasant time chatting with you, let me take care of that. My treat."

Hesitating, I looked up at the cook. He smiled again, shrugged his shoulders and nodded. It was okay with him, he figured she was good for it. I thanked her warmly and said meeting her was the highlight of my stay in New York City, adding that I'd never forget her.

Her largesse must have been contagious. When the cabbie got us back to the hotel at 6 a.m. and we prepared to settle up, he said, "Forget it. I had a great time. I had nothing else on tonight, anyway."

"What about the cab? We put on a lot of miles, won't the owner...?"

"I own it. Many of the New York cabbies are independents. I only answer to myself. You guys take good care. Pleasure. And thanks for the coffee." And he drove off.

A Little Friction

WHEN I RETURNED to Laurentian in 1975 to complete my BSc, I had quite a different attitude from the first time. I applied myself and had no problem doing well despite working full-time managing my two pizza franchises. Plus, life was becoming more complicated. My wife was pregnant with our first child, due to be born in early October.

In fact, the pregnancy is what led me back to school. The news that we were going to have a child brought home to me that life was moving on and I had no plan; I was just taking it as it came. I began to consider whether I wanted to spend my life slinging pizza. That was a no-brainer. Life in the pizzeria brought no intellectual stimulation or satisfaction, no feeling of accomplishment. Thus, the question invited a resounding 'no.'

So what did I want to do with my life? And there, waiting for me to acknowledge its presence, was the answer. I wanted what I had always wanted: to be an invertebrate paleontologist and study the ancient life that once inhabited this planet. So I enrolled as a mature student.

I admit I was nervous in the fall term, concerned that I had shot my wad the first time around and I no longer had what it took. My first set of exam results put all my doubts to rest. I graduated at the top of the class and qualified for the direct PhD (skip the Masters) program at the University of Saskatchewan beginning in the fall of 1978.

§

UNDERSTAND THAT saying I took my studies seriously is not to say that I didn't have any fun during those years. I somehow found time to lead a field trip of thirty students to see the reefs in Florida, to spearhead the revitalization of the geology club, to play 'old timers' hockey once a week—and get into a little mischief.

A very close friend to this day, Bill Elford, had been eyeing a pretty nice looking babe. At the time, we were in fourth year and final exams were approaching. A bunch of us spent late nights studying in the fourth-year room, a room set aside for fourth-year students writing a thesis. I attended the sessions any night I wasn't working.

The fourth-year room was opposite and one door down from the elevator, so we had a view of everyone coming off the elevator headed to the study carrels in the library. That is how this young lady caught Bill's eye in the first place. He quickly ascertained that she sat at the same long table every night and he usually found some excuse to go to the library and eyeball her.

I got the bright idea that it would be funny to ambush him, steal his pants and put them over the back of the chair across the table from her. He would have to go into the library in his boxer shorts and retrieve his pants right in front of her. Hilarious!

I organized it with Peter Nenadov, Dan Jerica and Jim Ireland. We fell on Bill in the corridor as he returned from his evening ogle. None of us were man-mountain, including Bill. We were all pretty lean and reasonably fit, however, so we thought we wouldn't have much trouble, four on one. We hadn't counted on Bill's wiry strength or his determination not to give up his jeans.

What should have been a brief scuffle—hold him down and pull off his pants—turned into a marathon brawl that worked its way up and down the carpeted second-floor hallway of the Science II Building. Bill was a hellcat and we needed all our resources and more than ten minutes to get his jeans off him. As soon as he lost them, he quieted down and we all laughed. Jim left with the jeans as soon as we had them off and took them to the library.

Our balloon of anticipated fun, however, suffered a leak. When he found out what we had done with his jeans, Bill walked nonchalantly into the library straight over to her table in his boxers. Standing across from her and looking right at her, he took his jeans off the chair and put them on, taking his time getting his shirt tucked in just right and tying his belt. Then he smiled at her, which she returned, and he came back out. How anticlimactic!

The next morning, the moment I saw Bill come out of the stairwell, I knew. He was obviously stiff and in pain, walking gingerly, as if he didn't want his legs to rub together. He laughed and said, "Wait'll you see this."

In the privacy of the fourth-year room, he slowly lowered his jeans. He was one massive friction burn, all scabbed over from hip to knee on one side, with a smaller one to match on the other hip. All that thrashing on the synthetic hall carpet with his jeans half off had nearly skinned his legs raw. We still joke about that episode and I never fail to feel a guilty twinge.

§

THAT SAME BUNCH of guys had done a number on me a few months earlier. I always took the stairs, refusing to use the elevator just to go up one floor. Coming out of the stairwell the morning of my birthday, they pounced on me. I was not the fighter Bill was, so they had no trouble holding me down. I was wearing a blue gingham shirt with snaps, which they pulled open. And Jim wrote 'Happy Birthday, Iggy, from the 4th year room' on my chest in indelible wide black magic marker. It would take more than a month for all the traces to finally wear off.

We had quite a laugh about it, then went to class. After the afternoon lab session, I had to run some errands for work before returning for our once-a-week night class. Some of the magic marker, still wet when I re-snapped my shirt, had bled into the material. Since I was going right past home, I stopped in to change shirts and tell my wife about the 'birthday card.' I had a quick bite and put on my second blue gingham, this one with ordinary buttons. Then I was off to my night class.

On those evenings, we traditionally went to the pub for an hour to wind down after the seminar class. Bill and I would nurse cans of Pepsi while the rest had a few beer. We'd joke, discuss our classes, generally enjoy each other's company. That night, two other tables in the pub were held down by geology students, all of whom we knew. Several yelled birthday wishes across the tables and toasted me the wish for many more.

One of the ladies called over, "I hear you got a special birthday gift from the fourth-year students."

When I smiled and nodded, she added, "So, are you going to show us the artwork, or not?"

I shook my head and said it was just black magic marker, no big deal. But she wasn't going to let me off the hook and soon her table was chanting, "Show us, show us."

Bill leaned over to me and said, "They won't quit until you show them."

I decided to make a show of it. Standing up, I said, "All right, are you ready? Here it is."

And like Superman in his phone booth, I gripped my shirt and pulled it open to bare my chest. Only as the buttons streaked off in all directions did I remember I had changed shirts and this one did not have snaps. This apparently cavalier gesture was a huge hit, making a bigger splash than the birthday memento on my skin. The crowd thought I had done it on purpose and I did not deny it. Going to class the next morning, I found the story had made its way around the entire department.

Cortina

Points In Between

Scotty

WHY IS IT THE CRAZIES, the belligerent customers, the inebriates looking for trouble, seem to come out of the woodwork on Friday and Saturday nights more than at any other time? Yeah, yeah. The easy answer is that those nights are the only two in the week when most people don't have to be concerned about getting up for work in the morning. They can go out and let loose.

But anyone that has worked in the late night hospitality services knows that there is no shortage of people who overindulge every night of the week. For some reason, however, they seem to be more prone to looking for trouble on those two nights.

That particular Friday night proved no exception. Not that it turned out altogether usual either.

Just before eleven, three big bruisers, all well-over six feet tall and muscular, came into the pizzeria. They were all dressed in the trademark style of blue collar workers: work boots, blue jeans and some sort of rugged jacket, open to expose gingham, flannel or denim shirts with snaps. The tallest and most vocal was wearing a jean jacket with the sleeves rolled halfway to his elbows. Another wore a black and red deerskin shirt/jacket, while the third had on a well-worn suede jacket that reeked of leather waterproofing. For the purposes of this narrative, I'll refer to them as Jean Jacket, Deerskin and Suede.

Their accents immediately gave them away as being French-Canadian and their breaths were strong indications that they had been partaking of more than a few suds. This last was one of the penalties of the restaurant being situated walking distance from a couple of the sleaziest bars in town. I don't object to either condition: I am of French-

Canadian heritage myself and, although I don't drink alcohol, I have no problem with anyone who does as long as they do it responsibly.

That night I was working the ovens—cooking, slicing, packaging, dealing with the customers. I had three teenaged boys working in the preparation area behind a vertical half-wall. With the rolling machine running, they were generally unaware of goings-on at the front counter. At that time of night, between the supper/early evening rush and the after movie/bar rush, business was steady, but not busy. When the three came in, we were able to get to their orders right away.

These guys were by no means falling down drunk, but they had enough alcohol in their systems either to release or create antagonistic attitudes. We couldn't do anything fast enough or well enough to suit them. They complained loudly about how long it was taking, the fact that they couldn't get a couple of beer while they waited and how small the place was. Although they had been using gruff language sprinkled liberally with obscenities, violence had just been a threat to that point. The situation deteriorated without warning.

The first pizza was no sooner cut and in the box, when Jean Jacket upturned it onto the floor on my side of counter. They began yelling so loudly—part French, part English, part some hybrid—that I couldn't tell exactly what was wrong with the pizza. They began knocking the furniture around, banging on the counter and threatening to come over the counter and beat me up. A young couple seated at one of the tables hastily got up and left, abandoning their half-eaten pizza.

Screwing up my courage, I told them that they would have to pay for the ruined pizza and leave or I would call the police. Well! That was like waving a red cape in the face of a raging bull. Jean Jacket reached across the counter to grab me, but only managed to grab the front of my apron. As I was about to be dragged over the counter, Scotty came in.

Now, Scotty, a friend and long-time regular customer, was no little guy either. He was about six-foot-two and hard—all over. He worked on bonus in one of the mines and moonlighted as a bouncer at a couple of the local hotels. He liked to fight!

Scotty had just stopped to pick up a meatball sandwich on the way to dealing with the rowdy late-night crowd at one of his hotel jobs. The three fellows giving me grief didn't seen him enter, their backs being to the door. Scotty immediately recognized two opportunities—a chance to help pull my fat out of the fire and get a little enjoyable exercise in the process.

"What the hell are you ugly frogs croakin' about, then?" He said loudly in the heavy burr that explained his nickname. "Why are you givin' the wee lad here a hard time?"

All three turned to look at Scotty. Still holding onto my apron, Jean Jacket told him, "Mind your own goddamn business, you fuckin' foreigner. We can treat this ass'ole any damn way we want. He's gonna get a hell of a beatin' for treatin' us like shit and, if you don't butt out, we'll kick the shit out of you, too."

Ever fast on his mental toes, Scotty came back with, "You and what army, you fuckin' dumb Frenchman?" That's when the trio's spokesperson made his mistake—he let go of my apron and lunged at Scotty.

A lot happened in the next minute or so. Scotty sidestepped the big brute's lunge, grabbed his arm, swung him around and slammed his back into the 6 x 6 upright that stood in the center of the small room, stunning him for a second. Deerskin took advantage of Scotty's diverted attention and grabbed him from behind, pinning his arms. Suede stepped in front of Scotty, presumably to pummel the captive, but he didn't get the chance. Scotty kicked him in the side of the knee, buckling his leg and he went to the floor. At the same time, Scotty drove his head back into his captor's nose, breaking it as it turned out, and drove his elbow into the kidney area of his side.

Free once again, Scotty stepped towards Jean Jacket who, stepping away from the upright, was making menacing motions with his clenched fists. Scotty ducked under a punch (right, I think), came up and grabbed his opponent by the hair with his left hand. Pulling the big guy's head forward, Scotty drove his ham of a right fist into Jacket's jaw and cheekbone. Left standing there with a handful of hair, Scotty watched his opponent go down, out cold, a large hairless patch of his pate bleeding profusely.

Deerskin pushed off my counter, against which he had been leaning for a few seconds, feeling his swelling and gushing nose, and tried to hit

Scotty from behind. Scotty was lucky this time. He stepped aside to kick the legs out from under the third assailant who was in the process of getting up. Down he went again.

Off-balance from missing with his punch, Deerskin stumbled into Scotty. Using the man's own momentum, Scotty accelerated him forward and around to slam his head down sideways on the top of my counter. Now bleeding from his ear as well, the guy collapsed on the carpet and stayed there.

Suede, finally having regained his feet, decided to cut his losses and ran into the back room. In there, the only potential avenue of escape was through another door that opened onto the stairs to the second floor. He didn't know the second floor contained only the washroom and four empty bedrooms—no escape. But that didn't matter anyway. Scotty caught him halfway up the stairs, grabbed him by the crotch from behind and dragged him down the stairs on his face. He left him semiconscious at the bottom of the stairs, bleeding from several abrasions on his face.

As they say in the movies, it all happened so fast! I had forgotten about calling the police. In the stillness that seemed loud after the mayhem, it once again occurred to me. I turned to the preparation area to find one of the prep guys just hanging up the phone. He said the cops would have a car there in a couple of minutes. It was two cars, actually, and more like five minutes.

For such a short fight, the cops kept us occupied for quite a while. The three instigators were in no shape to make a coherent statement, so they were hauled off to the emergency ward of the General Hospital and then to jail, where they were booked based on the statements of the witnesses.

What took so long? The officers had a problem with one detail in our statements. They were convinced we were protecting someone for some reason. The shape of the three, combined with the fact that Scotty hadn't a mark on him, in fact hardly had a hair out of place, led them to suspect Scotty had help. After some discussion, I suggested they wait and get a statement from the three in jail. The matter would be settled if they gave a compatible account of the incident.

As it turned out, the only thing we ever heard about it was that they pleaded guilty, thus making a trial and our presence in court as witnesses unnecessary.

Oh, and of course, Scotty got his meatball sandwich, on the house, and went off to work. He was a little late, but in fine humor.

Joe

JOE CAME TO WORK in the preparation area of the original Cortina location about a year after I moved inside from delivery. By then, I was working the ovens and front counter as often as I worked prep in the back. Joe never aspired to take on greater responsibility, happy to do his work well and take his money.

He played high school football at Sudbury High at the time and looked the part. He was about six-foot-two, 210 pounds and not an ounce of fat. His friend and line-mate, Bob, although he was at least two inches taller and fifty pounds heavier, wasn't near as strong. They also differed in temperament. Bob was the big, soft, jovial, seldom serious teddy bear; Joe, the sharp-witted, fit, physically hard and hard-working student of mankind. I only mention Bob here because he was with Joe so often when Joe wasn't working and the contrast between the two big guys was startling.

The rest of the teenage boys working at Cortina at that time, me included, were shorter, lighter and less muscular. Somewhere along the line, it became our playful pastime, when business was dead, to gang up on Joe in the back storage room and try to subdue him. Our simple ambition: to wrestle him to the floor.

Never happened.

The back room in earlier days had been used as a seating area with four tables to seat customers. Our business, however, was at least 90% takeout or delivery, so when business got so good that we needed more storage room, the tables went. Stock was now stacked along the walls with an open area in the center that grew and shrank in inverse proportion to the stock.

At different times, as many as four of us lighter dudes would trap Joe in the stock room, usually on his way back from the bathroom upstairs. The more we tried and failed, the more committed we became—we had to take him down! It was always a joke to Joe.

He would plant his feet about shoulder width apart and let us come at him. We'd throw ourselves on his back, grab his waist, hanging off his arms, his legs, his neck. You'd swear we were fleas bothering a big dog.

These little wrestling matches were all variations on a theme. Joe would reach down, pull one of us off his leg and hold that person pinned to the floor. He'd reach over his shoulder with the other hand, grab the guy clinging to his back, pull him over his head and press him at some angle on top of the guy already on the floor. Then he'd pull one of the others off his waist, turn him upside down and stack him on top of the pile. Usually, because holding that many down at once was not easy, one or more of us would wiggle out of the pile, regroup and attack again. This went on for a few minutes until he had all four of us stacked like cord wood under him. Then he would let us up and, if we had anything left, away we'd go again. He was never the one to call it quits.

Often these sessions resembled tag-team bouts. We always had to have an ear to the front counter in case a customer came in. One of us would have to pull out of the melee and go to serve the customer. As soon as the customer was gone, if the match hadn't broken up yet, he would rejoin the fray. And just to emphasize: *we never beat Joe!*

§

SOMETIMES YOU ASK someone to do something not doubting in the least that it will get done, but completely unprepared for how the person performs the task. Joe was like that. His straightforward approach commonly led to simple but surprising solutions.

One rainy Tuesday, I was presented with a problematic situation and asked Joe for his assistance. I didn't expect and will never forget how he chose to solve it.

The original Cortina location was on Brady Street in an old house that most recently served as a house of ill repute. It stood alone in the middle of the block, all the other old dwellings having been demolished to make room for the municipal carpark. Workers at City Hall, the Police Station, the Public Health Unit, the Fire Hall and others parked in this lot. It was huge and held hundreds of cars. Tom Davies Square occupies that space today.

The parking lot was not paved, just loose gravel on a clay base, as was our own small parking lot. Actually, the only entrance to the municipal lot was through our lot. So we had quite a bit of through traffic everyday. When it rained, both parking lots got pretty sloppy; and a lot of rain, enough to soak down into the clay base, meant a sea of mud. Watching the public servants in their business attire trying to negotiate the mud without ruining their outfits could be quite humorous, if we had nothing else to do. Of course, we were watching from the dry comfort of the pizzeria. Not so funny when we had to go out in it, especially the guys on delivery. And the mess in the entrance and the carpeted area in front of the counter!

The rain had been coming down pretty steadily since late Sunday, so the parking lot was long past treacherous. Many of the cars leaving at shift-end around 5:30 p.m. slewed sideways as their tires spun in the mud. And all were covered in sprayed layers of the stuff.

Around 7:30, the daily delivery van arrived from the main branch. Cortina now had four locations and all the pastas (ravioli, lasagna, macaroni, rigatoni, etc.), the sauces and the dough were made in the basement at the largest branch on Martindale Road. Following the tried and true formula used by so many successful restaurant chains, Cortina's owners realized the best way to maintain quality control was to have as much of the product standardized and centrally manufactured, then delivered to the various locations. The pasta even came divided into measured individual servings so that all portions were the same at all Cortina locations.

New product was delivered daily in the evening. This served two purposes. The women at Martindale had the entire day shift to do their work without interruption by the delivery staff. And evening delivery took pressure off the ladies that worked the day shift at the other locations. A lot of the containers, especially the sauces and the dough, were quite heavy, difficult and potentially hazardous for the ladies to maneuver. Day shift was primarily devoted to cleaning the premises and preparing produce destined to be pizza toppings, such as chopping onions and green peppers, something that could not be done in advance and shipped. Aside from a short lunch rush, business was generally slow until around 4:00 p.m. and that's when the evening crew arrived. Mainly teenage boys and young men, they were better able to handle the heavy deliveries.

When the delivery van arrived at Brady Street, the Ford Econoline long-box was fully loaded because we were the first stop, after which the delivery boy headed to the Barrydowne Road and Kathleen Street locations. As usual, the van backed up against the short wooden porch in front of the door, although the driver had a little trouble getting the alignment right in the mud. This delivery boy was relatively new; I had only seen him a couple of times and this was his first experience with our muddy lot.

By the way, I use the term 'delivery boy' as it was used by the staff in a non-pejorative sense. All of the delivery drivers for Cortina were male, most in their late teens, some their early twenties, but the label was applied to all.

A couple of feet left of the door was the window looking in on the pizza ovens. Standing in front of those ovens, I watched him back in. Joe and I were working alone, a bit of a challenge during the rushes, but we worked well together, no real problem. I had just put a couple of pizzas in the oven, so I had a few minutes to help Joe and the delivery boy unload our stuff. The transfer only took us a couple of minutes and I was back tending the ovens when the delivery boy left.

A few seconds after he went out the door, my arm deep in the oven, I was distracted by what sounded like hailstones hitting the window and door. I got quite a nice burn on my forearm as I hastily pulled the pies out of the oven and looked out the window, which was half covered in mud. A short pause later, more mud hit the window. The driver, trying to accelerate away faster than conditions allowed, had spun the rear tires and was sinking into the mud while spraying a generous layer of the mud and gravel all over the side of the building.

I made the request: "Joe, would you go and give this douche bag a hand getting out of the mud?"

Joe laughed and headed for the door. By the time he got outside, the van was irrevocably stuck, sunk to the axles! The task wasn't going to be easy, but I expected Joe to get the driver to start rocking the van with little touches on the accelerator while Joe pushed. Most likely, I would have to go and help once the customer came to pick up the pizzas I had just taken out of the oven. I watched their efforts through the mud-coated window.

Joe went to the driver's window, said a few words and went to the back of the van. Later he would tell me that he'd said, "Put it in neutral and don't touch a damn thing until I tell you."

He walked to the back of the van, but he didn't put his shoulder to the corner as I expected. He went to the middle where the rear doors came together and turned his back to the truck. Leaning against the doors, he bent his knees and lowered himself until he could get a good grip on the bumper. A real, honest-to-goodness metal bumper, not your modern plastic pseudo-bumper.

He adjusted his grip, took a deep breath and began to straighten his legs. Nothing happened for a couple of seconds. Then, even inside the building, I heard a gross, wet sucking sound as the wheels pulled free of the sticky mud and Joe straightened up. I stood there, unbelieving, probably with my mouth open. That van was still two-thirds full!

He paused, to gain his balance, then took four or five slow steps backward and lowered the rear of the truck gently onto the mud. He walked once again to the driver's window and said, as he told me later, "Okay, now, low gear and really light on the gas, okay?" As he came back inside, the van pulled out slowly, still spinning a little in the mud.

And Joe? He didn't say a thing. Obviously he had done nothing unusual. Go figure. But his shoes were a mess. Making humorous remarks about the new guy's driving skills, he cleaned his shoes, put his socks to soak in soapy water and went back to chopping green peppers.

§

I WASN'T SURPRISED to find out Joe was into motorcycles, particularly chopped Harleys. Somehow he looked the type—maybe the way he dressed or the way he carried himself or his build, I don't know. He just did. What *did* surprise me was that he was chopping one himself.

He was already two years into the project when he started working at Cortina in early 1970. He had been rebuilding and modifying an old Harley Davidson in the garage at home and, that summer, was in the final stages of the chop. He was tweaking the engine and drive train, and sending the last of the parts out for chrome-plating, as finances allowed.

Several Saturdays that summer I went over to his place in the morning to give him a hand. I'd bring the tunes on my five-inch reel-to-reel tape recorder—you know, *Beatles, Steppenwolf, Three Dog Night, Cream*, like that—and we'd work until time to clean up and get to Cortina for 5 p.m. Not that I had a clue about what needed doing or how to go about it. I mostly acted as gofer, like the nurse in an O.R., handing tools to Joe as he called for them. As soon as he explained what the damned tool looked like, that is. Occasionally, he'd give me some small actual job to do.

For instance, "Hold the head of this bolt with this wrench, while I attach this gizmo to the other end of the bolt and torque it down."

One time, my inexperience nearly led to disaster. He was ready to work on the kickstand and asked me to hold the bike upright while he removed the temporary piece and attached the newly chromed part. No problem. Until I became engrossed in what he was doing and forgot my job for a second. Some small movement of my body, perhaps, caused the bike to over-balance away from us, Joe being crouched beside me. The bike started to go over and I couldn't hold it. Not that I would have let go. I'd never just let Joe's bike fall!

No, I held on. I just didn't have the strength or the weight to pull it back to vertical. It was going over and taking me with it!

Without thinking, I am convinced, and without comment, Joe reached up from his crouch, grabbed the frame of the rear saddle and righted the bike. I was okay after that, maintaining full concentration for the five or six minutes he needed to get the kickstand positioned to his liking.

About mid-summer, the last of the chromed parts came in. Perfect timing. His brother, an artist/illustrator who worked at Inco, had recently finished hand-painting the gas tank. One more morning's work and the bike was complete. The overall impression was shiny chrome, lots of it, resting on jet black tori, accented by the abstract deep mauve and purple of the tank. It was beautiful!

Time for the test ride.

No helmets—keep in mind the time frame, 1970. Joe already looked the part in his usual attire: worn work boots, blue jeans and, that day, a white T-shirt with black sleeves and lettering on the front. For the life of me, I don't recall what was written on that shirt. All he needed to add were his leather biker gloves with the cut away fingers and his aviator sunglasses, *de rigeur* among Harley riders, and we were ready.

Never having ridden a motorcycle before, I felt privileged to be invited to accompany him on the inaugural run. He spent a few minutes coaching me on how to lean into corners, put my feet down when stationary and avoid the muffler with my legs. Then we were off.

What a feeling! The freedom, the sense of independence, the intimate connection with the road, were all feelings I had never experienced driving a car. And the vulnerability. The in-my-face awareness that absolutely nothing separated us from the asphalt. No protection whatsoever. It was exhilarating and more than a little frightening.

Once the wheels started to roll, Joe was the consummate biker, sitting straight, leaning back, arms stretched to the high-rise handlebars. Gear shifts were so smooth I seldom was aware of them. Cornering had this eerie sense of being almost parallel to the road (of course, we weren't) and wrapping around the corner. Cool!

We took a brief lap around the downtown area, to show off the bike, then headed out of town to open her up.

The Kingsway is Sudbury's version of the fast food/car dealer strip that every city seems to have on at least one major access highway. We were cruising down the inside lane doing just over the speed limit and gradually overtaking a station wagon from Iowa. Mom and dad in the front, three children occupied the back, probably aged 8 to 13, maybe. The kids goggled at us and pressed up against the back window, then the side windows as we drew abreast. They waved, talked excitedly, did the 'fish' as they oohed and aahed, yelled at mom and dad to look.

Joe pretended he didn't see them. Only we and the road existed. Shades of *Easy Rider*, man. We were the biker dude with his wimpy city sidekick on his chromed and gleaming chopped hog. The sun was shining, the sky was blue—pretty damned near perfect.

He eased back imperceptibly on the throttle so that we kept pace with the station wagon for perhaps 3/8 of a mile along that straight stretch of commercialism, letting the kids get an eyeful. Then, with the economy of the experience biker, he dropped her down a gear, gave her a little throttle and we laid about 100 feet of rubber, leaving the gaping kids and the wagon behind. Gone, eating up the road, out-of-town.

Epilogue: Less than two weeks later, a number of brewing financial difficulties came to a head and Joe needed $1500 *immediately*. He went to his brother for a loan. No problem, with a proviso: his brother would take possession of the bike and use it until the loan was repaid. A double benefit, he got to ride around on this cool custom chopper and he was sure to get his money back *post haste*. Joe didn't like it, but he needed the money. A few days later, his brother hit a rock-cut, totalling the bike and nearly killing himself.

§

JOE WAS A LOYAL friend to a fault. He didn't make friendships easily, although he was quite friendly, but once he let you past his emotional sentries into his circle of friends, his commitment to the friendship was unshakable. Oh, he had no trouble recognizing your failings nor any compunctions about giving you grief when he felt you deserved it, but if you were in trouble or in need, he was there. And you didn't have to ask.

We became friends quite quickly, recognizing in each other qualities we admired and respected. Over time, we learned a lot from each other. I won't presume to try to describe what Joe learned from me. You'd have to ask him.

But I can tell you a couple of things he taught me. He taught me a little about standing up for myself when necessary, not letting myself be bullied. He also taught me something about loyalty and commitment to friends; you don't get to choose—you're either in or you're out, no half measures in friendship. To be honest, I knew these things intellectually, but had never put the first concept into practice nor had the second concept really tested by an extreme case. Luckily, Joe was there when both situations arose.

Two separate incidents come to mind about Joe coming to my rescue physically, leaving me with lessons about taking care of myself that have served me all these years. The first was a relatively minor affair that was quickly deteriorating into a dire situation, until Joe defused it.

This particular weeknight we were in our usual roles, Joe in the prep area, me on the ovens. A burly and, it turned out, surly laborer-type came in and ordered a couple of meatball sandwiches. While I was preparing them, he began to complain that the last few he'd had were substandard. I was unconvinced when he was unable to tell me how long ago he'd purchased them nor describe the person who had served him, but he was adamant.

By the time I had the sandwiches ready, he was convinced he should get these free. I refused to give them to him until he paid. He became outraged, started to yell at me and call me names. The gist of it was I could keep the damn things and he would take a refund for the earlier sandwiches.

Leaning across the counter he tried to get into the till. The cash register was positioned so that customers could reach neither the keys nor the drawer. He didn't seem to be aware that you needed a particular key combination to open the drawer without a sale. Try as he might, he couldn't get satisfaction from the till, which just fueled his anger. Now he decided, at the top of his lungs, that if I didn't give him the sandwiches by the count of three, he was coming over the counter to rip me a new one and take the damn sandwiches.

As if on cue, Joe stepped around the half wall that separated the prep area from the oven/counter area.

"Got a problem here, Iggy?"

We all knew the question was rhetorical. The place wasn't very big, it was empty save for the three of us and no equipment was running. Joe had heard every word.

Trying to bluff his way through, the customer, in belligerent tones, said, "He's trying to screw me. He refuses to give me the meatball sandwiches he owes me."

To which I responded, a little braver in Joe's presence, "You haven't paid for them." Turning to Joe, I added, "He even threatened to beat me up and take them."

Joe turned to face the customer and threw his own threat back in his face. "I'm going to count to three. If you're not on this side of the counter by then, I'm coming over there and we'll see who gets pounded."

The customer, a little uncertain, paused to size things up. Joe was as much larger than him as he was larger than me. And Joe was in much better shape. Deciding to cut his losses, he told us what we could do with our meatball sandwiches and that we just lost a good customer. He gave us the finger on the way out the door.

A few minutes later, after a mini-rush of five or six pizza orders, Joe was telling me that most of these types are cowards. The best way to handle them is to call their bluff, take it to them.

"Yeah, but Joe, look at you; look at me. Big difference. No wonder he ran."

"What's that in your hand, Iggy?"

I hadn't noticed that I still had the pizza knife in my right hand. At Cortina, we didn't slice pizza with a wheel cutter, we used a wide knife with a 16-inch blade. And we kept it sharp. Watching those of us who were skilled with this knife when it was busy was very entertaining.

Joe said, "Use it. Hold it up, make the threat, wielding the knife like you mean business. They'll choose not to try you."

I used the threat several times in the years to come and never had to follow through.

§

LOOKING BACK, the other lesson I mentioned earlier could almost be considered a corollary to the *take the threat to the bully* philosophy. I am pleased to say that I've been fortunate enough to need this particular advice only once and in a much less dramatic situation.

This would've been late fall, 1970, towards the end of the brief high school football season. One of the most prestigious achievements for the local high school teams was to be the winner of the annual East-West game.

The high schools in Sudbury and surrounding communities, for sports purposes, were divided into East and West divisions. At the end of the football season, the teams with the best records in each division played for the overall title. The game was played on neutral territory at Queen's Athletic Field, a sports venue near the downtown core in Sudbury.

Joe, playing as he did for Sudbury high, had a keen interest in the East-West game. He and a couple of his teammates were going to the game and asked me if I'd like to go. I had never been terribly interested in the game because it seemed rather elementary and brutish, but I liked being asked, so what the hell? We went as a small group and sat on the side of the field dominated by East fans.

I actually learned a little about the game and gained some respect for those who played. Joe and his friend, Big Bob, started by explaining that in every successful play either someone on offence did his job right or someone on defense blew it. Or a combination of both. The opposite was true of every failed play. Then, as the game proceeded, they described the role of each player and who was responsible for the success or failure of a given play. By the end of the day, still not a fan of the game, I no longer perceived it as a bunch of brutes senselessly throwing themselves at each other.

Mid-third quarter, Joe and I agreed that a trip to the water fountain was in order. Most of Joe's friends were surreptitiously sipping on beer or cider, as were so many of the teens in attendance. Being deathly allergic to alcohol, I abstained, as did Joe. He wasn't against underage drinking, but he preferred a much less public site. Evidently, his older brother had been caught a few years earlier, causing his mother no end of grief and Joe didn't want to do that to her again. One of the penances of being labeled, "My Joseph is a good boy and would not do anything to bring me shame."

So we went to get a drink of water. The fountain was on the far side of the field and, being mid-quarter, had no lineup. About 20 feet of railing led to the fountain, intended as a visual guide and partial physical barrier to keep lineups orderly when the fountain was in demand.

The railing was pretty primitive, made of heavy duty, threaded iron pipe about three inches in diameter. Various lengths were screwed into assorted connector joints to produce the horizontal bars and vertical posts. The posts were sunk in concrete piers. Durable, strong, cost-effective.

We walked straight up and each had our fill. Turning away from the fountain, we found our way blocked by a group of five teenage boys. Immediately obvious were the facts that they had taken in more alcohol than Joe's friends had and they had come to the game looking for sporting entertainment of a much more violent and personal nature.

I know this is going to sound cliché, but the cliché owes its origin to the fact that these things actually do happen. These guys were tricked out like movie gang members. Lots of denim and leather, brass knuckles, knives—even a chain. Not a bicycle chain, true, but a two-foot length of ordinary heavy-duty chain.

"We'll take yer money an' yer dope an' if ya don't give us too much grief, we won't hurt ya too bad." The speaker wasn't the biggest of the group, but he was very definitely the alpha male.

Joe said, "We don't have either one and, if we did, we wouldn't be giving it to you."

The look on Alpha's face flirted with pleasure, almost as if he had been hoping we'd resist. Now the posturing started. He reached into his pocket with his right hand and pulled out a flick knife, flipped it open. His left hand was already decked out with brass knuckles. As he stepped toward Joe, the other four started to fan out in a semicircle with the two of us at the focus. The one with the chain began to swing it to build a little momentum. Alpha and the others went into various styles of crouch, weapons forward.

"Yer smart mouth is gonna cause ya a lotta pain an' we're still gonna smoke yer dope, asshole," Alpha said, as they all took another step forward.

Honestly, I was in serious danger of losing control of my bowels. I was so scared, I couldn't have spoken or run or even stated my name if my life depended on it, which I was convinced it might.

It was over in a second. Joe's hand shot out past Alpha's cheek and I almost panicked. For a microsecond, I was aghast that not only had Joe tried to hit this guy, but he had missed! Before I could complete the thought, Joe had grabbed him by the back of the head. Wham! He brought Alpha's head facedown onto the pipe railing and let him go. Alpha collapsed, dazed but not unconscious, blood spewing over his chest, his pants, the ground. His face seemed to have changed shape. No wonder. His nose and one cheekbone were broken.

Joe turned to the others, "Anyone else?"

The others fell all over themselves and each other trying to vacate the area.

We dealt first with the ambulance and then with police, which the ambulance attendants insisted had to be called when they responded at scenes of violence. Walking home later, my body was still pumped full of adrenaline and I told Joe how scared I had been. He admitted to having been scared too.

"But you didn't look scared. And what you did to that guy, wow! I've never seen anything like it. I could never do that."

"Sure you could. It's the only chance you have in a situation like that. Let me ask you something. Did you think they were going to let us leave without a serious beating?"

"Shit, no! I knew we were going to get it. I was afraid they might kill us." The memory brought another rush of adrenaline.

Joe said, "Yeah. I knew we were in for it."

He went on to explain, "When you know there is no way out of it, that you're going to get a beating, you don't wait for them. You don't let them control the timing, come at you when they're ready. You beat them to the punch, literally. Pick the leader, go at him unexpectedly and as hard as you can. And you fight dirty, fight to win. Fighting clean is for heroes in the movies who are going to win no matter what. Usually, take the leader out, the rest turn into cowards and get the hell out."

In the years to come, I would hear that same advice from different sources in a variety of situations. I can tell you, it works.

§

I MENTIONED EARLIER Joe's loyalty to friends. I thought I'd close out my 'Joe' section with an incident that illustrates the depth of his commitment. I realize these last few accounts depict Joe in a pretty negative light. Truly, Joe was not violent; in fact, he was pretty much a pussycat most of the time. He was just confident in his abilities and was not afraid to fight if necessary, whether to defend himself, a friend or a total stranger unjustly set upon by the bad guys.

Joe had a good friend known to me only by his last name, Carruthers, and whom I met only a few times. They had known each other for years, went to school together and shared an interest in automotive repair and customizing, especially motorcycles. Carruthers' father was a mechanic and owned an auto repair garage, so they got lots of exposure and free advice growing up. They were both athletic, Joe into football and Carruthers into martial arts. He held a black belt in karate in the summer of 1971.

The two of them, plus Carruthers' girlfriend, were going to a movie matinee at the old Capitol Theater on Cedar Street on a Saturday afternoon. For movie lovers, working evenings meant seeing a lot of matinees. The warm August sun was beaming from an almost cloudless sky, so anyone that could arrange it was outdoors. Unfortunately, the warm weather also brought out some of the more unsavory elements in our society.

Three Harley choppers were parked by the sidewalk on the same side of the street and a couple of doors down from the theater. Loitering on and around the bikes, laughing and talking in tones louder than necessary, all decked out in their colors, were four members of the local bad-ass biker club, Satan's Choice.

Our three moviegoers had to pass right by this raucous group.

As they were passing the bikers, one of the Choice made an extremely vulgar comment about the looks of Carruthers' girlfriend and what she would be good for/at. And he said it so everyone within half a block could hear.

To be fair, to say the young lady in question was extremely good-looking would be doing her an injustice. But that sort of vulgar public comment was unacceptable.

Carruthers only hit him once; the biker didn't see it coming. The other bikers were stunned into momentary inactivity. Carruthers, feeling he had made his point, took his girlfriend's hand and the three continued on to the movie theater, leaving the rest of the Choice to attend to their unconscious brother splayed on the sidewalk. About two hours later when the movie attendees left the theater, the bikers were not in evidence. Joe and his friends parted company as he headed to Cortina for his shift.

Saturday was always the busiest night of the week, requiring the largest staff. That night I was working the front, Joe and two other boys were in the prep area and we had two guys on delivery. To ensure as smooth and efficient a flow as possible, everyone answered the phone when they could. Why have someone interrupt what they were doing to answer the phone, when you had a free thirty seconds?

I happened to take the call. A gruff, foulmouthed voice told me to pass a message to Carruthers. He was to be in the Canadian Tire parking lot at 2 a.m. to receive his comeuppance. He could bring any assistance he could muster. The penalty for no-show? The voice rhymed off the names and addresses of Carruthers' parents, his girlfriend's parents and his dad's garage. The voice went on to say that the majority of nasty accidents happen around the home and expressed concern that the buildings looked like fire traps to him.

The first thing Joe did when I told him about the call, of course, was to phone Carruthers. Then they canvassed for support. Several of the guys working at two of the other Cortina locations went to school with Joe and Carruthers, a couple of them played football with Joe. They were in. The two fellows working that night with us said they were in, as well. Eventually Carruthers had ten solid and two tentative commitments.

All of these arrangements were made between taking other phone orders, rolling dough, dressing pizza, etc. We were a dedicated crew!

Joe looked at me, eyebrow lifted.

"Don't look at me, man. You know I'm not a fighter. I'd be of absolutely no use to you and I'm not macho enough to need to get myself pounded to prove I'm a man. Sorry."

"S'okay, man. At least you're honest."

"What I will do—I'll do clean-up myself, so you guys can get out here right at two o'clock when we close."

Closing at 2 a.m., we seldom got out of the building before 2:30-2:45 working together to clean up. The Canadian Tire parking lot was only one street over, so they'd be maybe a minute late.

Carruthers arrived at 1:30. The guys from the other locations wangled to get off at 1:45, so they were at Brady right at two o'clock. Everyone piled into cars—Joe and Carruthers in one and four guys in each of two other vehicles. A couple of others never showed.

I did the clean-up, wondering what was going on, how bad it was. Leaving about 3:15, I decided to drive by the Canadian Tire parking lot to see what was going on.

Nothing! It was all over.

Several police cars and a couple of ambulances were in attendance, so I drove on and got the story the next day. I wasn't there, so I really don't know what happened. My information, however, comes from the two main participants and a couple of witnesses, so I trust I have the essentials correct.

Apparently Joe and Carruthers, leading the pack, pulled into the lot, shut off their engine and hopped out of the car. The two following cars slowed, saw what seemed like an army, all those damn bikes and all those colors, and didn't stop. They kept right on going, leaving Joe and Carruthers hanging.

In actuality, there were only (did I just say 'only') eight bikes, one rider apiece. Accounts of what was said are sketchy, but amount to our boys being told that no one humiliates one of the Choice, in public no less, and gets away with it. Apparently, Carruthers replied something to the effect that if they didn't want it to happen again, they should leave.

The fight was short, broken up by the arrival of the police, summoned by an overnight janitor at Canadian Tire. He also reported two other cars arriving with more guys, but could not swear that Joe and Carruthers were lying when they said they were alone. The gang members remained silent on the subject. Our two boys had several open cuts and abrasions. Four of the Choice needed medical attention: one dislocated knee, one dislocated elbow, one broken jaw, one concussion, some broken or cracked ribs, multiple bruises, abrasions, contusions. Our boys more than held their own.

They took a little pleasure in recounting the details. The dislocated knee resulted from a classic side kick to the front of the kneecap delivered by Carruthers. His karate was also responsible for the dislocated elbow, achieved by another classic move. As one of the Choice threw a leather-encased, brass-knuckled right fist at his face, Carruthers swayed the upper torso back, away from the punch. As he did so, he swung his hands, forearms vertical, in a scissor motion, his right wrist moving right to left and catching his opponent inside the wrist, while his left wrist, moving left to right, made powerful contact with the outside of the elbow, snapping the joint. Suddenly and painfully, the biker had a right elbow that bend in the wrong direction!

Both took credit for contributing to the rib trauma and Joe was particularly proud of the concussion. To better defend himself, Joe had positioned himself with his back to the wall of the parking ticket booth. One of the bikers got the bright idea to sneak up on Joe from around the little building and hit him from behind while he was occupied with assailants in front of him. Unfortunately for him, Joe saw him. To entice him to continue, Joe stepped a pace or two away from the building, allowing room for the biker to follow the wall and get right behind Joe. As soon as he was in position, Joe spun around and planted a right haymaker on his jaw, catching the biker's head between his fist and the wall of the booth, putting him out of action.

An interesting side note is the fate of the biker whom Carruthers had originally clocked in front of the theater. Six weeks later, he and three of his cronies attempted to rob an all-night gas bar on the Kingsway at three in the morning. They had robbed this particular gas bar a couple of times before, as had a few other local hoods, and the owner was fed up. That night, when they came in armed with their usual weaponry and demanded that he empty the till, he pulled a 12-gauge shot-gun from under his counter. He told the leader, Carruthers' adversary, that if the biker came another step closer, he'd blow his nuts off! Of course, the biker laughed and stepped forward into a hail of buckshot. The emergency staff at the hospital could save neither his genitals nor his left leg. His biking days were over.

Cortina Brady was awash in testosterone for a couple of nights! Carruthers and Joe never heard another thing from the Satan's Choice club. There *was* some fallout from the incident, though. Friendships dried up overnight with the guys who had turned tail, not because they had been afraid and left, but because they made a commitment and didn't follow through, leaving friends hanging in a serious situation.

Joe and I were fine. He told me one evening when just we two were working that what he valued was a person that was true to his/her word. Friendship is based on mutual honesty and reliability.

Memorable Customers

EVEN AFTER ALL the years that have passed, a number of customers still stand out fresh in my mind. Some for being consistently idiosyncratic, others for something they did or said only once. I'd like to share a few of these memorable people with you.

Almost everything about this fellow was odd. He was about six-foot-three, very slim and wiry, with black hair that was poorly trimmed. His goatee and pencil-thin mustache were sparse and scraggly, hardly worth growing yet didn't warrant the effort to shave them off. His skin was very pale, even in summer. He was partial to gingham shirts and black jeans that were much too short. His pants invited various comments like 'high water pants,' or 'must have water in the basement.' Sticking out of those jeans were a pair of black dress boots that zipped up the inside ankle. He always wore a straw cowboy hat and round glasses with pink lenses. He told me one time, "I wear pink glasses because they make the world look rosy."

He always came in alone. He always ordered a large Number Five—tomato sauce, cheese, pepperoni, mushrooms and green peppers—and ate the whole thing. He never had anything to drink. He took his time, always reading from the book he had with him: either the Bible or the Merriam-Webster dictionary. Hey, kudos for self-improvement, right?

A miner himself, he made an obvious effort to use English that was a little more eloquent than commonly encountered in our mining town. One evening just after the supper rush, as I was preparing his pizza, he remained at the counter rather than moving to his usual table.

"Pardon me, sir. If you would be so kind as to pay somewhat closer attention to the distribution of toppings than last time, I would be grateful."

Now, I am not boasting when I say I was scrupulous about how I and everyone working with me dressed pizza and I never got complaints about coverage of the toppings. So, puzzled, I asked him to elaborate.

"I do not relish a wide portion of crust around the edge *sans* toppings. Please make special efforts to ensure that all the toppings are evenly distributed along the peripheral of the pizza."

Aah. I had noticed that he carried his dictionary that afternoon. Obviously, he had learned a new word and was creating an opportunity to try it out. I assured him I would take special care, did nothing different than I normally did and, as he was leaving, he thanked me for careful attention to details.

Before he went out the door, I said, "By the way, I realize you are a student of the language, as am I, so I hope you don't mind. Peripheral is an adjective and inappropriate in the context in which you used it. The proper word is periphery, a noun."

"My goodness. I do apologize for the *faux pas*. I will be more diligent. Thank you."

And he left.

§

PICTURE THIS: A weeknight, about eleven o'clock, mid-February. The temperature was -34 Celsius and falling. We didn't do windchill factor in those days, but it was definitely balls-and-brass-monkey weather. I was at the oven checking on some lasagna and felt a cold draft that signaled the opening of the door just on the other side of the counter. Closing my oven, I turned to greet the new customer.

He was about 17, rail thin, long loose hair. He was wearing beat-up tennis shoes with no laces and no socks. His jeans were frayed and showed signs of attempts at tie-dying. There was a hole in one knee. His jean jacket was too small to button, in the style of the day. Under it he wore one of the half t-shirts that left the midriff bare, also the height of teen fashion. Hanging from his neck was a red and white scarf about three meters long, not wrapped but looped once over the back of his neck and hanging almost to the floor on both sides. His hands were bare, as was his head.

What do you think were the first words out of his mouth?

"Jesus Christ, it's cold out!"

§

YOU'LL NEED YOUR imagination a little for this one. I had a long-term customer that had a real phobia about hot food—at least that's how it seemed because he said the same thing every time he ordered, whether or not it was pizza or pasta.

He was always very nice, probably a laborer judging by his style of dress, but clean and neat. He had a thick French accent, so a lot of what he said had those typically odd pronunciations with accents in the wrong places. This is where your imagination comes in.

He ended every order with the exact same phrase:

"An' no goddam 'ot peppers, eh!"

The word 'peppers' had the accent on the second syllable instead of the traditional first, so the pitch of his voice rose as he said it. The 'eh' wasn't pronounced 'ay' but sounded like the 'a' in 'ant'.

All in all, a lyrical and amusing little phrase that I looked forward to hearing whenever he came in. He never disappointed me.

§

ANOTHER PIZZA topping that was the source of a lot of fun over the years was the anchovies. These are fillets of small herring-like fish native to the eastern Atlantic and imported from Spain or Portugal. The fillets bear a startling resemblance to bushy eyebrows when cooked. We didn't sell many pizzas with anchovies because most people don't like them. But the people that like them, *love* them.

Customers, for some reason, had considerable trouble pronouncing the word. These little fish were variously called Ancherries, Anchelobies, Ankovies, Anchobies and, quite often, simply 'those god damned hairy fish.'

Whenever anyone ordered pizza with everything, we always asked, "Including anchovies?"

The reply was usually, "Oh, hell no. Everything else, but no fish."

Particularly entertaining were the customers who obviously didn't know what anchovies were, but let on that they did. The conversation usually went something like:

"Including anchovies?"

"Yeah, I want everything. I like my pizza loaded."

"Have you had anchovies before? They are small fish…"

"Of course, I have. I love all that stuff."

"Very good. Be about 12 to 15 minutes."

And about 17 minutes later, we'd hear, "What the hell are these awful, salty hairy things?" Usually a demand for a refund followed. My response depended on the level of vulgarity.

§

I NEVER KNEW his first name. Everyone always called him Skilling. I am assuming that was his last name. He was in his early twenties and lived not far from Brady Street.

I was going to describe him as a petty thief, but considering the nature of some of his thefts and the number he committed, I think I'll drop the 'petty'. He was a thief.

He was also a frequent customer. You'll notice I didn't say 'good' customer. He wasn't. He was always trying to get something for free, such as pizza someone had ordered and never picked up. When broke, he tried to coerce us into giving him food on the cuff. For a while, we accommodated him, especially Moe Labre.

Moe was employed at Cortina before all the rest of us, one of the first hired when the pizzeria opened. He lived near Henry, went to the same high school with us and recommended Henry to the bosses when he was looking for a job.

Eventually, even Moe had to pull the plug on Skilling because he took months to pay off even the smallest of tabs. One time, he owed for two meatball sandwiches for three and a half months—a total of $1.90!

Skilling specialized in theft to order, primarily automotive. Whatever you needed. Tell him the make and model of the vehicle, the part and give him some time. The larger the part, the higher the cost. He had a large ugly scar on his chest from a caper that had gone bad. He had been under a car in the middle of the night helping himself to a transmission on his 'wish list,' when he miscalculated. He loosened the bolts more than he intended and the transmission fell on him.

The only time he dealt in entire cars, I was told, was when the owner wanted the car to appear to have been stolen, for insurance purposes. Money and keys were left under the seat, the car disappeared and was never found. Apparently he stripped the usable parts, torched the rest and buried the evidence.

He carried a few specialized tools for gaining rapid access to vehicles. The one he used most was a short piece of wooden broom handle with a thick one-inch screw embedded in the end, pointing outward. He would screw this tool into the trunk lock and rap the other end sharply with his hand, driving the locked into the trunk. All he had to do was stick his finger in the hole and pop the latch. On doors, he had to use an additional gizmo to reach the latch. He was in and out in seconds.

He came into Brady around 4:30 on a summer afternoon. Moe was working the ovens.

"Hey, Moe. Spot me a couple meatball sandwiches."

"No chance, Skilling."

"Ah, why not, man?"

"Takes you too damn long to pay. You always want cash on delivery for your work, right? Sometimes, even a deposit? So, COD here from now on."

"Okay. Need anything for your car?"

Moe thought a moment and said, "Yeah, I could use a radio. My car has never had one."

"Which one is yours?"

When Moe pointed out his old early sixties Dodge in the parking lot, Skilling said, "Make the sandwiches, man. I'll be right back."

Skilling went into the sunshine and the municipal carpark. He had to be quick. Civic employees started heading home right at five and by 5:30 the lot was nearly empty. Less then ten minutes later, Skilling was back. Not only did he have an AM/FM radio, he had lifted it from a Dodge of the same year and model as Moe's that he'd found parked in the big lot. Moe just had to slide it into the dash. Or, Skilling suggested, he could install it for Moe in return for a couple of cans of pop and a small pizza for later. Done deal.

Many of the young staff members had dealings with Skilling. I didn't because the association made me nervous. In the end, nothing bad happened to any of the Cortina boys. By the mid-seventies, Skilling was in jail for theft and I never saw him again.

Hot Stuff

AFTER I WAS PROMOTED (that sounds more auspicious than it was), working the ovens was pretty evenly divided between Moe Labre, Henry and me. The first few shifts were intimidating partly because of the pace when it was busy and the pressure to make sure everything was properly cooked. The biggest factor by far was the heat of the ovens. We kept the ovens at 550°F, so just working near them was a warm enterprise. Once a person became comfortable, however, working in the heat became second nature.

Interesting how the brain deals with stimuli. It receives impulses from nerve cells all over the body, interprets the messages, then sends instructions to make the body react appropriately. So, when part of the body touches something hot, nerves in that part of the body send a signal to the brain, which in turn sends at least two messages back—one making that part of the body jerk away from the heat and the second causing the person to vocalize some sort of reaction (ow! shit! or some such). For this reason, most of us who worked the ovens seldom got just one burn on our arms. Almost always, oven burns came in pairs. Here's what would happen.

We had two ovens, one above the other. When it was busy, the ovens would be full of pizza, naturally. They could hold five large pies each—one in each corner and one in the center. The bottom of the oven had a huge element covered by a one-inch slab of stone upon which the pizza plates sat. The top of the oven was lined with bare elements that were red-hot most of the time when we were busy. We had to check on the pizza several times during the cooking process. Bubbles tended to form in the mozzarella cheese and had to be burst to ensure uniform cooking. And, of course, we didn't want anything to burn!

Reaching to deal with the pizzas at the back of the ovens required having the whole arm inside the oven, usually up to mid-biceps, at least. In this extended position, the arm naturally is a little bent and the elbow tends to drop below the level of the hand. In a moment of inattention, the elbow would drop low enough to come in contact with the door, which was very hot. The automatic reaction to the *zzzt* and burn of contact, was to jerk the arm sharply upward—*slamming it firmly against the element above!* This chorus of *zzzt-ZZZT* left a small burn on the inside of the elbow and an elongated ugly weal across the top of the forearm. One lapse of attention—two burns.

§

THE HEAT OF THE ovens and the way the brain functions allowed Henry and me to have a little fun with customers occasionally. Working the ovens, we handled a lot of hot material, including the hot aluminum pizza plates. With time, our fingertips became tough and a little leathery. More importantly, done frequently over time, the brain recognizes the handling of hot material as 'normal,' so it begins to ignore 'danger-burn' signals from nerves in the fingertips. Yes, if we held a hot plate for 12-15 seconds, we'd get burnt just like anyone else. For short periods, though, we had surprising heat tolerance.

The time elapsed for a pizza from the oven to the cutting board and back into the hot aluminum plate was less than 10 seconds, so the plate was still very hot. I could pick the plate up barehanded and carry it to the customers' table. Putting it down on the center of the table, I'd invite them to enjoy their meal and warn them, "Careful. It's very hot."

I knew full well that at least one customer would be thinking, "How hot can it be? He brought it out barehanded." From a step or two away, on my way back to the ovens, I'd grin as I heard behind me the sharp *zzzt* and, "Yeow, (expletive deleted)! That's hot!"

Sex

I DON'T WANT THE reader to come away with the impression that the majority of my memories of the Cortina years revolve around violence or odd customers. As a matter of fact, a fair amount of sex and even a little love were associated with the place. The old building itself seemed to enhance the libido subtly. I am not exaggerating when I say most of the females who worked there were sexier, more enticing, more desirable during their shifts making pizza than they were elsewhere on their off hours. No, it wasn't only me. Everyone felt it, to varying degrees, although not everyone would acknowledge it.

Several relationships were kindled at work; some were initiated by the males, horny teens that they were, others by the females. Almost all of them fizzled the moment the budding romances were taken beyond those walls.

I experienced the effect myself a couple of times. I remember two in particular—Alda and Ellen. Both were so damned hot at work, I had a difficult time maintaining focus on what I was supposed to be doing. My eyes were always being pulled to the magnetic roundness of their butts and breasts, the smoothness of their necks, the alluring sway of their hips. No matter what they were wearing under their aprons, the effect was the same. We didn't have uniforms, so people in the prep area could dress pretty much as they pleased. Some hot summer nights, I was happy to be working! The people working the front had to pay a little more attention to attire, but rules were still pretty flexible.

Males greatly outnumbered females on the evening shift. We were still at the dawn of the eventual loosening of standards that led to the permissiveness plaguing us today. I know for a fact, parents were less inclined to allow their daughters to work so late at a job that could expose them to a lot of negative elements, coworkers and general public alike. As a result, the evening staff mainly consisted of males in their teens and early twenties. The atmosphere was free and easy, lots of joking and laughing, singing with the radio while playing various air instruments—adolescent boy stuff.

Add one or more girls. All that other stuff didn't stop, necessarily, but something new was thrown into the mix. An underlying current of sexual electricity colored everything a tad. An observer would have found it humorous to watch all the guys suddenly competing for those few females—not overtly, but in myriad subtle ways. That same observer probably would also say this is not unusual; it happens wherever the sexes are mixed. I concede this point as generally true, but I feel it does not explain the Brady Street phenomena. A case in point: *all* the girls that interested me when we worked together at Brady Street held absolutely no attraction for me when we were scheduled to work together at Martindale Road.

I seriously considered asking both Alda and Ellen out at different times. I needed some time to work up the nerve, though. I had lots of female friends and was quite open and honest with them, not in the least insecure. But the minute the idea of dating arose, I found I had no confidence. In the cases of Alda and Ellen, this worked in my favor.

By the time I was ready to ask one of them out, my common sense had kicked in. I had worked a number of shifts with both at Martindale, plus I spent some time with them outside of work, bowling after shift, playing in a golf tournament, going in a group to the midway. I realized in these settings I had no interest at all in either of them, not physically, not intellectually. So I reined in the urge, for the most part. In a moment of weakness, I asked Alda to go to the movies, but she turned me down flat. She was totally involved with Claude, our prize delivery boy.

Others were not so fortunate. Take Joe, for instance. He gave in to the Brady vibe and nothing good happened. Lee got the job through a recommendation from Henry. She and Henry had been close friends since they were about ten years old; nothing romantic, just friends. She lived in Garson, a small town just outside Sudbury proper, now part of the Greater City of Sudbury. Henry had lived in Garson a few years earlier. He and I would bicycle out to see her often during summer holidays.

So, now in their late teens and still good friends, when Lee needed a part-time job, he arranged for her to work at Cortina Brady. In short order, Joe became interested in her at work and started putting the moves on her. She seemed to reciprocate and they began seeing each other. Wouldn't you know, working with her at Brady, Henry had become interested in Lee romantically after all those years and he became quite jealous and petty about the situation. Working with the three of them on the same shift was uncomfortable for the rest of us, to say the least.

Witnessing the deterioration of the relationship between Henry and Lee was particularly painful for me. I had seen them share so many happy moments. I had been privy to their private, intimate thoughts and feelings. We would bike to see her as often as possible in warm weather and they would exchange letters during harsher seasons. They discussed everything in those letters, openly, in straightforward prose. Henry would get me to help him write his letters: he wanted them to be perfect. I could tell just looking at him as he arrived for work if he had received a letter from Lee that day. His feet didn't touch the ground. His face glowed as he read those notes to me, which commonly extended over several pages.

Over the course of about six weeks, I watched that relationship go down the toilet. Oddly enough, and in complete agreement with the overall theme we are discussing here, evenings that they worked together at Brady in the absence of Joe were better. By the end of the shift, they were laughing together, tensions had eased; the old relationship peeked out. Mystifyingly, in the short time it took to go for a hot pork sandwich at the truck stop on Highway 17, it would all start to fall apart again. A harsh word, a critical gesture, a rolling of eyes or a negative reference by Henry about Joe and they were at each other's throats again. In the end, Henry broke all contact with Lee and refused to work with her.

The relationship between Joe and Lee was hardly any better. They argued like cats and dogs, even at work. I couldn't believe some of the things they said to and about each other, both at work and during the off-hours. Impossibly, and surprising everyone, they got married. I went over to their apartment only a couple of times. Too uncomfortable. They were at each other constantly. To no one's surprise, they were divorced in very short order, victims of the Brady vibe.

§

SOMETHING STRANGE was very definitely going on in that building. The proposition has been made more than once, usually in terms designed to suggest the speaker was at least half joking, that the sexual vibe at Brady Street derived from the building's history. One of the first things I was told when I started working there was that the building had housed a brothel for quite some time and had stood empty only briefly when the Masotti brothers bought it and opened their pizzeria. The contention was that so much illicit sex had been sold on the premises that its very essence had soaked into the physical structure itself and that all subsequent human activity in the building was affected by the pervasive sexual aura.

I did a little research on the brothel claim during my early days at Cortina and found pretty much what I expected. Nothing. Prostitution being illegal, no one would be stupid enough to register property or a business as serving that function. That aside, when I bought into the franchise system, eventually owning three locations in partnership with Henry, I met a lot of businessmen in the community. Some of the older ones actually admitted having availed themselves of the services in the house in their younger years. Others vouched that they knew people who claimed first-hand experience.

Like most owners of businesses open until the wee hours, I also became acquainted with a number of law enforcement types, mostly patrol cops, but a few detectives as well. A couple of the older policemen said they knew city officials who were clients of that venerable establishment and attested to having been instructed to ignore comings and goings unless violence was involved.

In all cases, these people did not actually name names, which is quite understandable. It is not for me to cross that line either. Suffice it to say, the claim of a house of ill repute having operated out of the Brady Street building certainly seems tenable.

But the truth of the claim doesn't matter and doesn't alter the fact that something odd was happening in that building and sex was involved. Even attitudes about sex were little bit skewed. Let me give you a couple of examples.

§

HENRY AND I BOUGHT the franchise to the original Brady Street location in 1974. The organization had become so large and busy that the Masottis no longer had the time to run it. So we bought it. We also hired a long-time employee of the Martindale branch, Anna Rinaldi, on a part-time basis for the evening shift. She was one of the best workers Cortina ever hired—she did everything and did them all exceptionally well. She was in her late thirties, married, with a preteen daughter. Attractive and well-built without being stunning, she was one of the sexiest women I have ever met. Even when she wasn't at the Brady Street store. Imagine the effect she had on us when she worked Brady Street!

Henry was recently married to Vivien, whom we also employed part-time. May as well keep it in the family, right?

Okay, the stage was set. One weeknight, Henry was working with Anna. After closing, as he had done with so many girls, he propositioned her. And there was no possibility of misinterpretation because he came right out and asked, a technique he learned from his brother (see next note). Anna shut him down cold!

A couple of nights later, Vivien was working with Anna. She gave the older woman attitude for a while, too busy with the supper rush to talk. But at the first lull, Vivian yelled that Anna, "What the fuck is your problem? You think you're too good for my husband?"

Anna proceeded to tell her to grow up and ignored her the rest of the evening. From that night on, she refused to work alone with either of them.

Okay, bad enough Henry put the moves on Anna. What makes him go home and bellyache about the rejection to his wife? Worse, what makes the wife turn around and berate the other woman for rejecting her husband? I don't know about you, but I think that's weird.

§

FOR A FEW MONTHS in early 1970, Henry and I would go over to his brother Marcel's after work. Uncle Marcel was only a year and a half older than us, so nearly 22. He lived with Brian Brown, in a small house owned by Brown, just off Regent Street in the shadow of the water tower. Both were alcoholics and drug abusers of a serious nature. Marcel did not work, contributing his share of expenses by dealing drugs. The house was filled 'round the clock by people drinking and/or doing drugs of several types. Some were paying customers, some hangers-on. And the stereo in the living room was always playing.

We would arrive between 2:30 and 3 a.m. and leave at around 6:00. Henry would proceed to drink himself silly, never one into drugs, and try to put moves on some of the females. Me? I was there for the music. Marcel and Brian between them had a hell of a record collection.

In the end, I stopped going when I had multiple coincident revelations: I was the only one straight and did far too much chauffeuring drunks and stoners or running errands; these people were no fun, stoned into lethargy or near catatonia, or drunk to the point of silliness; they all eventually ended up passed out; the music didn't justify the loss of sleep just to be there. In short, I wasn't enjoying myself. Plus, I had to put up with my dad's scorn as I passed him going in as he left for day shift. My dad would say, "The only people still out at this time of night are whores and thieves. Which are you?"

One aspect of my time spent at Marcel's held my interest a little longer than all the rest. I never got tired of the endless stream of babes that came out of his bedroom—in all states of dress or lack thereof. Now, Marcel was a typical Fay, meaning nothing to write home to mom about, in the looks department. Plus he was a boozer and a stoner. So how did he coerce these great looking women into bed? And when he/they were done, how did he get them to willingly get dressed, call a cab and go home at their own expense?

Curiosity got the better of me one morning. I waylaid him on the way back from the washroom in his under shorts and asked him how he did it.

"Do you pay them in product?"

"I don't *pay* for sex," he said, affronted.

"So, how?" And he told me. You'll never guess!

"I just ask."

"Huh?"

"I just ask. I see a girl I want, I walk up to her and ask. I get a lot of slaps in the face, but I get a lot of ass."

I wasn't sure I fully believed him. Then about three months later, on a warm summer day, I saw what I interpreted as evidence. Walking down Elm Street from the courthouse where I had just paid a fine for a speeding ticket, I saw Marcel up ahead on the corner of Elm and Lorne streets talking to a gorgeous blonde. Without warning, she hauled off and slapped his face, hard! She was livid, while Marcel looked vaguely amused. They left in different directions.

§

THE TOP (SECOND) floor of the Brady Street building was almost empty in our time. The washroom had an old-style sink and toilet, and a claw-footed cast-iron tub. The rest of the floor comprised four small, almost square bedrooms. The first on the left as you came off the stairs contained the only furniture on the floor—an old aluminum steamer trunk. Can you guess its function? You got it!

I lost count, very early on, of the number of girls who went upstairs and had sex on that trunk with one of the boys. Even more astounding, a surprising number agreed to having sex with other members of the male staff, waiting upstairs on the trunk while the guys switched places. Don't ask me about positions, but a number come readily to the imagination. I never partook myself.

What motivated these girls? Why would they do this willingly? And on the trunk! Granted, the boys took an apron up as a covering, but come on. It wasn't like they got anything, other than sex, out of it. They weren't paid, not even in meatball sandwiches! And some of them were truly nice, and nice looking, young ladies.

This scenario played out often enough that the phrase became part of the Brady street jargon.

"Where is (insert name of male employee who is supposed to be working, but not in evidence)?"

"Upstairs on the trunk."

§

TONY, THE OLDER of the Masotti brothers, possibly under thrall to the Brady Street aura, branched out into a small side venture. Three or four times a year, he'd bring a prostitute from Toronto and set her up at the Sorrento Hotel. Over the next few days, he would market her to certain of his business cronies, in addition to using her services himself.

Discrete is not a word I would use to describe Tony, but he knew enough not to openly broadcast his little enterprise. We had no inkling of what was going on, until the Friday night he called us from Martindale. He told us what was up, where she was and how to identify ourselves.

"She's all paid for. Take each your turn and enjoy yourselves. One at a time! Don't leave the restaurant shorthanded! Oh, and call me when you're done."

The staff was all male that night, five of us. Through the middle part of the evening, the other four went. Those that remained were only too happy to work a little harder to pull up the slack. The atmosphere was more 'up' than usual. Each, when he got back, raved about the girl and strutted like cock o' the walk. You'd think they'd done something no one had ever done before—and done it well.

Then came my turn. I told them I wasn't interested, so they could call Tony and say we were finished. They began to give me the gears, joking about me being queer.

"Don't tell me you're a virgin," said Claude, the delivery boy, thinking he was being funny. Neither embarrassed nor ashamed, I openly admitted I was. I again told Henry to call Tony, which he did.

I wasn't aware that he had shared with Tony the fact that I had not gone and why. So I was surprised twenty minutes later when Tony came through the door.

"Figgy (his variation on my nickname), get in the car. We're going to get you laid."

"I'd rather not, Tony. I appreciate the offer, but I'm not interested."

"Bull shit, you're not. You're just scared because you ain't had none yet. We'll fix that. Get in the car."

And I did. Why? Well, in front of all the guys, I was still male enough and immature enough to resent the idea that they might agree and think I was scared. And Tony, six-foot-four and, until recently, a worker on bonus at Inco, didn't take no for an answer. And, really, what young man at twenty doesn't want to lose his virginity?

We arrived to find an empty hotel room, one of adjoining rooms forming a suite. Tony told me to sit down and he'd go talk to her, explain the special circumstances. He came back in a few minutes with a double armful of the girl next door, wearing nothing but a black, see-through, shortie negligee, and put her in my lap.

"Have fun, you two." And he left.

I'm not going to describe her ministrations. I will say, she was very attractive, in a fresh, wholesome, unpretentious way. She was gentle, soft-spoken, and seemed like a really nice girl. I know how that sounds, but it's the truth. I liked her right away. I couldn't help but wonder what led her to this. And no matter what she did, I could not respond physically. After three quarters of an hour, she gave up.

Needless to say, I was a big disappointment to Tony. He did, however, promise that we'd try again in a few months. When he dropped me off and I walked into Cortina, all the guys cheered.

"So, how does it feel to be a man?"

Not one to accept unearned accolades, I said, "I don't know. Didn't happen. I couldn't get it up." Henry and I were different in a lot of ways and this was one. For me, if nothing was happening upstairs emotionally, nothing was happening downstairs physically.

You can imagine I was a rich source of humor around Brady Street for several weeks. I have often wondered what might've happened if Tony had brought *her* to *me* and we had gone upstairs to the trunk!

A Little Lovin'

BOY/GIRL RELATIONSHIPS at Cortina Brady weren't all just about sex. The goddess of love made rare and brief appearances as well.

Claude Poirier, head delivery boy, and Alda Stapely, pizza maker, were already an item when I arrived on the scene. Everyone recognized their mutual commitment and exclusivity immediately upon seeing the two together. They were completely devoted to each other. He was in his early twenties, Alda was nineteen and they were living together in a room at her mother's place. Her mother adored Claude.

Neither of them was even a hair above average intelligence nor had any lofty ideas about careers. They had gone to high school together and both dropped out in Grade 10. They wanted nothing more than to get married, have some kids and earn enough money to eventually buy their own house. Claude was always the gentleman. He didn't curse, not even just among the boys, and was scrupulously honest. Alda was his mirror image. Always the lady, she didn't use foul language and was always willing to help. They seldom got angry and I never heard either of them talk badly about someone behind his/her back.

When Claude found out I had asked Alda on a date, and he did because she told him, he thanked me.

"What? You're not angry I might've tried to steal her away from you?"

"Nope. I know she loves me. But she was really flattered you asked her. That made her so happy. So, thanks."

A few weeks later, when the new musical *Oliver* was in the last two days of its run in Sudbury, Claude came to ask me a favor. Alda had said she was not interested in seeing it, but recently, hearing everyone raving about it, she had changed her mind. Claude couldn't take her because he was working both nights and they needed the money. He knew I really enjoyed the movie and, in fact, had seen it several times with different people, so he wondered if I'd take Alda to see it. I did and we had a very enjoyable evening.

Claude and Alda—genuinely good, down to earth, honest, simple people. I was proud to know them.

A few months later, they were married, continuing to live at her mother's. And in less than two years, they had two children, both boys I think. All still at her mom's. Sure, they were crowded, but they made do and were happy.

Shortly after the second child was born, Claude took Alda to Toronto for a weekend getaway, leaving the kids with grandma. This was in January or February. They got caught in a major snowstorm on the way down. The pileup involved 40 vehicles. Claude walked away without a scratch.

Alda was not so lucky. A piece of metal pierced her throat and her skull was fractured. She survived with some damage to her vocal chords and permanent brain damage. From that time on, her short-term memory only extended over minutes and most of the long-term memory was gone. She didn't know her kids when she got home, or even that she had kids, who her brother was, where she had met Claude. She had to be told repeatedly who these people were and her role in their lives; she would soon forget again. From one minute to the next, she would forget the conversation and repeat herself or do the same chore she'd just completed.

Claude was the soul of patience. He worked hard to support her. He encouraged her, never seem to tire of explaining yet again some simple detail of their life together. I lost track of them about ten years later, in the early eighties. He was still with her, spoke lovingly of her. The world needs more men like Claude.

Clodet

ONE MORE IMPORTANT journey down Lovers' Lane I have to mention before leaving the topic. This one had nothing to do with the aura surrounding Brady Street. The young lady involved never worked for Cortina and, although she stopped in at the Brady location several times a week for a while, she was seldom there for more than a minute. At first. No, this one is a tale of true love, with all its joys and sorrows. I should know. This one's mine.

Again a cliché, I know, but I truly never will forget the first time I saw her. The weather was warm, early in July and it was 4:30 p.m. on Saturday. She was dressed in an almost-mustard waitress uniform and wearing an open blue jean jacket. And she was beautiful. To me.

She was slender with almost boyish hips, legs that just kept going, small breasts and attitude—just the way I like them. By now you have figured out that I have a thing for legs. Her hair was short and blonde. Her hands, almost masculine, were working hands with shorter fingers than her body plan suggested. Not elegant hands by any means, but I liked them right off.

With a hint of French accent, she said she had just come in to use the pay phone. Could I give her change for a dollar? We had a pay phone on the wall just to the right of the counter. With her change, she called Empire Union Cab, one street over. Destination: China House. And she was gone, outside to wait. I watched her through the window in the door until she got in the taxi and watched it until it turned off Brady Street and out of view.

Hmm. The China House. One of the most popular of Sudbury's several Chinese restaurants, situated on Elgin Street.

I'm not going to try to tell you it was love at first sight because it wasn't. Neither was it lust. There was something about her that attracted me. I could not explain it then and I can't now. I just wanted to get to know her.

I began to see her regularly, same time of the day, same scenario except she usually didn't need change. I wanted to talk to her, ask her name, what she did, but I was shy and had to work up to it. The only situation in which I am insecure and tentative is when trying to initiate contact with a woman that interests me beyond friendship. So I stood watching her wait for the taxi, saying to myself, 'As soon as she comes in next time, I'm just going to ask her name.'

I figured she couldn't live very far away. She was on foot and came in to call a cab to take her all of six blocks. So she must live nearby and not have a phone. I began to watch at that time of the afternoon to see if I could get a clue. I already knew that she came west along Brady from the direction of Notre Dame Blvd. A couple of days later, a dull, rainy afternoon, I was looking up the street wondering if I'd see her that day and there she was, coming out of an old house, similar in style to our building, right on the corner of Brady and Notre Dame. Seconds later, she rushed in from the rain.

After making the call, she asked if it was okay if she waited inside out of the rain.

"You're welcome to wait inside, rain or no rain." Screwing up my nerve, not giving myself a chance to second-guess, I added that she wasn't too wet, so she must not live too far away. And I was over the hump. She told me where she lived, I introduced myself and she reciprocated.

"I'm Clodet Francis, nice to meet you."

"Claudette," I repeated.

Something in my pronunciation gave me away and she added, "Not the traditional spelling. I have never felt traditional, so I changed it to C-l-o-d-e-t," spelling it out for me.

"Good for you," I said. "I like it."

That was all it took.

From then on, she would wait inside and we'd chat, starting with the basics of who we were, where we came from, what we wanted to do with our lives. One day, she arrived fifteen minutes early, so we'd have more time to talk. And, finding out what time she had her breaks, I began stopping in at the China House for late suppers on my nights off.

Relatively early on, she revealed that she smoked a little marijuana and dropped acid (LSD). This in addition to her obvious use of ordinary tobacco; she actually smoked quite a bit. The drug use didn't give me pause because, although I never did drugs of any sort, most of the people I knew did. It was, after all, 1971. And only a very few people I knew had serious drug problems.

Like me, she was a night owl, seldom going to bed before five or six in the morning. She didn't work as late as I did, since the China House closed at 1 a.m. Most nights she went home after work, smoked a joint, sometimes dropped a tab of acid and played tunes until the sky started to lighten. I was and still am a music lover to the core, so the news that music was a big part of her life was music to my ears.

One afternoon, while she waited for her cab, I asked her if she wanted to go somewhere with me after work.

"Where?"

"A surprise. But you'll like it."

"Okay. Want me to come here after my shift?"

"No. Go home and I'll pick you up after cleaning up."

She agreed and at 3 a.m. she found herself at Ramsey Lake. I took her to a favorite spot, a ledge cut into a rounded rocky cliff that fell about thirty feet to the lake. Sand had blown into the ledge and covered the bottom, making it pretty comfortable. The ledge was just wide enough for two people to lie on side-by-side. Which is what we did.

The night was warm, starlit, a light breeze. We talked about a bunch of things and, at one point, she asked me if I came here a lot and why.

"I love it here. It's a great place to think, clear my mind of the crap, talk to myself and listen to what I have to say. On top of that, if you are quiet, the lake will talk to you."

"What does it say?"

"The lake has been here since the last Ice Age and the water is much older yet. If you're really still and listen, the lake will talk to you about how the Earth formed, the evolution of life, where we came from. Be really quiet now. Hear it? Hear the waves? They're talking to us."

"What are they saying?"

Right up my alley. I had just finished my first year at Laurentian University. I would be going back in the fall to study geology. I intended to become a paleontologist and had been reading natural history for years. So that night, the lake explained to her how the Sudbury basin was formed, how the mineral deposits developed, how this area was repeatedly flooded by shallow seas. The night was magic—the first of several we shared over the next year.

I began spending nights in her apartment, talking with her and listening to music, while she got stoned. The more time I spent there, the more I became aware of just how great a role the drugs played in her life. When she was home, she was stoned. All the time.

Aside from me, all of her so-called friends were heavily into the drug culture. Far too often, some addict was at her door at 5:00 a.m. trying to score some dope to maintain his/her high. And she would supply it if she had it because, when she was short, she did the same thing. Much of the money she earned went to pay for drugs.

She was dealing, no pun intended, with one of these stoners at the door early one morning, *Born To Be Wild* playing on the portable record player, when I realized I was in trouble. She was witty, she was intelligent, she was kind, generous, fun, gentle, romantic, supportive, interested and interesting. She was a serious drug addict. She smoked ordinary tobacco heavily. And I was in love with her.

At 7 p.m. on Tuesday evenings in the early seventies, radio station CHNO played an hour of listeners' requests, with Steve Reagan as the D.J. He would introduce the song, make the dedication to so-and-so, from so-and-so, then play it. Feeling particularly good about an afternoon with Clodet, I called in a request one Tuesday. I asked him to play The Look Of Love *by Lesley Gore, a particular favorite of mine. The dedication was 'to Clodet, working at the China House, from her pizza guy.' Before he hung up, Reagan asked where I worked and commented on the quality of our pizza.*

Then I called the China House and talked to the manager, who generally answered the phone himself. The man had a real problem with the English language, but I finally got him to understand. I asked him to tune the radio to CHNO at seven for an hour. The song dedication aired at 7:10 and I got the call at 7:14. She was ecstatic! No one had ever done that for her.

The evening shift at Cortina listened to the radio a lot. So we heard the request show every week. I had noticed that seldom did Reagan ever play the same request; possibly people seldom made the same request or, maybe, the idea was to give everyone a chance. I wanted to do it again the next week, so I decided to try a little bribe to get around that second reason. I called, asked Reagan if he was in the mood for pizza, an offer that he jumped all over. After taking his order, I made the request, which he said was no problem. The pizza went out with the next deliveries.

Another hit! And a routine was established. Every Tuesday, I sent him a small pizza at 6:30, he'd make the dedication and play the song at 7:10. Even if we were tuned to another station, everyone knew to tune to CHNO at seven until we heard it. Reagan even raved about the great pizza made by Cortina a couple of times.

I ran into a roadblock at week twelve. Tony, one of the owners, mentioned hearing the dedication to one of the part-time staff at Martindale. The employee also worked at Brady occasionally and, not knowing Tony was not in the loop, made a comment about the song being played so often that Reagan was gaining weight on all the free pizza. Oops.

I got the call. Tony wasn't actually angry, but enough was enough. No more free pizza for Steve Reagan. The next Tuesday I called, explained the situation and made the request.

"Sorry, kid. No pizza, no tunes." And he hung up on me! What a jerk. I thought that was not only rude, but a little unreasonable. It was not like he was giving away anything concrete, whereas I was feeding him and potentially putting my job at risk. From that time on, when I was working, Cortina Brady did not listen to the Steve Reagan show.

Over the next year, Clodet and I became closer. I had never felt that way about anyone and she said the same. We never tired of being together. I began sleeping with her—no, really sleeping. We did not make love, although there was a lot of heavy-duty foreplay. Several men had taken advantage of her in the past, professing love, until she began having sex with them. Then the relationships became only about sex and drugs; tenderness and caring went out the window. She was afraid to spoil what we had.

"Once sex is involved, everything changes," she'd say. I was in no hurry and sex was not my reason for being with her, so I was okay with that.

Drugs and smoking were the problems. The drug use, both the weed and the acid, increased in frequency. She'd get jumpy, agitated, had trouble focusing, if she abstained for too long. And *too long* became shorter and shorter with time. To complicate matters, the more time I spent at her place, the more obvious a truth I already knew became: I could not live with a smoker! I am extremely allergic to smoke. At that age, I was still young and stupid enough to be willing to put up with smokers so that I could be among people I liked. I just took more medication and got on with it. But I knew I could never live with a smoker, let alone one that smoked as much as Clodet. I already suffered through two or three bouts of pneumonia a year, plus all sorts of breathing problems due to asthma. Living with a smoker would eventually kill me.

Occasionally, she could resist them both for a day or two. Like the weekend we spent at my parents' camp on Windy Lake. Aware that they had no intention of going that weekend, I asked my dad if I could use the camp. It was the only time I would ever make that request. He didn't ask if I would be alone and I didn't say. I was impressed, though: he didn't give me the 'safety, careful with fires, secure the boats, lock the door, etc.' lecture that we always got even when they were going to be there with us.

We were in a different world that weekend. The weather couldn't have been better. We played, we laughed, we hiked, we even cried at one point because she was so happy. We had fun trying to find a bathing suit for her among my sisters' stuff. We had to mix and match because her butt fit in an older sister's bottoms, but her small boobs only fit the top of one of my younger sisters. In the end, she stayed in her bra and panties.

We lay on the dock and looked at all the stars of the Milky Way that can't be seen in the city. We played Tarzan inside, me climbing like an ape into the rafters, beating my chest and leaping down on her on one of the beds. The third or fourth jump broke the leg of the bed! After laughing ourselves to tears, we spent a couple of hours fixing it so my parents wouldn't know. They never mentioned it.

That weekend was the first time we seriously talked about marriage. The only small downer of the two days. We both wanted to get married. I reminded her that I could not live with a smoker and that her drug abuse was way past out of hand.

"I know. I have to quit. I will. Marry me and I'll quit the drugs and smoking."

"Doesn't work that way, Clodet. This is a big problem and if you can't do it before, you won't be able to do it after. So, you quit and I'll marry you."

We agreed we would both work on her problem and we'd be able to do it together. How naive we were.

After that weekend, her addictions only got worse. We had the marriage discussion a couple of times over the next few months, pretty much verbatim. It always came down to: marry me, I'll quit; quit, I'll marry you. I was beginning to get a bad feeling that I refused to acknowledge.

Then *the* Thursday. I slept over after working Wednesday evening. We had listened to music and talked, Clodet got high. I rose early and went to the university for my 8:30 class. I had my own car by then and was driving myself. My time with Clodet had made me re-examine my priorities and I was taking my studies more seriously. Too little, too late, for that year anyway.

Clodet only had to work at 3 p.m., so I was to call at one o'clock to make sure she was up. When I called, I got no answer. I assumed she'd woken early and gone out to run errands before work. But the more I thought about it, the more that didn't ring true. Usually, after a trip like she had been on the night before, she only got up at the last minute. Thank goodness it didn't happen every night.

By 2:30 I was decidedly uneasy. Still no answer. I skipped the lab that was starting and drove to her apartment to check. Yes, of course, I had a key.

Walking into her bedroom, my first impression was that she had been murdered. The bed was full of blood. She wasn't dead, but I couldn't rouse her. I called an ambulance. They determined she was hemorrhaging from the vagina and was in a coma due to loss of blood. They hooked her up and we rushed to the hospital.

Hours later, the doctor informed me that the drugs in her system were near overdose levels and the hemorrhaging was directly related to drug abuse, smoking and inadequate rest and diet. He asked me her history, then made the decision to keep her for a week after they had stabilized the present situation, to give her body time to rest from the drugs and to try to talk her into rehab.

"She is so far gone, I'll be surprised if she remembers anything much after the LSD took effect. She certainly won't remember what has happened today."

He recommended that I go and clean her place as best I could. We would tell her what happened, of course, but the shock of seeing the physical evidence when she got home was potentially very psychologically damaging.

One of the last things he said to me: "She's a very lucky young lady. To have you, I mean. If you had waited until after your lab, you would have found her dead."

I went to clean her bedroom. I don't think she ever really believed the story, preferring to believe she had nearly OD'd and we were trying to frighten her into rehab.

Clodet refused rehab. I was working the evening she checked herself out of the hospital and she was already stoned when I arrived at 3 a.m. That was the last night I stayed with her. I told her I loved her, but I could not watch her do this to herself. She cried and once again asked me to marry her. I said I couldn't, because I loved her.

Two days later I took her to the Greyhound bus station and put her on a bus to Toronto. She was going down to stay with some friends, ostensibly to try and get herself together, but I knew it was to get away from a painful situation. At the bus door she smiled and asked if she could have the belt that I was wearing. She always loved that belt. I took it off and gave it to her.

Then she kissed me.

"You still have such an innocent kiss. I'll always love you." I believed her because I knew I would always love her.

Mischief

I'VE MENTIONED THAT pay phone on the wall beside the counter on Brady Street. The bosses had Bell Telephone install the phone six or seven months after I started at Cortina. Customers asking to use the phone had become a pain, plus the bosses thought it would be good for business. Anything that got people in the door had to be good for business.

For nearly a year after it was installed, we had a lot of fun with that phone due to a series of unlikely circumstances. The Prospect Hotel was a sleazy flophouse two blocks from Brady Street. It was the type of hotel that catered to lowlifes with next to no money, drug users who needed a place to get high or people who only needed a bed for an hour, if you get my meaning. Just off the lobby was a pool hall, Prospect Billiards. They had a pay phone that had been there forever, a convenience for customers, but its usage had gotten out of hand. Too many people were making shady deals of all sorts over that phone. Worse, they gave the number to people as a contact and the staff spent half their time playing secretary for these drug pushers and petty thieves. Oh, and let's not forget the girlfriends and wives looking for their guys!

So the owners of Prospect Billiards had the number changed, but left the old label on the phone. They did not give out the new number. Customers could still use it to call out, but they couldn't arrange to receive calls on that phone.

Right around that time, the pay phone was installed at Cortina and didn't Bell assign the old Prospect Billiards number to that pay phone! Very soon after installation, we started getting calls from people expecting to reach someone at the Prospect.

At first we didn't know what the heck was going on. "What? No, this isn't the Prospect, it's Cortina Pizza on Brady Street."

Often they didn't believe us and would argue, "Don't you lie to me. Did Chuck tell you to say that if I called? That S.O.B. You put him on the phone right now."

We got a lot of variations on that theme. When we clued in, the guys decided to have fun with the girls and we started answering the phone 'Prospect Billiards' or just 'Prospect.' When some babe asked for some guy, we'd run a number on her. And we had several numbers we could run.

"Phil? Nope, haven't seen him all evening. Actually, haven't seen him since last week. What? No, ma'am. I don't care what he told you, he wasn't here on Tuesday and he ain't here tonight."

Or

"Brian? Brian who? Brian Duchesne! Yeah, he was here, but he just left. Where? How the hell do I know where he went? No, Julian wasn't with him. His girlfriend came to pick him up. What do you mean, that's impossible? I was standing right here when they left. How do I know it was his girlfriend? Okay, an assumption, but she's the same girl he's been meeting here almost every night that he comes in. For about the last four months. Pretty good looking, too. What? You got me, lady. If you say you're his girlfriend, I believe you, but then I don't know who this other babe is."

Or

"Doug Mancini? Yeah, he's here, but he can't come to the phone. He told you he wasn't coming here anymore? Well, what can I say? No, he's busy, he can't come to the phone. Why? Well, you ought to know why. He's upstairs with his pusher, doing their business. You know Doug. After the deal is done, he'll probably use a little product and get shit-faced. Listen, you want me to get him to call you? I'll tell him and if he ain't too wasted, he'll probably call."

And so on. Oddly enough, some of the girls began to talk to us, unload their problems, starting with their relationships and eventually talking about their lives in general. They'd start calling specifically to talk to one of us. The Cortina boys, some of them anyway, would open up a bit and damned if some pretty steady telephone relationships didn't develop—and continue even after we told them the truth! I know three relationships that even extended to dating, and one that almost got that far. This last was between two girls, best friends, and Henry and me.

Henry had been chatting up this girl named Jess (Jessica) on a pretty regular basis and it was sounding promising. She shared an apartment in Lively with her girlfriend, they were 19 and first-year university students. According to her, they were both pretty good-looking.

Henry decided to bite the bullet and asked her out. She thought that would be great, but did he have a friend that could double date with her friend? We thought that was reasonable; she was being cautious. Not a good idea to set up a first date to meet a total stranger alone. Henry asked if I'd like to double date. Sure, I was game.

Getting a night off together took a little arranging, so the date didn't happen until two weeks later. In the meantime, I started talking to Irene, the friend, on the phone occasionally when Jess called Henry at the 'Prospect.' Well, when we finally met them, they were both pretty and they lived in Lively. That's where the truth ended, pretty much. They were 15, in high school and lived at home with their parents.

I certainly couldn't be offended that they lied to us. Hadn't we done the same to them? I did decide that the date wasn't happening. Henry and I were 20 years old and a dating relationship with these young girls could get us into a mess of trouble. Henry was not convinced, not wanting to give up voluntarily the potential for sex. His wavering on the issue led the girls to believe I might reconsider.

Don't get the wrong impression. These girls were not smitten with *us* so much as the idea of going out with older 'men.' They were almost gushy and giddy with the contemplation. I remained firm that night. No date. We went for coffee and donuts, then took them home.

The girls weren't deterred and began calling the 'Prospect' even more often. Henry continued to spend time talking to Jess if we weren't busy, only making matters worse. I even told them the truth about the phone and who we were, to try to turn them off. They thought it was cool that we were in charge of Brady Street when we worked. They started dropping in on Friday or Saturday nights to talk to their 'boyfriends,' even bringing other girls from school one time to meet us.

At this point, even Henry had had enough. He was tired of being pestered and their immaturity made him realize just how young they were. He was finally convinced that getting involved with them could lead to real trouble.

How to get rid of them? We decided to scare them away. Not in the sense of physical threat or anything. We had pretty good relationships with a number of police officers, a big fellow named Wayne in particular. He was a great guy. But at 6'4" and very solid, he was intimidating. He agreed to help us out.

We told the girls that, if they were serious about being our girlfriends, they could meet us after work Saturday night and we'd take them to an all-night party. There would be booze, pot, maybe some acid—whatever they wanted. They were a little hesitant and we hoped they would decline, but they said they'd be there. We arranged for Wayne to show up about half an hour after closing on a routine drive-by check of the building.

The girls had arrived, and Henry and I were finding nonexistent cleanup jobs to do, giving Wayne the chance to make his appearance. When the cruiser pulled into the lot, the girls became tense.

I said, "Don't worry. They check all commercial buildings a couple of times on night shift. He probably won't even get out of car."

But, of course, he did. He knocked on the door and, acting as if he didn't know us, asked who we were and why we were there so late. And who were these girls? I explained that we had just finished cleaning up.

"The young ladies work here as well?"

"Uh, no. We are going to a party after work, so they met us here."

"Really. These young ladies strike me as being a little young to be out this late, let alone going to a party in the middle of the night with boys obviously so much older."

Now Jess and Irene were becoming recognizably nervous and fidgety, moving to stand closer together.

Wayne asked, "How old are you two?"

Jess blurted, "Eighteen," not willing to push it to the 19 they told us. Still, Wayne acted unconvinced and said, "I'm going to have to ask to see some ID—from all four of you."

Good touch. Our drivers licenses established Henry and me as 20; Jess actually had a laminated birth certificate that indicated that she was 15, while Irene had nothing but a Grade 11 student card. Wayne looked at them and frowned.

"Eighteen, eh? I make it more like you're both 15 or thereabouts. Seriously underage."

Taking out his notebook, he asked them for their addresses and phone numbers. As they had nothing on them to substantiate their information, Wayne asked for a telephone book and made a show of looking up their parents. Satisfied that they had given him the correct addresses, he asked how they expected to get home.

"Iggy and Henry are going to drive us."

"Not anymore, they're not. Here's what's going to happen. The boys here are going to pay for a taxi to get you home right now (news to us!). I'm going to keep an eye on things around here for the next few weeks and asked a few other officers to do the same. If I see you here again, or hear that you've been here, I will pay a visit to your parents and we're all going to have a long talk about your dating habits."

He turned to me and continued, "And you boys are going to stay right here and we're going to have a chat about the impropriety of dating underage girls. Henry, call a taxi."

The girls gone, the three of us had a good laugh. We decided a couple of meatball sandwiches were in order. Wayne's was on us.

The traditional motto of police forces in North America is 'to serve and protect.' Wayne certainly did both that night, serving the general good and protecting the four of us from potentially big mistakes. I sometimes wonder how things worked out for Jess and Irene.

§

FOR ABOUT A MONTH in the summer of 1971, an eleven-year-old negro boy hung around the Brady Street location. Off school, bored, nothing to do, he would drop by, lean on the counter and chat with whoever was working. He was a nice enough kid, although he tried to act older and more worldly than he was. We would put him to work running the odd errand or sweeping the customer area—simple jobs—and pay him with food or drinks. We never let him stay more than about an hour. We didn't want him to think he could loiter around all day nor did we want to run the risk of the restaurant becoming a hangout for listless kids. Not good for business.

He was standing at the door to the prep area talking to me while I made spaghetti sauce. He was never allowed into the business area of the restaurant. He stopped mid-sentence and exclaimed, "Shit, man. Look at all the weed!"

I looked at him, then to the shelving that had his attention and back to him. "What are you talking about?"

"You've got a gallon jar nearly full of Mary Jane, man." He pointed to an old pickle jar that we used to store oregano. We used the herb in both pizza and spaghetti sauces.

"Naw, that's oregano for the sauces."

"Don't try to shit me, man. I know marijuana when I see it."

"You do, do you? And how would you know that?"

"My brother smokes a lot. He lets me smoke with him sometimes."

I was pretty sure he was just acting the big shot, so I let that last comment slide. "Well, that ain't marijuana."

"Sure it is. Can I buy some from you? I won't tell nobody where I got it. I promise, man. Just between us."

I refused, once again telling him it was oregano. Then told him it was time he went home.

He became a nuisance. Every time he came by, all he wanted to talk about was our stash and why we wouldn't sell him any. After more than a week of this pestering, I decided to teach him a lesson. I agreed to sell him a couple of ounces. He was just so proud of making his first big drug score, even though he let on that he did it all the time.

He left running. And came back two hours later barely dragging himself. The brown had drained from his skin to be replaced by a sickly gray-green. He reeked of vomit. Man, he looked awful. And miserable.

Weakly, he accused, "What kind of shit did you sell me? Who sold it to you? Man, this weed made me sick. I been pukin' my guts up. You could kill someone with that stuff. I wan' my money back."

"I told you it wasn't weed. It's just oregano. Learn to tell the difference before someone dumps something really dangerous on you."

He was none the worse for wear by the next afternoon. I heard no more about weed and, in a few days, he just stopped coming around. Yeah, I returned his money.

§

THAT LAST LITTLE anecdote was about an unintentional ruse. Here's one that was a little more deliberate.

Henry and I bought into the Cortina franchise system in 1972 and within eighteen months had three locations: Val Caron, Hanmer and Brady Street. Right from the beginning, the partnership was in trouble. We had worked extremely well together as employees of the Masottis, but as owners we had very different philosophies about managing money, staff and customers. By 1975 we had parted company. He took the more lucrative Brady location and I kept the other two.

When I went back to university in 1975, I kept the restaurants for two more years. I went to school during the day and worked the evening shift at one of the locations. During the dead period of January-March, I often worked alone on weeknights.

On a Sunday night in late March, 1976, I was working at Hanmer with Gabby (Gabrielle)—17, attractive and petite—a relatively new employee. New enough that she was still a little shy and tentative around me, but a good worker and learned quickly. Still not completely familiar with everything, she took advantage of a lull to check things out. I used the same time to try to get some homework done.

She came from the sink area carrying an old pickle jar (handy things, those jars) that was two-thirds full of a thick, partly translucent, white liquid—floor wax. It had been stored at the very back of the cupboard under the sink, so she'd really been digging.

"Excuse me, Iggy. What's this?" The innocence and trust on her face sparked an idea and I couldn't resist.

"Um, I'd rather not say. I'd hate to offend you." Just the right hesitation to pique her interest. No way she wasn't going to ask.

"No, really. You won't offend me. What is it?"

Trying to look reluctant, I said, "Semen."

Shock and embarrassment colored her face red and she blurted, "What?! What's it doing here? Where did it come from?"

I give her credit for not going 'yuck' and trying to get rid of the jar as quickly as possible. My mouth opened and the story just told itself.

I reminded her how hard I'd been working, both at Cortina and at the university. I was seldom home, saw very little of my wife and new daughter. Certainly the time that my wife and I had for intimacy was limited and brief. But a man has his urges. I went on to say that many of the slow weeknights working alone, I often wouldn't see a customer for as much as an hour. So I occasionally used some of that time to relieve the pressure and masturbate. A silly thought occurred one night: I wondered how long it would take me to fill a jar. Stupid, I admit, but there it is—four months' worth.

Throughout the telling, I kept expecting her to stop me and say something like, "Very funny. Now what is it, really." But she didn't. Her expression kept shifting from something like disgust to something very like pity. Without saying anything further, she put the jar back.

She was rather quiet the rest of the evening. I was ready to let her off the hook if she brought it up, but she didn't. The next weekend, she worked Friday and Saturday with me and two others. She was fine with them, but was even more tentative than usual around me. She was scheduled to work Sunday night with me again. I asked her before she left on Saturday if she could stay a little later Sunday so we could give the floors a much-needed scrubbing. Since we closed at midnight on Sundays, she didn't feel it was too much to ask, so she agreed.

After cleanup the next night, we tackled the floors. I took the customer area, the part that got the most abuse and needed more elbow grease, while she worked on the preparation area. When I had finished scrubbing, I went to get the wax. Timing was perfect. She was occupied changing the water in her pail, so she didn't see what I was doing. I went out front and started waxing the floor.

Finished her mopping, she climbed up to sit on the counter to wait for the floor to dry. She watched as I poured more 'semen' on the floor.

"What the hell are you doing? That's disgusting!" she shouted. I couldn't hold the laughter in and I couldn't talk for minutes. Through it all, she kept saying, "What's so funny? How could you be so gross?"

When I got myself under control, I explained. For a minute, she was offended, thinking she was really naive (which, I guess, she was) to have fallen for such an obvious prank. Then she started to laugh.

It mustn't have traumatized her too badly. By the next weekend, she had told all of my teen staff how she'd been fooled—including the other girls.

§

I WAS NOT MUCH of a hunter myself, but I had a couple of small groups of friends who liked to get away in the fall to hunt moose, breathe a little unpolluted air, drink a little beer. I would go because I enjoyed their company and had no objection to a share of fresh meat that hadn't had all the flavor and nutrition processed out of it.

When Henry asked me to go moose hunting for a couple of days one fall, I agreed only because he would be insulted if I said no. And Henry insulted was a belligerent, pouting, non-communicative Henry for days. I asked where he wanted to go and if he had a moose tag. He had a tag. I figured one was enough; we'd be lucky to get even one moose. But he had no specific location in mind, just up north somewhere.

I had the perfect spot. A couple of years earlier, I had cruised timber around Foleyet for a forest management company. I knew a fellow that had a hunting trailer on the Ivanhoe River in the heart of moose country. He was happy to let us use it.

Never having hunted moose before, we made planning decisions based on what we'd heard from other hunters. Apparently the best time to hunt moose was at first light or a dusk, near a marsh. We decided to get all our gear together and take it to work with us. That way, we could hit the road right after work. The two and a half hour drive would get us to the trailer shortly before dawn, so we could get a full day's hunting.

I had a surprise coming. Just before closing, Henry's Negro friend, Al, came in with the brother of the girl Henry was seeing. Henry had arranged for these two to come with us. I didn't know the girlfriend's brother, so I had no opinion there, but I didn't like Al. He was a womanizer, had fathered a child with a girl named Maria, then badly mistreated her. She was a good, if naive, soul and I had come to like her. But I bit my tongue, deciding not to create a problem.

The four of us piled into Henry's Mustang and we were in the trailer about an hour before dawn. We were killing time, waiting for first light, drinking coffee and talking. I took advantage of the time to clean my Winchester lever-action 30-30. It was fairly new, had only been used in target practice and I kept it in immaculate condition. I emptied the rifle and began using the ramrod on the bore of the barrel.

The conversation turned to girls and sex, as it often did. In due course, Henry told Al that Maria had been dropping by to talk to me at work lately. She didn't look happy, was everything okay?

Al responded angrily, "Ever since she had the kid, she thinks she owns me. She even expects me to marry her. Why would I marry a slut like that? All she's good for is tail. I think she got pregnant on purpose, to try and trap me. To hell with that. The kid's her problem. She's even trying to get me to pay her support. No way. Not my problem."

The conversation moved to whether Maria was any good in bed, whether Al could get her to go to bed with the other two.

"Yeah, she's just a slut. The whore will sleep with anyone and she'll do anything for me. I'll set it up."

That was enough for me. I liked Maria, she certainly was not a slut and I thought Al was an irresponsible asshole. I decided to use a joke to lighten the mood and change the focus of conversation—and maybe get just a little bit in Al's face. Standing up, I stuck the barrel of my empty 30-30 right into Al's crotch and, in my poor imitation of John Wayne,

"Listen, pilgrim. 'taint seemly a galoot like you should be bad-mouthin' the little lady. You best apologize for calling her them names or I'm gonna to have to blow yer nuts clean off."

Al went pale under his dark skin and everyone went quiet. After a heartbeat, Al said, "Hey, man, that's not funny! Sorry, okay? I didn't mean nothing."

"That there's more like it, pardner." I pulled the rifle out of his crotch and, with a John Wayne flourish to complete the image, I cranked the lever. A 30-30 bullet was ejected across the little trailer!

My turn to go pale. I was positive, I am still positive, I had emptied the rifle. I began to shake and got weak-kneed, had to sit down. I was really shaken. Not just because I was mistaken about emptying the rifle. Much more terrifying was the knowledge at the core of my being that, had Al decided not to apologize, I would've pulled the trigger.

§

YOU KNOW HOW some people are just so naturally gregarious that shortly after meeting them, they talk to you as if they've known you for years? And sometimes, you wish they didn't feel quite so comfortable?

Gordon was like that. I had never seen him before he walked into Cortina one evening. He was staying at the YMCA until he found a place to live. From Timmins, he had come to Sudbury because he heard Inco was hiring. He wasn't keen on being a miner, but he liked the money and the benefits. He became a steady customer for about two years, at which time he decided to move back to Timmins.

Gordon liked to talk. And if he had nothing particular on his mind, he would wheedle his way into the conversations of people around him. In addition to the obvious irritation of his butting into your conversation, he had that annoying 'been there/done that' attitude. No matter what you'd done, seen, bought, driven, etc., he had done, seen, bought and driven it bigger, faster, more often, more expensive. A very annoying posture and it turned out to be his nemesis.

This particular evening, when he arrived, he noticed me preparing two orders of spaghetti for delivery. Saying they looked appetizing, he ordered a plate for himself. And, for a change, he was going to eat at one of our tables rather than take it with him. As I prepared to put the lids on the two to go, ready to put them in the bag, Henry reminded me the customer had ordered chili peppers. We offered parmesan cheese and chili peppers as complements to our pasta.

"I know. I put them on the side in a folded napkin. I'd hate to put too much and have the customer unhappy and complain."

"I just sprinkle on what I figure is okay and close the lid," Henry replied. "Never got too many complaints."

"Well, I figure the customer might prefer to add it to taste."

Gordon piped up from the other side of the counter, "Henry, when you bring mine out, you can go ahead and add as much as you like. Never too hot for me."

While waiting for his meal, he went on and on about how he loved hot food, it was never too hot. He had a cast-iron stomach. His spaghetti, when it arrived, had a liberal sprinkling of chilies. One taste and he said, "Hell, this ain't hot. Henry, wanna bring me the shaker of chili peppers?"

From my side of the counter, I said to him, "Maybe you should try a few more mouthfuls before you add more. Those chilies are pretty hot and they can sneak up on you."

"Naw, I've had a lot hotter. You have no idea. I've had people try, but no one has been able to make it too hot for me."

Henry said, "That plate would burn a hole right through me and fall out my butt."

"Aw, you just can't take it. As a matter fact," Gordon said, picking up the large spoon by his plate, "I could eat this spoon heaping with chilies and not even break a sweat."

The spoon he held was one with an oversized round bowl intended for use when rolling spaghetti on your fork

"No damn chance," I said. "That could kill you, man."

"Naw, done it before. Betcha twenty I can do it."

He was starting to get on my nerves with his bravado, so I decided to make an easy twenty bucks. I made the bet. We put our money on the counter, he heaped the spoon with chilies and down it.

The chili peppers almost did burn right through him. He turned beet red, began to sweat profusely and gestured for water, unable to talk. He ended up sitting on the floor against the counter, only semiconscious. His heart was racing, so we called an ambulance.

He couldn't make sounds for over three hours. The ER doctor told him not to speak at all for at least three days. He had permanently damaged his vocal cords, as well as burning his mouth and throat.

When Gordon moved back to Timmins, he was completely healed, yet his voice was still harsh and raspy. I continued to put chilies on the side with my spaghetti orders.

§

HENRY AND I, Joe and Lee were working a busy Saturday night. Claude Poirier and another fellow were both kept hopping on delivering. Mid-evening, about 8:30, pickups had slowed a little, but the deliveries were piling up. Henry, who was working the oven, told me to take over for him—he was going to make a few deliveries in his own car to help get caught up.

To be truthful, he'd recently had his 1965 forest green Mustang repainted black with a bright orange hood (my idea) and he just wanted an excuse to drive it. He loaded up with four orders and off he went.

Halfway through the deliveries, two pizzas left, a car cut him off at an intersection and he had to jam the brakes. One of the large pizzas, which were on the passenger seat, slid out of the box and onto the floor. Pizza boxes were pretty flimsy in those days, not the stiff corrugated jobs used now. Henry just put the pizza back in the box and made the delivery.

Once more, timing is everything. He had just come through the door into the prep area, when the phone rang. Being closest, he answered it.

The customer had a complaint about a delivery he had just received and wanted to talk to the person in charge.

"You're speaking to him." Technically true.

"I just got two large pizzas delivered and one of them is full of gravel."

Henry, in very calm businesslike tones, "Did the delivery boy charge you extra for the gravel, sir?"

"Well, uh, no, but..."

"Then what the hell is your complaint?" Henry yelled into the phone and hung up.

Auto Woes

RAISE YOUR HAND if you've seen the movie *Bullitt* with Steve McQueen. Those of you with your hands down, go out and rent it. The movie, a little dated now having been shot in 1968, is a very good action police drama. And it boasts arguably the all-time best car chase scene ever filmed, Steve in his green 1968 Mustang GT being chased by the baddies in a 1968 Dodge Charger. Even if chase scenes are not your 'thing,' I defy you to watch it and not get a surge of adrenaline.

I saw *Bullitt* at the drive-in with my girlfriend and another couple. We all loved it and were excitedly reliving the best parts as we hung up the speaker box and cleaned the remnants of popcorn from the upholstery preparatory to leaving. I was pumped, man. I *was* Steve McQueen and my 1967 Chev Biscayne had transformed into a 1968 Mustang.

We headed into the line of cars inching towards the exit. I was talking excitedly, playing the role, anxious to get to the open road. We were going to tear up some asphalt, man! I let a couple of feet open between us and the car ahead, then popped my clutch briefly so the car leapt to close the gap. Then I did it again. All the time, I was making fast driving noises. Yeah, I know. Not too damned immature!

But I quieted down in a hurry. I popped the clutch one too many times for a fraction of a second longer than I should have and 'Bam!' Right into the rear end of the car ahead of me. My first accident with my first car. Pretending to be Steve McQueen. In a drive-in parking lot. How humiliating.

The guy in the car ahead of me was younger than my 19 years and driving his mother's car. So, although the dent in the bumper was quite small, I didn't argue when he insisted I replace the whole bumper rather than repair it. An expensive movie; great, but expensive.

That chase scene still gives me an adrenaline rush. Perhaps it is fortunate I no longer have a driver's license.

§

BRUCE GATES WAS one of the all-around nicest of my high school friends. He was polite, well mannered and easy-going. He didn't have any of the vices so many others had—he didn't curse, smoke, drink to excess or do drugs. He was just a nice guy.

We went to high school together, then both went on to study geology at Laurentian. When we started second-year, Bruce bought a late fifties Ford (Fairlane or Galaxie 500) from his father. The car was 12 or 15 years old and his dad's pride and joy. It was immaculate. Having grown up with the car and being very close to his father, Bruce loved the car as well. His dad was reluctant to sell his Ford, even to his son, but finally gave in to Bruce's coaxing. When the deal was done, his father cautioned him to take good care of the vehicle.

And Bruce did. He was so proud to be able to say he owned the beautiful classic. He washed and waxed it regularly, kept the interior spotless, didn't allow anyone to smoke in it. When he started driving it to the university, he figured he'd defray some of the costs by taking on three paying passengers. For a very reasonable rate, about half of bus fare, we were picked up and dropped off at our doors. This was during my early Cortina years when I was spending so much time sleeping in the student lounge.

One Friday afternoon about 4:30 in early spring 1970, we were headed home as usual. The streets were bare and wet, the snow banks having been reduced to black, gravelly mounds about 30 cm high and the temperature was just above freezing. There were four of us: Bruce and me in the front; Don Bouffard was in back with another student whose name I cannot recall. We were joking and laughing, looking forward to the weekend. With the onset of rush-hour, traffic was slowing; it was pretty much stop-and-go by the time we got onto Notre Dame Blvd.

As we approached the intersection at Kathleen Street, pressure eased a little and the pace picked up. We were the fourth car from the intersection when Bruce rolled down his window and did something completely out of character. He had noticed a young man wearing a blue leather Laurentian University jacket walking on the far side of the street. He stuck his head out of the driver's window and, as he drew alongside the student, yelled out, "Laurentian bum!"

At the same time as he was rolling his window down and turning his head, the light at the intersection turned amber. The driver of the third car ahead of us, on the edge of the intersection, decided not to run the amber and stood on his brakes causing the next two cars to brake suddenly as well. Bruce didn't see these developments. As he yelled his derisive remark, his car slammed into the vehicle ahead, badly crumpling the trunk of that car and making an accordion of his own front end.

We were all stunned. We had been watching Bruce, so we hadn't seen the accident developing either. As we got out of the car, the guy in the leather jacket smiled and gave Bruce the finger. Bruce didn't even notice. He looked at me and said, "My dad is going to kill me!"

Of course he didn't, but he was *some* upset. On the upside, he had been working on that car so long that he was familiar with it and they had it repaired in short order. The downside was that, given family dynamics, although it was Bruce's car, bought and paid, he was not allowed to drive it for a month! Had he known, I guess the 'Laurentian bum' would have had the last laugh.

§

CLAUDE POIRIER was the only delivery driver at Cortina who didn't have any car accidents on the job. Yet, he was the fastest, most efficient. He could make as many as 60% more deliveries on a given night than any other delivery person. I remember one particularly busy Friday, after I had been delivering for quite a while, when Claude did $215 worth of deliveries and I could only manage $135. This may not sound like much, but at the time a large #5 pizza was $2.95; the same pie is worth about $17 today. He delivered a lot of pizza in nine hours that night. Somehow Claude was particularly suited to be a delivery person.

When I first started on delivery, I worked on busy nights as second delivery to Claude at Brady Street. If we happened to be at Brady to get our next deliveries at the same time, he would get his orders straightened out, then take a look at mine and make a few comments to help me out.

He would say things like: "This house is halfway down the block. It is a pale yellow, not very noticeable, but the house on the right has purple eaves troughs."

The first few times he did that, I said to myself, "Yeah, sure. Who's he trying to kid?" He was always right.

When the busy time of the night was over and there were no more deliveries for me, I would often ride with him just to kill some time, holding his deliveries on my knees. Many times he would be driving, chatting with me, apparently not paying any real attention to where he was going. Then he would just pull into a driveway seemingly at random. I would look at the bill on the first order and find we were sitting in the driveway at the very address.

I'd turned to him and say, "How do you do that?"

"I don't know. Just a good memory, I guess."

Claude didn't speed, but he knew every shortcut, lane-way and parking lot that could be used to shorten the trip. Of course, cutting through private property or public parking lots was illegal. At least once a month, we got a call at Brady from the police dispatcher saying,

"Tell your young Mr. Poirier to stay on public thoroughfares or we'll have to ticket him." We all knew that the reason they called was because they couldn't catch him and it was easier than coming to wait for him at Brady Street.

Through all my years at Cortina, I don't recall Claude ever having even a close call. The rest of us were not so lucky. Accidents were relatively common among the delivery boys at Cortina and we were usually at fault. We had a couple resulting from equipment failure and a few were caused by the other drivers.

§

WHEN I WAS HIRED, Vito, the younger of the two owners, gave me the cautionary indoctrination. "You can't waste any time on this job, but you can't be rushing so much that you get into an accident. Take your time, just don't *waste* time. If you have an accident, it costs me money in insurance and repairs and unhappy customers. Plus, while you're dealing with the cops, deliveries get backed up. If the car is so badly damaged it can't be used, I have to get another car. So accidents cost money, waste time and disappoint customers. Pay attention, keep a safe steady pace."

I recognized the truth in what he was saying, but it was difficult not to feel pressured to perform, when you are just starting out. I was afraid, if I got too far behind, he might decide I wasn't up to the job and let me go. Against 'common sense,' when we were busy, I pushed a little.

I had two accidents that were my fault, both soon after I started delivering and both because I was rushing. The accidents were minor in terms of damage, but dealing with police officers took time and put me further behind than if I'd taken it easy. The first happened on my third weekend, so my *sixth shift*. I was working at Martindale Road and taking four or five deliveries at a time because it was busy. A cool September evening, driving conditions were perfect. About 11 p.m. I was rushing back to Martindale along Walford Road. Martindale Road became Walford Road as it crossed Regent Street. Walford was almost four lanes wide, but was restricted to two-lane traffic, the outside portions used for parking. Two public schools sat on opposite sides of the street, so the speed limit was only 30 km/h. And I was stuck behind a woman doing just that. Two cars approached in the opposite lane.

Impatient, I decided to pass the lady on the right, where there was lots of room for the Volkswagen (VW) bug I was driving. I pulled over and stepped on the gas. As I came up beside her, I sneezed without warning. The body jerk caused by the sneeze made me wrench the wheel slightly and briefly to the left, enough to broadside the lady. Damn!

I called the police and the boss from a house across the street. I was occupied with the police for over an hour, getting back to Cortina just after midnight. The boss had been delivering himself in his own vehicle in my absence. I received a reprise on the safe driving lecture.

Three months later, on a Friday night, conditions were terrible. It was cold, freezing rain mixed with snow was falling and only the most traveled thoroughfares were reasonably navigable. All others were coated with ice, the least traveled being the most treacherous.

Lousy weather always means busy on delivery—who wants to go out in such weather? My last delivery before heading back to Martindale was five pizzas to a party at the University of Sudbury Residence at Laurentian University. The residence was a long curving building with the access road curved parallel to the convex side. Although I wasn't going fast, I was going too fast for the conditions.

I came around the curve to find a Peugeot parked at the end of the drive. I applied the brakes and began to slide on the ice. I pumped the brakes to no apparent effect. Over a matter of seconds, almost in slow motion, my VW bug closed the twenty meter gap and came to rest against the rear-end of the Peugeot. The only damage was a broken lens on the left rear tail light.

I went in with the pizza and waited in the foyer while the person who had ordered was called down. When we finished our transaction, I asked if he knew who owned the car. The owner was a math professor who was upstairs.

I asked the fellow to give the professor a note with my name, address, the fact that I was an LU student and saying that I would come by his office on Monday morning to arrange repairs. He agreed and I left.

The police were waiting for me at Martindale Road when I got back. I was charged with leaving the scene of an accident. Apparently, a female student had been looking out the third-floor window and, seeing the accident, told the math professor and he called the police. I figured that was before he got my note and everything could be straightened out on Monday.

Saturday afternoon, I went to Harvey's, an automotive parts store in Sudbury at the time, and bought the replacement lens for the Peugeot. Monday morning, on my way to the math prof's office, I stopped by the parking lot and replaced the lens. Done.

When I talked to him, he said he hadn't gotten my note and despite the fact that I had already repaired the damage, I deserved to be taught a lesson. He refused to request that the police drop the charges.

From his office, I went back to the dorm and found the guy to whom I'd given the note. He had become sidetracked with distributing the pizza, then by a girl and a bottle of beer, and never delivered the note. He ended up tossing the note in the garbage. He agreed to testify that I had given him the note if I needed him to do so.

Next thing was to get a lawyer. Leaving the scene of an accident not only carries a hefty fine, but is a permanent blot on your record, one I wanted to avoid. In the lawyer's opinion, I *had* left the scene, but the judge might be lenient in the face of mitigating circumstances.

Two months passed before the court date. On the day, the lawyer for the prosecution presented their case first. When he finished, the judge said, "Let me summarize: you have a witness who saw the VW hit the Peugeot, another that saw the defendant taking pizza out of the VW after the collision, another that watched the VW pull out and leave. Is that correct?"

"Yes, your honor."

"You do not have an eyewitness that saw the defendant in the VW at any time. So you cannot actually place the defendant in the VW at any time, let alone support your contention that the defendant was driving the VW at the time of impact, is that correct?"

"Yes, Your Honor, but…"

"No 'buts' about it. I am dismissing this case due to lack of evidence." Turning to me, he went on, "Your affidavit indicates you replaced the taillight on the Peugeot at your expense. I can rule that he has to reimburse you for that, if you choose."

"No, Your Honor, I was never trying to deny responsibility for the accident. I admit breaking the taillight and have no problem with replacing it, sir."

"Case dismissed."

As it turned out, I didn't even need a lawyer. But I learned my lesson. From then on I paced myself on delivery. I became the tortoise who knew 'slow but sure wins the race.'

§

NORTHERN ONTARIO can be treacherous in winter, as witnessed in the previous account. For good reason we have a 'no fault due to conditions' category available to police officers investigating winter accidents. Under some conditions, you are completely helpless and all you can do is sit tight and watch events unfold.

I had been delivering at Cortina for a few months and was feeling comfortable with my duties. The job was beginning to be routine. On a cold night of intermittent snow and freezing rain in January, 1970, the routine was broken.

I was driving a little box of a car, a green Toyota. I loved it—four-speed, small and quiet, easy to park. That night, with the streets so slick, deliveries were taking much longer than usual and we were backed up. I was taking extra orders to try to catch up.

Martindale Road makes a shallow s-shaped curve as it crosses Regent Street to become Walford Road. Regent is a long, curving, moderate slope for quite a distance from the left that continues through the intersection. Although I had eight orders in the car, I was in no rush, taking my time. I approached the intersection cautiously but, when the light went amber with me still a distance away, I found I couldn't stop at the corner. I pumped the brakes, but slid the length of the little car into the intersection.

To my left and uphill, headlights demanded my attention. There, still a distance away, was an eighteen-wheeler moving down-slope toward me and braking.

But it wasn't stopping!

I put the Toyota into reverse, but it just sat there spinning on the ice. Same result in first gear. By then, the eighteen-wheeler was sliding, all wheels locked. Too late it occurred to me to get the hell out of the car. All I could do was sit there and watch the grill of this International slowly skidding closer. Above that grill, I caught a glimpse of a ghostly white face, a face in shock. I wondered how mine looked.

The truck was slowing down, but not enough. With an almost gentle jar, the grill and bumper of the big rig made contact with the driver's side of the Toyota and we were both sliding down Regent. A little over a hundred feet farther, as Regent turned left away from us, we ran into the snow bank. Before we came to a halt, the Toyota had folded like an accordion to about one-third its original width.

I walked away without a scratch! The pizzas, however, didn't fare quite so well.

§

TONY MASOTTI had a real problem with automobiles. In those days, he bought new cars more often than most people wash theirs. And when he was finished with a vehicle, it was *finished*. Most went directly to the junk yard.

His problem? Heavy on the gas pedal? Careless driver? Negligent at maintenance? None of the above. His failing was that he couldn't say no to his staff. Most of us were in our late teens and early twenties, and few of us owned cars. Once an employee had worked at Cortina for a bit and met with Tony's approval, he was willing to lend his car to that employee upon request. Many nights he'd come into work and lend his car to an employee that had the night off, the only stipulation being that the car had to be back by closing. It was not uncommon for that stipulation to be broken; he'd be mad, then lend it again next time to the same employee.

He had more than one car, so we could even borrow one of them to, say, go to Toronto for the weekend. He also used his vehicles to substitute for delivery cars that were being serviced or as a supplement when delivery was extremely busy.

All those different young drivers rapidly took their toll. The cars took a beating. They got into minor fender-benders and serious collisions; they had their bottoms torn out by being driven over obstacles; they fell through the ice and ended up on the bottom of Minnow Lake; they were rolled; and they had utility poles fall on them. These vehicles suffered broken windows, sprung hoods, seats broken off their foundations, motors seized by being driven without oil. In short order, they were wrecks.

Tony finally came to his senses. His Ambassador was on its last legs, so he ordered a new Tornado with all the bells and whistles. The dealer expected delivery would take a week. Tony used the time to let everyone know, and to repeatedly emphasize, that no one, *no one*, but Tony was going to drive the new car. *No one!*

The Tornado came in on Friday. Undercoating and a few other things had to be done, but the dealer promised Tony he would have it that day. As so often happens, the dealer ran late and finally called Tony at work at 8 p.m. The car was ready. The dealer was willing to have it dropped off at Cortina so Tony wouldn't have to wait until the morning.

Tony excitedly agreed, a kid in expectation of a new toy. He had one minor problem. He was at work now with two cars to drive home. He enlisted one of the delivery boys, Lorne, to follow him home in the old Ambassador, where another delivery boy could pick him up.

All evening, every time Lorne came in to pick up new delivery orders, he bugged Tony to let him drive the new car home. Just that once. Just to Tony's house. Tony kept saying 'no.' No one was going to drive his new car. In the end, when 3:00 a.m. arrived, he gave in. Just once. Given Lorne's past performance with vehicles, this was not the wisest decision. They left Cortina, Tony leading in the old Ambassador, Lorne following in the new Tornado.

All right, bad enough that the young fellow was partly distracted by all the neat gadgets, but he stupidly lit a cigarette. Tony lived near the General Hospital and the most direct route home went right past the Emergency Entrance with its ambulance bays. As they approached the traffic lights that controlled access to the Emergency Entrance, their green light suddenly went amber and then red, as an ambulance roared out of a bay with its lights flashing. Tony jammed on the brakes.

Didn't the delivery boy pick that moment to lose control of his cigarette and drop it on the seat between his legs. He panicked. He couldn't burn a hole in the new car's seat! He glanced down, unaware of the situation developing ahead of him, and frantically groped between his legs for the butt. He inadvertently stepped on the accelerator and rammed right into the rear of the Ambassador.

No one was seriously hurt, although Tony had a sore neck for more than a week, but the Tornado was so badly damaged that he sold it to a wrecking yard for parts rather than repair it. And Tony had never even gotten to drive it!

§

ABOVE I SUGGESTED that Lorne was not the most reliable driver among the young men working at Cortina. And, indeed, he wasn't. In his tenure of a few months, he had more accidents with more vehicles than anyone else in their entire employment history with Cortina. How he got away with such conduct can only be attributed to the fact that he was a gifted con artist. Physically, he looked like a nice guy. He presented as honest and trustworthy. He was well spoken and knew what to say to flatter the bosses' egos. He was quite a different fellow around the rest of us.

Lorne liked to race. He and a couple of the others would occasionally play a game they called *Lose the Tail* in the early hours of the morning when the streets were relatively empty. It was, essentially, a chase game. The lead car had to try to lose the following car, the 'tail,' while the tail had to stay with the lead. If the lead did succeed in getting away, he tried to maneuver so that he came up behind the other car and now the shoe was on the other foot. The former tail was now the lead.

About 4 a.m., he and Henry were playing *Lose the Tail* on this particular night. Lorne was lead, driving the Cortina Econoline delivery van and Henry was tail in his 1965 Mustang with me riding shotgun. Twenty minutes into the chase, Lorne had yet to shake Henry. We had tailed Lorne, at high speeds, all through the south-end, through Minnow Lake and into the downtown area. We tore along Durham Street going North and ignoring the traffic lights.

When we reached Elm Street, Lorne decided to make a sudden left, figuring we were so close behind him that Henry would be unable to react fast enough. Henry didn't even try, we were going way too fast.

So was Lorne, as it turned out. As he entered the intersection and turned left, the van went up on its right wheels, balanced there for a second as it tried to negotiate the corner, then went over on its right side. The van slid across the right-hand lanes, over the sidewalk and into the Bata Shoes store through its main display window. What a mess!

For the rest of its service until they got rid of it, the Cortina delivery van had the logo and phone number only on the left, driver's side. The right side was blank, slightly mismatched green panels.

The incident that put the final nail in Lorne's coffin happened a few weeks later. Despite his bad reputation, he was still delivering. At the end of one shift, he wheedled the use of the delivery VW beetle overnight. Tony gave him a lecture, then let him take the bug.

This was mid-December. The weather had been colder and snowier than usual. Of the two lakes situated right in the middle of Sudbury, Lake Ramsey was still open, but the smaller and shallower Minnow Lake had frozen over.

Lorne and one of his friends, not a Cortina employee, decided it would be fun to go bumper riding on the snow-covered ice of Minnow Lake. In this sport, one person drives the car, the other holds on to the rear bumper and surfs the snow on his boots. I always found it was far more fun when we hitched a tow on the bumpers of city buses when the streets were snow packed.

Lorne and his friend decided using the bug was safer since it was much lighter than the friend's Pontiac. They only got about 40 feet out onto the lake when the thin ice cracked and the front end of the bug dipped down into the water. Lorne scrambled out of the car, got to a pay phone and called Henry and me, still at Brady cleaning up. When we were done, we went to Henry's apartment, got a length of chain and arrived at the scene just in time to see another crack develop and the VW beetle go to the bottom in about 12 feet of water.

Lorne never worked another shift. Considering his wages and the vehicle repairs he had incurred, he had been an expensive employee.

§

SUNDAY MORNING, just after 11:00, my girlfriend and I were headed home to her parents' place after church. She was still trying to convince herself that she should embrace the Catholic religion into which she'd been baptized as a baby. You couldn't ask for a better June day—warm, sunny, hardly a cloud in the sky. We were in a white VW beetle with the Cortina logo and phone number painted on the side. I had worked Brady the night before and Tony allowed me to take the delivery car home. I had to work again at 3 p.m., so this made getting to work much more convenient.

We had attended mass at St Anne's Church in downtown Sudbury. Joanne and her parents lived on a hill overlooking the Kingsway, on the way east out of town. Exiting the downtown heading east, Elm Street became the Kingsway, the transition consisting of a relatively sharp left turn followed by a sharp right. The seedy Kingsway Hotel sat in the middle of that second turn and a gas station was located next to it as the road straightened out. In front of the gas station stood three wooden Hydro poles about two feet apart.

I have no recollection of the accident. One moment we were keeping pace with traffic and enjoying the morning, the next I was regaining consciousness in a badly battered VW bug. I was still in the driver's seat, the side window was gone and the windshield was shattered, but still in place. My face ached like hell. My right hand was stretched out and holding Joanne in her seat. The tummy of her dress had an almost perfectly circular hole torn out of it matching the clump of material clutched in my right hand. My wrist was sore and bent at an odd angle. Joanne's right eye was bloodshot and a bruise was developing on the right side of her forehead.

I clued in to the fact that I was bleeding profusely from my face at about the same time that an attendant from the gas station gave me a greasy rag to put on it. I couldn't get the rag closer than an inch because of the large shards of glass sticking out of my face. By the time we got out of the car, the ambulance had pulled up, so I must have been unconscious for at least a couple of minutes.

Eyewitnesses reported that our VW came around the corner and, instead of straightening as the road did, continued to turn and ran straight into the Hydro pole without braking. Later, a mechanic determined that the front right tie rod in the steering assemblage had snapped due to metal fatigue. So, as I tried to straighten from the turn, the right front wheel stayed angled to the right, pulling us into the pole. I put my face through the side window; somehow I reflexively reached across to hold Joanne in her seat. On impact, she rocked forward, smacking her forehead on the windshield and breaking my wrist against the dashboard. My face received several stitches and left another bunch of manly scars.

Epilogue: Failure due to metal fatigue in auto parts such as that tie rod is extremely rare. I haven't bothered to calculate the odds of it happening twice, but they must be long odds indeed.

Eight months after that first tie rod failed, it happened again. At 2 a.m., I had just left Joanne at her parents' and was driving west on the Kingsway. This time I was driving a used Oldsmobile Delta 88 that I had purchased in the fall of 1971. Typical of February, it was cold and snowing, but the Kingsway was well lit and the snowplow had just passed, so conditions were acceptable. And that stretch of the Kingsway is almost arrow straight. As I approached the lights at Bancroft Drive, thinking about the pleasant evening, the Oldsmobile abruptly veered right, up over a three-foot snow bank and into the parking lot of an auto body repair shop. Luckily, that part of the lot was empty. No damage, not even to my fragile soft parts.

On inspection, a mechanic found that the front right tire rod had failed due to metal fatigue. Not too freaky!

More than one person, hearing this story, quoted the old adage, 'bad things come in threes,' and I admit to having thought it myself. For at least a year, the thought would occur to me while I was driving. When would the third tie rod break? I eventually put it out of my mind.

Just over three years would pass before that specter reared its spooky head again. But this time was a little different.

§

MARCH, 1974, and I was home quite ill with pneumonia. Joanne and I had married the previous June and were living in an apartment in Sudbury. I had gone in to work that evening, but was just too ill. I called an employee to cover for me and went home. At 1:45 a.m. I got a call from work: I had forgotten to leave the keys, so they couldn't lock up after closing. I would have to drive back to Hanmer, about thirty kilometers from the apartment, to lock up.

Snow was falling steadily and the temperature, although below freezing, was in that zone where snow on the highway was constantly melting and freezing due to the friction of tires. Very slippery.

We took our time, in no hurry. I was in no mood to rush.

Just before Hanmer, after a straight stretch, the highway turns ninety degrees to the East at a four-way intersection. The Hanmer

Hotel sat on that corner in those days. The hotel was pretty lax in checking the age of their patrons, a circumstance well known and used to advantage by local underage drinkers. That night, leaving after closing, an intoxicated 17-year-old boy got behind the wheel of a Datsun, a friend in the passenger seat. A second friend, passed out, was slated to ride home in the backseat, but another patron volunteered to take him. Lucky for him.

Driving a cautious 30 km/h, we were in the middle of the straight stretch when we saw the lights of a car approaching well over the speed limit. As it got closer, it began to slew sideways, first one way, then the other. I kept expecting it to slow and straighten out. And it did, just long enough to convince me all was okay. A few car lengths in front of us, the car slewed once more and was sliding towards us, side-on in our lane. The road was much too slippery to stop in time or to try to steer around the Datsun.

The front of our Volvo hit the Datsun in the middle of the side panel just behind the front passenger door. I was flabbergasted that Joanne and I weren't hurt. We'd been wearing our seat-belts and, as advertised, the front end of the Volvo had crumpled, but the passenger compartment was undamaged.

Getting out of the car, I found the Datsun totaled. It had been cut completely in half, frame and all, behind the front seats. The rear axle, trunk and mangled backseat were upside down in the ditch on the opposite side of the highway about forty meters away.

The front of the vehicle was about ten meters directly behind the Volvo. The weight of the engine had pulled the engine compartment down to the ground, so the driver, still behind the wheel, was sitting high in the air. Before he attempted to do anything else, he had the drunken presence of mind to turn off the windshield wipers that were still working in the absence of a windshield. He turned out to have a fractured right leg.

His buddy was lying face down on the road, blood staining the snow around his head. I thought he was dead because I couldn't find a pulse in his neck. He was alive, however, albeit with a fractured back. The young driver was not only driving under the influence and underage, he had no insurance. His mother had bought the car with his father's life insurance, but didn't have enough money to insure it.

Did he learn anything from the incident? Yes, but all the wrong lessons. He was charged with several criminal offenses and two misdemeanors. His mother hired a well-known shyster lawyer who managed to get all charges dropped except the misdemeanor 'failing to yield half the roadway.' The next Saturday, he showed up at my restaurant on crutches, his leg in a cast to the hip, with three other teens. They were all drunk and he was driving his mother's sedan.

Oh, and yes, the front right tie rod on the Volvo turned out to be broken!

Joanne

I MET MY FUTURE wife, Joanne, on a cold Sunday afternoon in the winter of 1970. Henry and I were scheduled to work at 3 p.m. because Cortina opened at 4 on Sundays. We had to be there an hour earlier to get things ready, primarily to turn on the ovens and put spaghetti sauce on the stove. As usual, we'd been out until all hours of the morning and only got out of bed in time to go to work. He picked me up at 2:30 and we took the Kingsway toward downtown.

Halfway up the Kingsway, seeing the sign, Henry suggested we get 'breakfast to go' at the Deluxe Drive-In, a popular hamburger joint. I loved their Chicken on a Bun and I could always eat, so in we went.

She was working the front counter, serving customers. She took our orders and chatted with us and the other customers, while she waited for the cook to prepare the food. She was quite attractive and friendly, but her vivacity is what really stood out. She was full of life. She moved quickly and efficiently, no wasted motion. And she was always talking, but not nonsense, not just banter with the customers. She asked questions as if she truly wanted to get to know you. Smiling all the while.

Every so often, she would assume this funny childlike cartoon voice for a minute or two. In that voice, she'd address the men as 'Mister' in a slurred pronunciation that made the 's' sound like 'sh.' The effect was both charming and vulnerable. Hmm. Attractive and interesting. I'd have to check her out again sometime.

That sometime came the next Sunday and a habit was formed. For the rest of the winter, about every second Sunday, we would stop at the Deluxe on the way in to work, more than half the time at my suggestion. Sometimes Henry and I were alone, other times accompanied by one or two others of our young coworkers that Henry was giving a lift to work. They didn't seem to notice that, despite the fact that I usually suggested the stop, I often didn't get more than a drink. I preferred to eat at work where it didn't cost me anything. I was there just to look at the babe.

During this period, we didn't have any real conversations. We were never in the restaurant more than a few minutes. Joanne *did* act increasingly familiar with all of us as we became regular customers.

One Sunday, late in the spring, she wasn't there. Nor the next three weeks. Oh, well. It had been entertaining while it lasted.

About a hundred yards west and on the opposite side of the Kingsway, was the Dairy Queen. Almost as if fate were intervening, I took my sister, Christine, for ice cream one afternoon less than a week after I'd accepted I wouldn't see this young lady again. I was driving the Cortina VW delivery car and Christine waited in the car, while I went to the counter. Of course you've already guessed who was working there. She seemed genuinely glad to see me and we chatted as she prepared our orders.

"So, you work at Cortina?"

"Yeah. They sometimes let me take the bug home from work. We decided to come for a treat before I have to go in. When did you quit the Deluxe?"

"I didn't. We have this arrangement: I work winters at the Deluxe, when the Dairy Queen is closed, then I work here summers. It's really convenient because I live on the hill right behind the Dairy Queen."

And she meant 'right behind.' Her parents' house was literally on the rocky cliff immediately behind the restaurant. She went on to say she worked most days, rotating day and evening shifts. Through the course of our conversation, I finally volunteered my name and she told me hers: Joanne.

I wasn't quite comfortable dropping by alone yet, not confident enough to have her think I liked her and was stopping just to see her. For a couple weeks, on evenings off or in the afternoon, I took Christine or my youngest sister, Rosanna, for ice cream. By the way, Christine knew exactly what was happening and kept pushing me to stop dragging my feet. Joanne asked about Rosanna, I guess because she was so much younger, but never about Christine. Later she admitted that seeing me with Christine put a downer on her evening because she was interested in me and it bothered her that I was coming to the Dairy Queen with my girlfriend! Christine and I still laugh about that.

In the end, I went alone one evening because I had the evening off, but couldn't find anybody to accompany me. I started going alone on a pretty regular basis and, depending upon how busy she was, we'd talk for a minute or ten. Sometimes when I wasn't busy at Cortina, I'd take the bug and run over for a few minutes. I always bought a Strawberry Shortcake without the ice cream, so the fact that I was there just to see her wasn't too obvious. Why that particular order? I am not a fan of DQ ice cream, so I needed something palatable without it. I would like to point out, though, that their Strawberry Shortcake was not shortcake at all, but sponge cake.

I don't really think I was fooling anyone. At times I'd stop and find she wasn't working. By then, I was on first-name basis with the other girls and they would greet me with, "Strawberry Shortcake, no ice cream, right? By the way, Joanne is off tonight, but I'll check her schedule and tell you when she's working next." Other times, she might be working in the back. As I approached the counter, one of the girls would notice me and go to get her. After serving me and talking a minute, she'd return to the back and I'd leave.

The summer passed with us getting to know more about each other: interests, attitudes, goals. I kept telling myself I was going to ask her. I thought I'd start out small, ask her to go for coffee after work some Sunday night. We both got off at midnight on Sundays, so I could pick her up shortly after cleanup. Perhaps we could go to Country Style Donuts for coffee, where we could really talk without being interrupted by customers. I let three Sundays slip by, almost but not quite asking her. Finally, one Sunday towards the end of fall, I took a mid-evening run from Cortina. I was to bring back a banana split for Henry and a sundae for Joe.

I got to the Dairy Queen and, like Cortina, they were not busy. I gave Joanne the order and we chatted while she was preparing it, most of the time with her back to me. I decided 'now or never.' She was putting the toppings on the banana split when I took the plunge.

"Uh, Joanne? You have to go straight home after cleanup tonight?"

"No. Why?"

"I thought, maybe, I could pick you up and we could do something. Grab a coffee, go for a ride."

She turned around so fast that she spilled strawberry sauce all down the front of her uniform.

"Well! It's about time!"

§

SPONTANEITY IN relationships has been a guiding principle for me throughout my adult life. I find too many of the things we do as part of relationships are so rote, done out of habit or to suit societal expectations, that they lose all meaning. Being spontaneous revitalizes, requiring a return to conscious decision. I believe, and have seen plenty of evidence, that a mother generally is touched far more deeply by a special gift from her child out of the blue, for no reason, than she is by the same old card and flowers on Mother's Day, when they are expected.

Shortly after Joanne and I were married, I had a large bouquet of flowers delivered to her at Uptown Cleaners, where she had been working for over a year. No reason, no occasion. I sent them to her at work because of the surprise factor; it simply was not expected. What woman doesn't like to have flowers delivered to her in front of friends or co-workers?

The manager, a middle-aged woman who'd been married for about fifteen years wanted to know what the occasion was.

"No occasion. He just sent them because he was thinking of me and decided to surprise me."

"Oh, come on. Not your birthday?"

"No."

"Not your anniversary? Are you pregnant?"

"No."

"Are you doing something new, like buying a house?"

"Okay, stop it. It's none of those things. He just wanted to surprise me."

The manager, unconvinced, let the matter drop, but not for long. Later, during a lull, she started again.

"Well, if that's true, there is no special occasion, then he's cheating on you. Or at least, he's done something wrong, or is planning to, and he's feeling guilty. He's buttering you up and easing his conscience by doing something nice for you. No man does this sort of thing for no reason. There's always a reason."

Joanne didn't know how to respond. And after listening to that tune all afternoon, the value of my surprise was almost completely lost. When I picked her up, she had been more than half convinced that I was hiding some transgression.

I wonder what it's like to filter the world through such negative lenses as those of her manager. I fear that outlook is all too common in our society.

Non-Conclusion

WHEN I BEGAN TO write this chronicle, I had to decide when I should draw that arbitrary cut-off line 'the end of my early years.' I chose 1973, the year of my marriage to Joanne because it was such a pivotal time representing a major period of transition into adulthood. Admittedly, I have included a couple of anecdotes about events that actually took place after that date. They were so intimately tied into earlier events that I felt this small breach was warranted.

I am happy to be here to acknowledge that 1973 was not the final destination on the bus trip of my life. Perhaps I will continue this travelogue sometime in the future. And I sincerely hope, wherever your bus is heading, you are enjoying the scenery.

www.ingramcontent.com/pod-product-compliance
Lightning Source LLC
Chambersburg PA
CBHW052034090426

42739CB00010B/1900